THE BOOK OF PRACTICAL

WITCHCRAFT

A COMPENDIUM OF SPELLS,
RITUALS AND OCCULT KNOWLEDGE

THE BOOK OF PRACTICAL
WITCHCRAFT

A COMPENDIUM OF SPELLS, RITUALS AND OCCULT KNOWLEDGE

PAMELA BALL

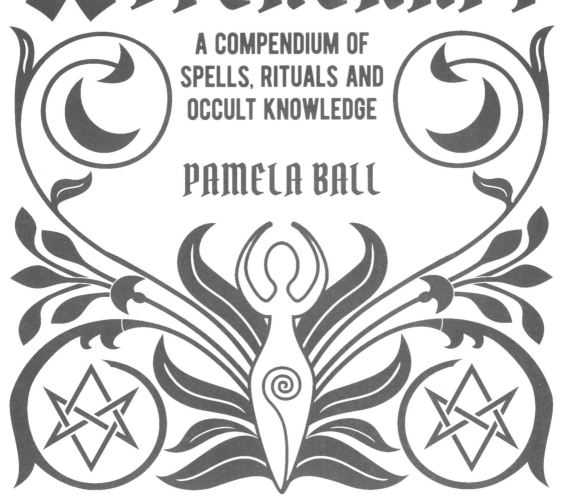

SIRIUS

All images courtesy of Shutterstock.

SIRIUS

This edition published in 2022 by Sirius Publishing, a division of
Arcturus Publishing Limited,
26/27 Bickels Yard, 151–153 Bermondsey Street,
London SE1 3HA

Cover design: Peter Ridley

ISBN: 978-1-3988-0883-6
AD010752US

Printed in China

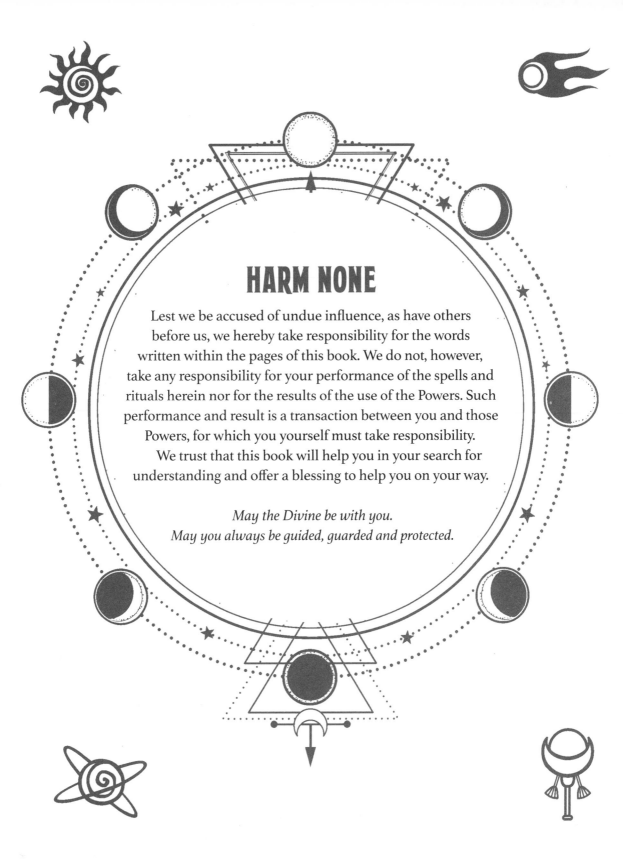

HARM NONE

Lest we be accused of undue influence, as have others before us, we hereby take responsibility for the words written within the pages of this book. We do not, however, take any responsibility for your performance of the spells and rituals herein nor for the results of the use of the Powers. Such performance and result is a transaction between you and those Powers, for which you yourself must take responsibility. We trust that this book will help you in your search for understanding and offer a blessing to help you on your way.

May the Divine be with you.
May you always be guided, guarded and protected.

CONTENTS

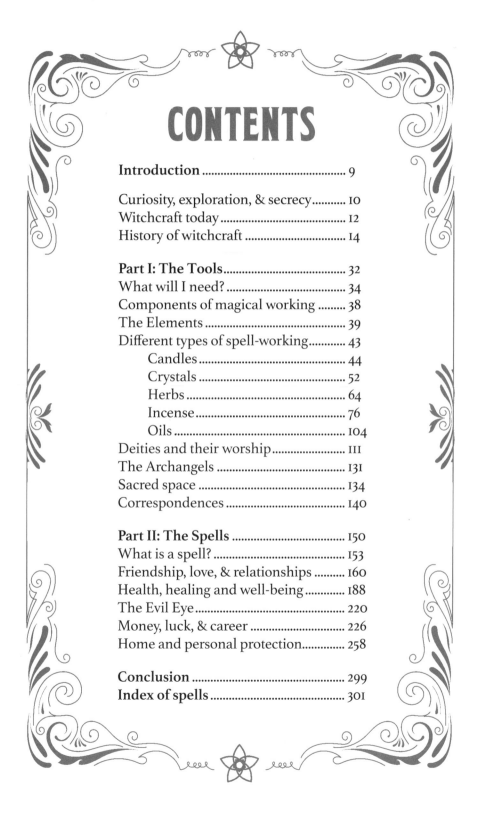

Introduction 9

Curiosity, exploration, & secrecy 10
Witchcraft today 12
History of witchcraft 14

Part I: The Tools 32
What will I need? 34
Components of magical working 38
The Elements 39
Different types of spell-working 43
      Candles 44
      Crystals 52
      Herbs 64
      Incense 76
      Oils 104
Deities and their worship 111
The Archangels 131
Sacred space 134
Correspondences 140

Part II: The Spells 150
What is a spell? 153
Friendship, love, & relationships 160
Health, healing and well-being 188
The Evil Eye 220
Money, luck, & career 226
Home and personal protection............. 258

Conclusion 299
Index of spells 301

INTRODUCTION

The desire to change and improve that which we have has been around for many thousands of years, if not since humans first walked the earth. Magic and spell-working have always been a part of that, and indeed still are today. Anyone who practises any form of magic, including spell-working, needs to be grounded. This means having both feet firmly planted in reality and also having a basic knowledge of what magic is and is not, what spells can and can't do, and what – with practice – you can do with the tools, information and knowledge you have. This book sets out to give you that information in as succinct a manner as possible.

It is sometimes best not to attempt any definition of ancient magic and magical belief. However, in any discussion of magic and its practitioners we must take account of a period in which the magical traditions of several different cultures coalesced and merged into a type of international and even multicultural magical practice, with its own rituals, symbols and words of power. This occurred in the Mediterranean basin and the Near East from the 1st to the 7th centuries and is the basis of most of the early, more intellectually based, systems of magic.

The pursuit of magic is, in part, the result of the human desire for control. In this period there was a need to control the natural environment, the social world, and the outcome of those forces we did not fully understand. This underlying desire for control comes to the surface most often in times of change, as we have seen repeatedly over the last fifteen centuries. During this time the techniques may have been modified, but the goals have remained the same. The basic laws of magic, of control, still apply today just as they have always done.

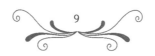

CURIOSITY, EXPLORATION AND SECRECY

One of most interesting characters from early times was Abraham Abulafia (1240–95), who made available much arcane knowledge, which ultimately formed the basis of Kabbalah. Believing in the divine nature of the Hebrew alphabet, he held that God cannot be described or conceptualized using everyday symbols. He therefore used abstract letter combinations and permutations (tzeruf) in intense meditations lasting for hours to reach ecstatic states.

These were spells in the real sense of the word since they literally "spelt out" the keys to altered states of consciousness – failure to carry through the keys correctly could have a far-reaching effect on the careless practitioner, resulting in madness and other states of illusion. Again, these beliefs have been brought through to the modern day and used to great effect. Controlled use of altered states of consciousness, backed up by empirical evidence, is still one of the most potent tools a magical practitioner can have.

The Renaissance period in Europe saw the coming to prominence of many secret societies and scholar-magicians. Because of the burgeoning natural curiosity encouraged by Renaissance principles, a new importance was placed on the actual controlling of the forces of nature. The basis of magic-working had previously been seen as harnessing the power of spirits and demons. Now, additionally, the human mind was a factor to be considered and magical working was geared to gaining power, not only over external forces but also over internal states. Much good work was done in understanding the interaction between the spiritual realm and the physical, and how changes can be brought about within the latter. Both Kabbalah and alchemy, one of whose objectives was to transform baser metals into gold, became very popular.

By the 17th century, folk magic and witchcraft were being used side by side, often with little differentiation between them.

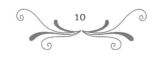

Most people were alternately fascinated and frightened by energies that offered control of nature coupled with opportunities for enormous wealth. However, witchcraft then became more widely identified with demonic or satanic entities opposed to God and therefore was deemed to be wholly evil. A heretic was defined as a traitor – an offence punishable by death – and the persecution of those who did not conform to the so-called religious thought of the day became relentless. Suspicion alone was enough to ruin a life. This caused the practice of witchcraft to go underground, not just in terms of secrecy but in actuality, for example in the use of caves and secret places, such as Wookey Hole in Somerset, England.

The practice of magic survived, however, and by the 19th century there is evidence that many secret societies, each surrounded by its own unique mysteries, still survived. They were often formed by highly creative people who were searching for new and different ways of self-expression. Many of the beliefs of these societies were based on the old traditions, though some differed widely from those of the old alchemists. Rituals and invocations were developed that were supposedly based on the ancient rites, often with a very strong bias towards melodrama. Secret societies have also survived into the present day, though not always with full awareness of the fact that their rituals are based on magical practice.

WITCHCRAFT TODAY

Today there is a rich heritage of magical practices and beliefs on which we can call to satisfy our need for control over our own lives. Where conventional religion no longer offers an outlet for our sense of belonging, we can turn to magical rituals and spell-making to honour our origins. We can make use of the knowledge and practices that have been handed down to us and have survived, often in the face of adversity. The principles that form the basis of magical practice still operate today, as do the various belief systems associated with them.

Many of these belief systems take their names from the Greek word *theo*, meaning "god". One can be polytheistic (belief in many gods) yet see all things as being part of one great mystery, or monotheistic (belief in one god) yet recognize that for others there may be many gods. Again one might be atheistic (with no belief in god), with simply a belief in one's own power.

In the working of magical spells no one can tell you what to believe – you must make your own decisions. The words "Paganism" and "Pagan" come from the Latin *paganus*, meaning "rustic" or "belonging to the country". Largely, ancient Paganism was pantheistic (believing in all gods) but today the word has come to mean someone who does not recognize the God of the main religions of the world, such as Christianity or Judaism. Irrespective of what you choose to believe, magic and spell-making is aligned closely to a belief in the power of nature and there is the need for love and respect for all living things. How we express that will be mirrored in our spell-making.

Spell-making is such an individual craft that nobody can, or indeed should, be so bold as to try to tell others how to cast their spells. However, in some areas it is useful to receive guidance as a starting point from which you can devise your own ways of working. This book is divided into two parts; in the first we look at what you will need to begin working with spells. This includes the tools you will need, how to create sacred space, and the best times and correspondences for spell-working. Finally, in this first section, we advise on the best ways for constructing your spell and rituals and how to record your methods and results.

The spells in the second part of the book are divided into the following four categories: Friendship, Love and Relationships; Health,

Healing and Well-being; Money, Luck and Career; Home and Personal Protection.

Each spell has an introductory paragraph with information as to what type of spell it is, the best time to carry it out, and which discipline it comes from (if known). We then tell you what you will need and then give you the method to use. Some spells require incantations, some invocations and others simple actions to make them work, and this is laid out for you. Lastly, we tell you what to expect – results can be unpredictable, and sometimes conspicuous by their absence.

If a spell doesn't work for you in the way that we have suggested, it might be that your intended result does not fit into the overall scheme of things. Do try it again on another occasion and use your intuition to decide what might be changed or adjusted to suit your personality. Have confidence in yourself and never be afraid to experiment.

Popular acceptance of magical powers and spell-making will always be mixed. Some people will accept unquestioningly, others will search for alternative causes and others still will remain concerned by the manifestation of such powers. For some people these powers are part of everyday life and it is for each individual to decide whether or not they wish to develop and use them.

It now merely remains for us to wish you health, wealth and happiness and the hope that you enjoy your spell-work and its results!

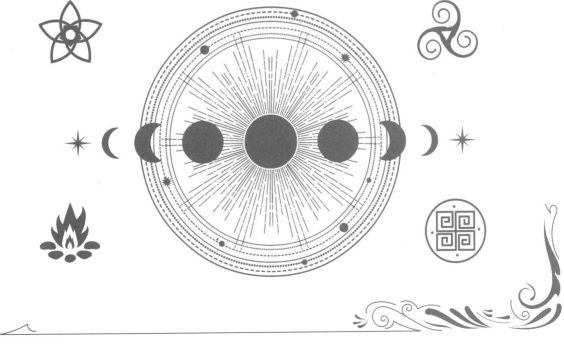

HISTORY OF WITCHCRAFT

The word "magic" comes to us from *magea*, the Greek word which itself derives from "magoi". The Magoi were a caste of Persian priests who studied astrology and practised divination. It was not just in Persia (modern-day Iran) that these arts were practised thousands of years ago. All over the world, in every primitive society, men and women looked to the stars for guidance and the spirit world for inspiration. Our ancestors worshipped gods who, they believed, looked after the spirits of those who had died and gone to live in the spirit world. In most, if not all, of these societies there was one person, usually a man, who was regarded by the others as being able to communicate with ancestral spirits. Today, we call such a person "the shaman". There are many parts of the developing world in which the shaman continues to play a major role in small communities.

As part of his (or very occasionally her) role, the shaman performed rituals and made magic. Rituals help to demarcate the ordinary and the extraordinary, focusing attention on aspects of the cosmic process, which were believed to control every aspect of life. Magic was an integral part of these rituals and it is fair to say that some magical elements survive in the religions of today and that most of these religions have their roots in some aspect of shamanic practice. As an example of the former, some Roman Catholics believe that during the Mass, consecrated wine turns into the blood of Christ and bread into His body (although the majority have now come to see the bread and the wine as symbolic rather than actual). And to exemplify the latter, Sufis believe that in entering a state of ecstasy brought about by intense physical exercise, their holy men can communicate with God.

As "civilization" dawned, first, according to archaeological evidence, in Mesopotamia and from there spread east into India and west into Egypt, religions developed in which magic played a central part, and both magic and religion depend on ritual. The religions of Ancient Egypt, of Classical Greece and Ancient Rome, those of the Celtic world and the Scandinavian countries, all had magic in some form at their roots.

Magic has no one homeland, but Ancient Egypt can be said to be its cradle. There it

Egyptians believed that two things that had been connected could continue to react on each other even when separated and that like has the power to affect like.

Thus, a burn could be cured by the recitation of the words used by Isis over her son Horus when he was once burned, and that one may cause one's enemies pain by mistreating a wax image of them. From these, and similar conceptions, arose the belief in protective amulets which assumed huge importance for both the living and the dead.

Egypt was an extremely stratified society, in which everyone knew their place, but there was no professional class of magicians – indeed, there was not even a general word for magician. Magic was the domain of priests and others who studied sacred books. But magic on a small, personal scale was within the reach of anyone who was willing to observe the conditions laid down, and judging from tomb paintings and papyri that have survived the many thousand years that have passed, magic played a very large part in everyday life. There are records of spells being cast to escape death, to drive out disease, to avert the evil eye, to cure snakebite, to drive out rats from a barn and to prevent the approach of a storm. There was even a spell to secure the various advantages summed up in the phrase, "to be blessed every day."

was believed that the sun god Ra died in the western sky every night to spend the hours of darkness in the underworld and to be magically reborn every morning in the eastern sky. Many later magicians believe that nine-tenths of the world's magic comes from Egypt and the Old Testament depicts Egyptian magicians as so powerful that they could reproduce the magic that Moses used to convince the Pharaoh to allow his people to leave Egypt.

In Ancient Egypt, magic was known as "hike," which was a spoken formula that had to be reproduced exactly as prescribed if it was to work, and an act or gesture that had to be performed at a particular time and place and under special conditions. The

In the Graeco-Roman world, the gods were duly worshipped and tales of them

looking down from where they lived and using their magic powers to help those whom they favoured, and hinder those whom they frowned upon, became part of common belief. And the same can be said of the Germanic and Scandinavian people.

All of these peoples honoured the same things – rivers, trees, plants, animals, the wind and the rain, the sun and the moon. But perhaps it was for Pagan Celts that they played the most important part in religious ritual, although little is known about the Celts for they left no written records and archaeological records of them are scant. A number of votive sites have been found, suggesting that religious rites were performed at sites of natural significance – on the banks of important rivers, in clearings in woods and on the tops of hills and mountains.

Paganism

It is the oral rather than the written tradition that makes many people believe that nature played a significant role in Celtic religious ritual and it is this oral tradition that suggests to many that modern witchcraft has Celtic roots. Away from the world of fairytales and wicked witches, modern magic and its spells have their roots in Celtic times – 700BCE–100CE. The deeply spiritual Celts were artistic, musical, fine farmers and brave warriors, feared by their adversaries. As pantheists, they honoured the "Divine Creator of all Nature" and worshipped the "One Creative Life Source" in all its many aspects. They believed that after they died they went to "Summerland" where they rested and awaited new birth on Earth.

Celtic rites and rituals (the names of which will be familiar to those who study witchcraft today) were supervised by the Druids (the word translates from the Celtic phrase for "knowing the oak tree"). It is believed that it took twenty years of hard study to become a Druid.

Druids were regarded not just as priests: they were judges, teachers, astrologers, healers, bards and ambassadors, passing from one warring tribe to another to settle disputes. Nature and the passing seasons governed the Celts' religious year. At the end of summer, they celebrated Samhain – the final harvest of the year, which marked their New Year. This was the time when they honoured their ancestors, their loved ones who were resting in Summerland. Many of the customs that we now follow at Halloween have come to us from the Celts' Samhain rites and rituals.

Samhain was followed by the Winter Solstice, the annual rebirth of the sun, which the Celts celebrated as jovially as we celebrate Christmas today, and in some respects in not dissimilar fashion!

The time when spring was just around the corner and when domestic animals were about to drop their young was called Imbolg, followed shortly afterwards by the Spring

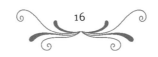

Equinox and Beltane – both of which were regarded as fertility festivals.

Lughnassa, the Summer Solstice and another harvest festival, celebrated the sun's glory and the power of nature. It was now that the sacred mistletoe used by Celtic priests was harvested, cut down with a golden sickle from the oak trees on which it grew and caught in a white cloth so it would never fall to the ground.

The Autumn Equinox, or Mabon, was the final harvest festival of the year.

These religious beliefs and practices grew into what later became known as "Paganism". The word derives from the Latin for "country-dweller," and as the wheels of the year went round and round, Paganism's beliefs and

Druid rituals blended with the ways of others and such practices as concocting lotions and potions, performing works of magic and casting spells developed.

The Coming of the Bad Times

Further south, Rome was fast becoming the dominant power in Europe and as its empire spread north into and beyond the Alps, the number of Druids dwindled as the conquering armies brought their own ways and beliefs which spread far and wide.

Around 2,000 years ago, in Palestine, the Christian religion was born. Like those who followed the Jewish faith, Christians believed in one god. The main difference between the two faiths being that while many Jews came

to believe that Jesus Christ was a prophet, followers of Christ believed that he was the son of God and part of the "Holy Trinity" a triad made up of God the Father, God the Son and God the Holy Ghost.

Christians believed that the way to communicate with God was through Jesus Christ. The Christian faith spread from Palestine, eastwards into Europe and in 317CE, the Emperor Constantine declared it to be the official religion of the Roman Empire. All over Europe old gods were banished and the new religion imposed in their place.

Of course, followers of the old ways persisted with their traditions, despite the fact that it was not uncommon for the priests, including the Druids, to whom people looked for spiritual leadership, to be persecuted and in some cases put to death. But old traditions die hard and they continued to be handed down from generation to generation.

Two hundred years later, Pope Gregory I (540-604) did a great deal to consolidate the power of the Catholic faith. Tens of thousands of people were baptized into it, forswearing their old ways and giving themselves to Rome. Gregory was cunning. He realized that people are unwilling to change their ways. He saw that they would continue to gather to honour the one god in places where they, and their fathers, and their fathers before them had gathered to worship the old gods and perform the rituals and ceremonies attendant with traditional

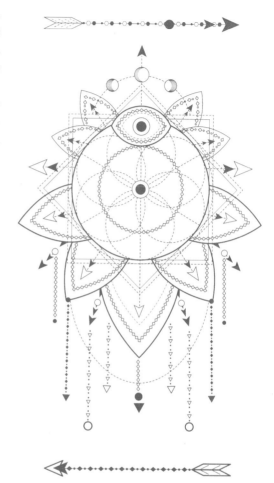

worship. So wherever it was possible, he decreed that churches be built on the sites of existing Pagan temples. Pagans believed in an entity called "The Great All" who was formed of "The God" and "The Goddess". Sites dedicated to The Lord and The Lady were common, and when churches were

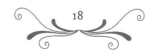

built on these sites, they were often dedicated to The Virgin Mary and called "The Church of Our Lady," "Our Lady" being another name for the Holy Virgin. In simple ways like this, the old ways persisted.

In any organization, the larger it grows, the more difficult it becomes to control. So it was with the Catholic Church. Centralized in Rome but spreading north to Britain, west into present-day Spain and Portugal and east into Greece, it was hard for the Pope in the Vatican to stop variations in doctrine and ritual creeping in. To discourage this, inquisitors were employed to search out Christians whose beliefs and practices were not in line with official dogma. Anyone who did not follow the true path was branded heretic and if they did not immediately recant when the accusation had been made, they were imprisoned and in some cases put to death.

An Infamous Bull

In 1484, Pope Innocent VIII issued a papal bull concerning the practice of witchcraft. He was not the first to do so: several of his predecessors had written on the subject and what should be done about it. Innocent's was different in that it was much more widely read than earlier ones. Thanks to the European invention of movable-type printing by Johannes Gutenberg around 1432 (it had been used in China many centuries earlier) it was easy for the Church to issue many copies of Innocent's bull. Without it, each copy would have had to be laboriously handwritten by monks.

All over Europe, priests read that clergy and laymen and women were not treating the threat posed by witchcraft seriously enough. Innocent insisted that it was the duty of every Roman Catholic (and that meant almost everyone, for the Church was so powerful) to help his inquisitors search out witches.

While it is true that there were men and women who were practicing witchcraft as an evil art – worshipping Satan and weaving malevolent spells – most of the people who came under the inquisitors' suspicious eyes were innocent men and women. They were people who believed that remedies that had been handed down from generation to generation worked. They were often country people who were more in tune with the forces of nature than their urban cousins. It is more than possible, in fact it is almost certain, that some of these folk remedies and the way that nature's powers were harnessed were survivals of Druid customs and rituals.

Innocent's bull encouraged two monks, Heinrich Kramer and Jakob Sprenger to publish the *Malleus Malleficarum*, or *The Hammer of Witches*, which was essentially a witch-hunter's manual. It explained why witchcraft was such a terrible thing, why it was the duty of all good Catholics to stamp it out and how to tell if someone was practising the evil arts.

In their rant against witchcraft, Kramer and Sprenger, who were inquisitors themselves, list the types of witch. They accused witches of having sexual relations with the Devil and working with him to spread his dark ways. The book detailed how a trial should proceed, beginning with a notice that was to be fixed to the walls of the parish church (or town hall). It was worded:

Whereas we, the Vicar of . . . do
endeavour with all our might
and strive to preserve the Christian
people entrusted to us in unity
and happiness of the Catholic Faith and
to keep them far removed
from every plague of abominable heresy
. . .
Therefore, we the aforesaid Judge to
whose office it belongs, to the
glory and honour of the worshipful name
of Jesus Christ and for the exaltation
of the Holy Orthodox Faith, and for
the putting down of the abomination
of heresy especially in all witches in
general and in each one severally of
whatever condition.

The book went on to inform on how proceedings should be initiated against alleged witches; the manner in which they should be arrested; how witnesses should be questioned; the use of torture; and the sentence. Judges were warned not to touch an

accused person with their bare hands and to wear a bag around their neck containing salt that had been consecrated on Palm Sunday. In the same bag there should be herbs, similarly blessed, enclosed in consecrated wax. Witches should be led backwards into the court and if the judge had to approach the suspect he must first cross himself and approach her "manfully". In this way, the two monks wrote, "with God's help the power of that old Serpent will be broken."

The Witch-Hunts

The book led to thousands of men and women being accused of witchcraft all over Europe and, later, European colonies in the New World. Torture was often used to force a confession out of an innocent person. Some were deprived of sleep and became so disorientated that when they came to stand trial they were in no state to argue their innocence. Others were tortured in more physically painful ways. In some parts of Europe the "strappado" was used. This hideous machine was a sort of pulley that raised an accused person off the floor and held him or her hanging by their arms, feet off the ground, the weight of the body dislocating the arms and causing terrible pain. In other places, the accused was subject to torture by instruments of compression – thumbscrews, leg screws and head clamps.

In Germany, suspect witches were made to sit on the "witches' chair" – a metal seat

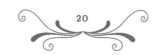

below which a fire was lit! In Scotland, confessions were forced out of suspects by an instrument called "the bootes" which "chrushte the legges and beaten them together as small as micht be" and "made the bones and flesh so bruised, that the blud and marrow sputed forth in great abundance."

Almost inevitably the accused confessed and was sentenced to death. Some did not even get the "opportunity" to stand trial and plead their innocence in whatever mental or physical state they may have been in. "Swimming the witch" was widely practised in several parts of Europe. The suspect's ankles were bound to the wrists and he or she was thrown into water. If they sank, they were innocent: if they floated then witchcraft was

confirmed and sentence duly pronounced. In Scotland, suspect witches were pricked for the "Devil's mark" – a spot where no pain was felt. If such a spot was found it marked the place where the Devil had consummated a pact with the accused.

The fact that most people accused of witchcraft were innocent did not deter those who searched them out. Witchcraft was thought to be the most heinous of all crimes because it represented those who were working against society in general and God in particular. Those who sought it out were acting on God's behalf and on behalf of their monarch who ruled by divine authority.

Witch-hunting was more intense on mainland Europe than in the British Isles, especially in England where the Witchcraft Act was passed in 1563, giving the State rather than the Church the responsibility of seeking out and punishing men and women who practised the evil arts. There were probably less than 5,000 trials, less than half of which resulted in the accused being executed.

Two of those who came under the scrutiny of the court were Elizabeth Francis and Agnes Waterhouse. Elizabeth Francis was tried for bewitching a child and making her ill. She told her judges that her grandmother had introduced her to witchcraft when she was twelve. The cat, she told her accusers, had helped Elizabeth become rich and killed her lover when he refused to marry her. She confessed to allowing the Devil to

kill three of her parish priest's pigs, to drown a neighbour's cow and to slaughter three of another neighbour's geese. More seriously to modern eyes, she confessed to killing her husband: but it was for witchcraft as well as murder that she was hanged.

Agnes Waterhouse was lucky. She was accused of keeping a toad as her familiar – the supernatural spirit who takes the shape of an animal and assists a witch in her magic – and using it to bewitch a child who refused her request for bread and cheese. Fortunately for Waterhouse, the court accepted that the charges against her were based on the spiteful fantasies of an untrustworthy child and the charges against her were dropped.

The Salem Witch Trials

The 1563 Act and a subsequent one passed in 1600, after James VI of Scotland had acceded to the English throne as James I, were in force not just throughout the British Isles but in the colonies in North America. It was there that the spiteful accusations of not one but three children led to perhaps the most famous witchcraft trials of all time. It seems that, to get themselves out of trouble, the daughter of the minister and his two nieces accused their Caribbean slave, Tabita, and two others, Sarah Good and Sarah Osborne, of making them possessed by the Devil. When brought before the court to give evidence, the girls fell into (probably) self-induced fits – evidence that the Devil was within them – and the

three unfortunate women were found guilty. In the hysteria that followed, innocent men and women in the town and surrounding area found themselves accused of being in league with the Devil and forced to face their accusers in court. The first trial had set the course for all subsequent ones. The accused were presumed guilty, unless the townspeople could be convinced otherwise. Fortunately many were able to convince the court that the charges against them were based on little more than ill-founded, spiteful gossip. But several were not so lucky and were executed for their supposed crimes. Execution was mostly by hanging, but one man was sentenced to death by being crushed by boulders!

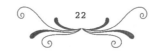

The Dawn of a New Age

With the gradual emergence of scientific, rational thinking in 18th century Europe, witchcraft became widely seen as little more than superstitious nonsense and, eventually, witch-hunts came to an end. The last person to be convicted of witchcraft in England was Jane Wenham, in 1712. The hunts lasted longer on mainland Europe where an unfortunate Polish woman swung her way into history when she was hanged for witchcraft in 1782 – the last officially sanctioned execution for witchcraft on record.

Witchcraft ceased to be a crime – or at least, where it remained one in the statute books, the laws against it fell into disuse. But despite the fact that logical thought was dispelling the ancient art as superstitious nonsense, the old ways did persist. All over the world, either on their own or in groups, men and women carried on making magic as their ancestors had done since the dawn of human civilization.

Among them was a woman called Margaret Murray, an anthropologist by profession and an Egyptologist by passion. Her book, *The Witch-Cult in Western Europe*, published in 1921, stated that the victims of the witch-hunts were practising an ancient religion: Paganism. She believed that a supreme deity had been worshipped and that he had taken the place in Pagan ritual of what Murray called "The Mother Goddess". Murray, who claimed that Joan of Arc had been a member of this pre-Christian religion, was dismissed as a crank. But her book was read by many, including plantation-owner Gerald Gardner who became interested in magic when he was working in Malaya. He retired to London in 1936 and moved to the New Forest in Hampshire in 1938 where he joined the Rosicrucians, a secret society formed in the 15th century to study the occult. In 1939 he claimed that a witch whom he called "Old Dorothy" initiated him into a local coven.

The Wiccan Way

In 1954, Gerald Gardner published *Witchcraft Today* in which he advocated the use of old, long-established rituals and introduced many of his own devising. Gardner venerated The Goddess and women in general. He believed in the power of nature and that men and women could tune into it to alter the course of things. Gardner's work has, according to several anthropologists, three direct links to ancient Paganism – the use of high magic, the use of plants and herbs in spells, and the involvement of folk rites and customs to manipulate the powers of nature.

Gardner's work led to a revival in interest of the traditions of witchcraft, not just in Britain, and he is credited by many as being the founder of what has become an officially recognized new religion – Wicca. Wicca honours The God and The Goddess (their names vary from group to group) as the two

main deities and followers worship them in their rites and rituals.

Wicca spread and, as it did, different groups developed their own rites and rituals. In England, Celtic practices and Gardnerian belief are blended together in the form of what has come to be known as British Traditional Witchcraft. In the United States, where Gardner's work was introduced and developed by Raymond Buckland, Wicca has now become an officially recognized religion.

Wicca has followers all over the world, wherever people feel a need to turn from traditional religions and return to a more Earth-based one. They practise various forms of magic and perform rituals to attune themselves with the natural rhythm of life forces, particularly those marked by the phases of the moon and the four seasons.

Wiccans belong to a wider movement – Neo-Paganism, which, as the name suggests, has its roots in Celtic Paganism. But not all Neo-Pagans are Wiccans: the term also refers to Druidism, New Age, shamanism, Ceremonial Magick, the occult sciences, Voodoo and the revival of any pre-Christian mystery tradition.

The Wiccan Rede

Wiccans live by the Wiccan Rede, a simple benevolent moral code that holds that as long as no one is harmed, "do what thy wilt." One popular version of the Rede, taught to her pupils by Dorothy Morrison, a leading American Wiccan and High Priestess of the Georgian Tradition, goes as follows:

Bide the Wiccan Law you must,
In perfect love and perfect trust.
(Keep the laws of Wicca lovingly and with perfect trust.)
Live and let live:
Fairly take and fairly give.
(Treat both nature and people as you would like to be treated.)
Cast the circle thrice about,
To keep the evil spirits out.
(When making magic, Wiccans usually cast a circle around themselves. They do this three times because the number three stands for the three phases of The Lord and The Lady.)

To bind the spell every time,
Let the spell be spake in rhyme.

(By speaking their spells in rhyme, witches believe it gives the conscious mind something to think about, while the unconscious mind taps into the energy of nature and the magic is done.)

Soft of eye and light of touch
Speak little and listen much.

(Wise magic-makers are gentle. They listen and learn.)

Deasil go by the waxing moon,
Sing and dance the Witches' Rune.

(When the moon is waxing – moving from slim crescent to plump fullness, it is the time to move round the ritual circle clockwise as this draws in good things.)

Widdershins go when the moon doth
  wane,
And werewolves howl by the dream
  wolfsbane.

(When the moon is waning is the time to move round the circle anti-clockwise as this takes away negativity. Wolfbane's toxicity makes it a feared plant.)

When the Lady's moon is new
Kiss thy hand to Her times two.

(Welcome the new moon – just visible in the sky after being dark for three nights – welcome her by kissing the index and middle finger twice.)

When the moon rides at her peak,
Then your heart's desire speak.

(When the moon is full, you can ask her for anything as she will grant the heart's desire.)

Heed the north wind's mighty gale,
Lock the door and drop the sail.
When the wind comes from the south,
Love will kiss thee on the mouth.
When the wind blows from the east,
Expect the new and set the feast
When the west wind blows o'er thee,
The departed spirits restless be.

(These lines refer to the elements with the four directions.)

Nine woods in the cauldron go,
Burn them fast and burn them slow
Elder the Lady's tree.
Burn it not, or cursed be.

(There are nine different magical woods burned in the witch's cauldron during various rituals – apple, birch, fir, hawthorn, oak, rowan, vine and willow. Elder wood is never burned because the tree is sacred to The Lady.)

When the Wheel begins a turn,
Let the Beltane fires burn
When the Wheel hath turned to Yule,
Light the log and let Pan rule.

(This refers to the cycle of the year. Beltane, the spring sabbath and Yule the winter one, sit at opposite ends of the wheel of the year.)

Heed ye flower, bush and tree,
And by the Blessed Lady be!

(For the Lady's sake, nurture and respect nature.)

Where the rippling waters flow,
Cast a stone and truth you'll know.

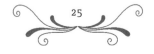

(Actions spread, like the ripples caused by a stone cast on the water, affecting everyone and everything around.)

Whenever you do have a need,
Harken not to others' greed.

(Never take money in exchange for using magical power.)

With the fool no seasons spend,
Nor be counted as his friend.

(Others associate you with the company you keep. If you mix with fools, that's how you'll be regarded.)

Merry meet and merry part,
Bright the cheeks and warm the heart.

(The company of friends is the best company there is.)

Mind the threefold law you should,
Three times bad and three times good.

(Always remember that whatever you do, good or bad, comes back to you three times.)

When misfortune is enow.
Wear the blue star on your brow.

(When trouble beckons, visualize a blue pentagram on your forehead for protection.)

True in love ever be.
Unless thy love is false to thee.

(Always be loyal in love: but if you are let down, move on.)

Eight words the Wiccan Rede fulfil,
"An it harm none, do what ye will."

(Feel free to do whatever takes your fancy, as long as in doing so, none are harmed.)

A Principled Group of People

When most people think of spells they think of witches: and when most people think of witches they think of gnarled old crones casting evil spells. For centuries, writers, and later filmmakers and television producers, perpetuated this view, although to be fair there were movies such as The Witches of Eastwick and television series such as Bewitched and Sabrina the Teenage Witch that showed witches in a more light-hearted, approachable manner.

To improve the witch's image, in 1974, the American Council of Witches set out to remedy this. The Chairman of the Council, Carl Llewellyn Weschcke, drafted thirteen principles of Wiccan belief to define Wicca and to help non-believers to realize that those who followed its ways were far from the wicked witches of the popular imagination. These principles are:

1. We practise rites to attune ourselves with the natural rhythm of life forces marked by the phases of the moon and seasonal quarters and cross-quarters.

2. We recognize that our intelligence gives us a unique responsibility toward our environment. We seek to live in harmony with nature, in ecological balance, offering fulfillment to life and consciousness within an evolutionary concept.

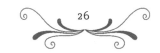

3. We acknowledge a depth of power far greater than is apparent to the average person. Because it is far greater, it is sometimes called "supernatural" but we see it as lying within that which is naturally potential to all.

4. We conceive of the Creative Power in the Universe as manifesting through polarity – as masculine and feminine – and that this Creative Power lives in all people and functions through the interaction of the masculine and feminine. We value neither above the other, knowing each to be supportive of the other. We value sex as pleasure, as the symbol and embodiment of life, and as one of the sources of energies used in magical practice and religious worship.

5. We recognize both outer worlds and inner, psychological worlds and see in the interaction of these two dimensions the basis for paranormal phenomena and magical exercises. We neglect neither dimension for the other, seeing both as necessary for our fulfillment.

6. We do not recognize any authoritarian hierarchy, but do honour those who teach, respect those who share their greater knowledge and wisdom, and acknowledge those who have courageously given of themselves in leadership.

7. We see religion, magic and wisdom-in-living as being united in the way one views the world and lives within it – a worldview and philosophy of life that we identify as the Wiccan Way.

8. Calling oneself "witch" does not make one a witch. But neither does the heredity itself, or the collecting of titles, degrees and initiations. Witches seek to control the forces within themselves that make life possible in order to live wisely and well, without harm to others, and in harmony with nature.

9. We acknowledge that it is the affirmation and fulfillment of life, in a continuation of evolution and development of consciousness that gives meaning to the universe we know.

10. Our only animosity towards Christianity, or towards any other religion or philosophy of life is to the extent that its institutions have claimed to be "the only way" and have sought to deny freedom to others and to suppress other ways of religious practice and belief.

11. As (American) witches we are not threatened by debates on the history of the craft, the origins of various terms, the legitimacy of various aspects of different traditions. We are concerned with our present and our future.

12. We do not accept the concept of "absolute evil" nor do we worship any entity known as "Satan" or "the Devil" as defined by the Christian tradition. We do not seek power through the suffering of others, nor do we accept the concept that personal benefit can only be derived by denial to another.

13. We acknowledge that we seek within nature for that which is contributory to our health and well-being.

(With thanks to the Council of American Witches for permission to reproduce these principles here.)

Other Traditions

As Wicca spread, various groups interpreted it in different ways. There are those, in Britain, who belong to the British Traditional Witchcraft movement, which blends together Gardnerian practices and beliefs with Celtic traditions. Others look to the Pictish tradition, which is based on Scottish witchcraft, focusing as it does on the magical energies of all aspects of nature with no emphasis (or very little) placed on religion.

Witches who follow the Dianic tradition look to Diana, the Roman moon goddess and worship only the feminine aspect of The All. The movement encouraged feminism and is involved in feminist issues. Many exclude men altogether from their rituals.

In some parts of Europe, a pre-Gardnerian form of Wicca is followed, sometimes called hereditary witchcraft. Membership is restricted to those who can trace their ancestry back to antecedents who followed "The Old Way". Members are usually introduced to covens by family members, usually a parent or grandparent.

The Alexandra tradition, founded by Alexander Sanders in England in 1963, puts a strong emphasis on Ceremonial Magic but is essentially Gardnerian in practice. One difference however is that followers of the Alexandra tradition perform their rituals either semi-clad or fully clothed whereas Gardnerian covens sometimes do their rituals naked, or sky-clad.

Celtic Wicca is based on the ancient Celtic pantheon and Druid rituals. Celtic Wiccans embrace ancient Irish myths and much of their magic is directed at natural healing. The Norse pantheon has its Wiccan

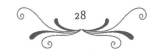

followers who look to the magical customs and ancient myths of pre-Christian Iceland and Scandinavia for inspiration, while those whose ritual and magic is inspired by the gods and goddesses of Ancient Egypt are said to follow the Egyptian tradition.

Low Magic and High Magic

Low magic, sometimes called natural magic, was widely practised in the Middle Ages and still is in some parts of the world. Also known as practical magic, it combines the arts of witchcraft, spellcraft, hexcraft and voodoo, which utilize herbs, amulets, wax images and other simple objects along with visualization and incantations to bring about the desired result. It is the folk magic of less developed parts of the world where it is often done for a fee, and in the developed world it is the magic of many spellcasters. In low magic, spells are cast for good or evil.

High magic, or Ceremonial Magic, on the other hand is performed to bring about union with the divine. In high magic, the powers of nature, conceived of as being either angelic or Satanic, are controlled in conjunction with spirits, using words and the names of sacred gods.

Typically, magic involves the use of elaborate rituals, the invocation of spirits (often in dramatic, theatrical fashion) and mystic sacraments.

Practised since ancient times, Ceremonial Magic is mainly the domain of those

seeking mystical power and enlightenment. Ceremonial Magic is still practised by those who adhere to Abramelin magic and study the Kabbalah.

Involving spirit communication, word magic and palindromic number squares, Abramelin magicians believe that the world was created and is maintained by demons whose work is directed by angelic spirits. The magicians believe that properly purified and using the correct prayers, formulas and tools, and with the help of the angels they can take control of the demons and bend them to their will.

The Kabbalah is based on unusual interpretations of the Hebrew scriptures. Despite its appearance as an elaborate system of magic, it is actually a tool to allow the magician to achieve mystical union with God.

The Kabbalah teaches that God is known by 72 different names and that the Universe is composed of four planes of being. There are several facets of the Kabbalah that make it compatible with the beliefs and practices of nature-orientated Wicca, but most Wiccans would find the monotheism and strict codes of behaviour imposed by Judaism, with which the Kabbalah is inextricably linked, hard to accept.

Some Curious Beliefs

Witchcraft, especially in its malevolent magical form, still exists in the beliefs of many African cultures and indigenous peoples around the world. In North America, for instance, the Navajo believe that witchcraft is an exclusively male practice, its initiates meeting at night to make magic, wearing nothing except a mask and jewellery. They sit among baskets of corpses and are said to "converse" with dead women.

Some African cultures hold that witches get together in cannibal covens. They meet, it is believed by some tribes in Guinea, in graveyards, sitting round a fire and feasting vampire-fashion off the blood of their victims.

Witches have the ability to take a person's soul and keep it until the victim dies. Witches here are believed to have made a pact with an evil spirit who grants them power that they exercise through a familiar, such as a dog, baboon or, as with witches in medieval Europe and 17th century North America, a cat.

The Zande, who live in the Congo area and some other central African peoples, believe that a witch's power comes from his or her own body.

They believe that the source of the capacity to cast evil spells is located in the witch's stomach and that as the witch ages, so their power increases. The witch can activate this power simply by wishing someone ill but the spell is made stronger by the use of potions and powerful magic.

In other parts of Africa, witches are thought to act unconsciously and might well be unaware of the ill that they cause until it is brought to their attention. Those who suffer at the hands of such a witch might have held that view until the witchcraft is turned in their direction. Then they are quick to change their minds and claim that the witchcraft was deliberate.

Witchcraft is still blamed in some developing parts of the world for disease and disaster, some as major as a fatal landslide or a devastating flood which has serious consequences for many people, others as trivial as failure in an exam or performing badly at a job interview. In parts of Brazil, for example, where job loss is thought to be due to witchcraft, whoever suffered the loss participates in a ritual consultation with a shaman, who, of course, expects to be rewarded for his efforts!

To be fair, many people who believe that witchcraft can be responsible for misfortunes do not lay the blame at its door every time misfortune strikes. If there is a logical explanation, it is often accepted: a badly built shelter that blows down in a gale was obviously not strong enough to withstand it. But if a seemingly well-built hut collapses for no apparent reason, then the blame may well be laid at witchcraft's door.

People in modern Africa and other areas where witchcraft is still part of everyday culture, usually also believe in local divinities and in the spirit world. If they are sick, they will often turn to conventional medicine

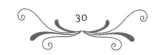

to cure their physical symptoms while also looking to the local "witch doctor" to explain and treat the hidden causes of the illness. The sick may wear amulets to protect them from illness, practice the divination advised by the witch doctor, and take the "medicine" that is prescribed.

Often when witchcraft is held to be responsible for misfortune the sufferer will try to discover the source. The bewitched might seek help from a diviner to establish the identity of the witch. The diviner may go into a trance and use a variety of props, often dice or animal bones, to do this. Among one African people, divination to find out a witch's identity is by administering poison to a chicken and mentioning the name of the suspect. If the chicken dies, the suspect is innocent: if it lives, guilt is pronounced and the appropriate action taken.

 # PART 1
THE TOOLS

WHAT WILL I NEED?

When performing your spells and magical workings, you will find that you need to understand why you use certain tools in specific ways. Before learning how to set up your altar (see page 134), here is a list of the most commonly used tools.

Altar Objects

This is a general term for the objects that you place on your altar – candleholders, flower vases, crystals and so forth – which do not necessarily have a specific magical use of their own; they are present to create an ambience. You should remember to dedicate them to the purpose in hand by presenting them to your chosen deity – you may find it helpful to consult the Deities section (see page III) which has a comprehensive selection for your information.

Athame

By tradition, the athame is a ceremonial knife used especially in the performing of spells. It is not intended for cutting herbs and so on: its role is ceremonial, for example indicating the quarters or directions. Ideally it should be of the best and purest metal available.

Its handle is usually black and sometimes carved with magical designs and symbols. Many experienced magical practitioners consider that the most powerful athame is one which has been inherited.

Besom

A besom is a different name for a broom, and is particularly associated with the easily recognizable so-called "witch's broom" of old. It is a particularly personal tool, and is often made specially for the practitioner, with twigs from the tree of her choice. It is usually kept specifically to be used in the sacred space or circle – this time for cleansing – and is also used both symbolically and spiritually.

Boline

The boline is a knife traditionally used in cutting plants, herbs, wands and other objects for spells and other magical workings. It is akin to the gardener's pruning knife as a useful, practical tool. It often has a white handle and a curved blade. It is consecrated because this is a way of honouring its purpose.

Burin

A burin is a sharp-pointed instrument used for inscribing candles and other magical objects with symbols, words and pictures in order to make spells more effective. In many ways, it is more effective than either the boline or the athame and is used much more as an instrument which pierces a surface rather than cuts it.

Candles

Candles are such an integral part of a spell-maker's work that they have become a whole branch of magic all their own. They represent the Element of Fire, but also light. Various colors bring different things to magical workings and they are an important part of any ritual (see pages 44–51).

Cauldron

Because cauldrons were easily disguised as cooking utensils in olden days, most people today tend to think of them as a large cast-iron pot. There has lately been a return to original materials and nowadays they can be made of almost anything. They are often of a size that can be stood on the altar, or in the sacred space. They are used mainly as containers for herbs, candles and other magical objects.

Chalice

Used as a ceremonial drinking vessel, the chalice is sometimes made from precious metal, although it can also be made from glass. An elegant object, the chalice will usually be beautifully decorated with elaborate designs – which may have magical significance – or jewels and gemstones.

Charcoal

Charcoal is a component of incense and oil burning. Nowadays, the best charcoal is usually found in compressed small discs of about 3 cm (1 inch). These give a burning time of approximately 45 minutes.

Compass

While this may seem a somewhat unusual tool, many spells, rituals and techniques require that you honour or face certain directions or compass points in their performance. It is also necessary to know the correct alignment in Feng Shui. Much the easiest way to work out the directions is by using a compass. It does not need to be particularly decorative, ornate or expensive, merely one with which you are happy to work.

Incense and Oil Burner

The choice of this tool must be a personal matter. An incense burner should give plenty of room to allow the aromas and smoke to disperse properly. Traditional material such as brass or clay may be used. The best shape is slightly flat rather than too concave. Oil burners should be of a sufficient size to allow

a long enough time to complete your spell. Burners which allow you to float the oil on water, which then evaporates, are probably the safest.

Paper

During spells you will often need to write your wishes or aims down and it is good to have some paper ready prepared. Parchment type is best, but heavier good quality is perfectly acceptable. You consecrate it by holding it for a short period in the smoke from your favourite incense.

Pen and Ink

Traditionally, quill pens were used for writing spells and incantations, but if you can't find a quill then use the best pen you can afford. Try to keep it especially for magical work and consecrate it by passing it carefully over the top of a candle or through incense. Also buy a good-quality ink and, if not already formulated for magical purposes, consecrate that in the same way. Neither pen nor ink should be used for other purposes.

Pentacle

The pentacle is a shallow dish, which is usually inscribed with a pentagram – a five-pointed star. It is used as a "power point" for consecrating other objects such as water or wine in a chalice, amulets and tools.

Pestle and Mortar

The pestle and mortar are so symbolic of the union of God and Goddess that they deserve a special mention within the use of magical tools. Mainly used to prepare herbal mixtures and incenses, they can also become part of your altar furniture when properly consecrated.

Scrying Tools

Scrying is the practice of using certain channelling tools, which should be consecrated before use – such as crystals, mirrors, colored water, runes and so forth – to try to gain an insight into external events. Any object can be used for scrying, though usually they are reflective, and they employ the arts of concentration and contemplation.

Staff

The staff is used very frequently by practitioners today, particularly if they are of the Druidic persuasion. Longer than the wand, it has the same attributes and uses. A staff is deliberately fashioned for the practitioner from wood taken from sacred trees, such as oak, hawthorn and hazelnut.

Wand

The wand should be no longer than the forearm and is often made from sacred wood. Since the wand is a very personal object, it should be chosen carefully and equally

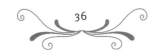

carefully attuned to your own energies. It cannot be used magically until it has been properly consecrated.

Obviously, you will not need to use all of your tools all of the time and you should develop for yourself some way of storing them, so that they retain their potency. You can do this by perhaps keeping them on your altar or in your sacred space. Use a specially dedicated box or other container or, if you know they are not likely to be interfered with, simply wrapped in black silk or velvet. Treat your tools with respect and they will serve you well.

COMPONENTS OF MAGICAL WORKING

Just as a recipe contains ingredients, so there are certain components that are needed in magical workings, in order to enhance the power and energy that is created. To the uninitiated some of these may seem strange, yet if we remember that much magic initially had to be performed with only what was immediately and easily available to the practitioner, the use of such items makes a great deal of sense. Candles, crystals, herbs and so on thus become an important part of modern-day spell-working.

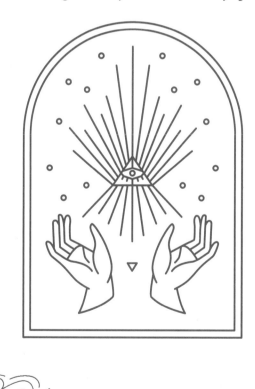

THE ELEMENTS

In most systems of magical working you will find mentioned the four (or sometimes five) Elements, often in conjunction with their directions or, as they are known in magic, quarters of the Universe or cardinal points. Together and separately, they are extremely powerful sources of energy and can give a tremendous boost to your spell-making.

The four Elements are energies, and manifestations of energy, that make up the entire Universe. They also influence our personalities and therefore what we do. Magical working calls to each Elemental kingdom and its ruler to protect each cardinal point and its properties. Each Element has an intrinsic power and is known for having certain qualities, natures, moods and magical purposes.

The four Elements are Earth, Air, Fire and Water and you may well find that you work best using one of them in particular. People drawn to candle magic, for instance, are using mainly the Element of Fire, while those who work with incense are using Air with a fair smattering of Earth in the herbs and resins. Oils used in baths for spell-work are using the Element of Water and Earth.

The fifth Element is that of Spirit which is the "binding principle" behind everything. Sometimes known as Aether, it is, on the whole, intangible, yet is that which makes everything happen. You are both its representative and its channel, so in magical working you have a responsibility to act wisely and well.

EARTH

Traditionally the direction of this Element is North and the color normally associated with Earth is green. It is represented on the altar usually by salt or sand. Crystals, because they are totally natural substances, can also be used.

When invoking Earth and the powers of the North, you are looking for recovery and healing and perhaps trying to find answers to questions. These powers deal with gaining knowledge, blessing, creating and shielding. When working within a magical circle, this is the first corner or quarter on which you call for protection.

The principal nature spirits of the Earth are called gnomes. They are said to live underground and guard the Earth's treasures. Other groups within the Earth's nature spirits ruled by the god Pan are brownies, dryads, earth spirits, elves and satyrs.

AIR

The direction of this Element is East and the color usually associated with it is yellow. Incense is often used to represent Air, since the movement of the air can be seen in the incense smoke.

When you are looking for inspiration, need new ideas or perhaps to break free from the past or undesired situations, you would use this Element. The quality associated with it is that of thinking or the use of the intellect. When working in a magical circle, Air is the second quarter on which you call for protection.

The sylphs are the Air spirits; their element has the most subtle energy of the four. They are said to live on the tops of mountains and are volatile and changeable. They are usually perceived with wings and look like cherubs or fairies. One of their main spiritual tasks is said to be to help humans receive inspiration.

FIRE

Fire is the Element of the South and is usually represented by a candle or a cauldron with a fire inside. Its color is red and its associations are to do with power, determination and passionate energy.

You would call upon this Element for protection from evil forces, cleansing and creativity. The quality associated with Fire is "doing" and it is a male principle. It is the third quarter or cardinal point on which you call for protection when working in a magical circle.

Without salamanders, the spirit of fire, it is said that physical fire cannot exist. They have been seen as sparks or small balls of light, but most often they are perceived as being lizard-like in shape and about a foot or more in length. They are considered the strongest and most powerful of all the elementals. As nature spirits they are greatly affected by the way that mankind thinks.

WATER

Water is the Element of the West and is represented by a bowl of water or a goblet of wine or fruit juice. Its color is blue and, because it represents the giving of life, is associated with the elements of sea, rain, snow and rivers.

When you need cleansing, revitalizing, the removal of curses or hexes or change of any sort, you will call upon Water. It is to do with emotions, right through from the most basic passions to the most elevated forms of belief. It is predominantly feminine. It is the fourth and final quarter that you invoke in any magical circle.

The undines are the elemental beings connected with Water and are beautiful and very graceful. The nymph is frequently found in a fountain and the mythical mermaid belongs to the ocean. Some undines inhabit waterfalls, others live in rivers and lakes. Sometimes smaller undines are often seen as winged beings that people have mistakenly called fairies.

SPIRIT

When you feel you are sufficiently adept at using the other Elements, you may begin to use Spirit – the fifth Element. This has no special space but is everywhere. It should never ever be used negatively because, particularly when you are weak and tired, it can rebound on you.

You may well find that you instinctively link strongly with the Life Force as Spirit, in which case you are probably succeeding in bringing all the Elements together within yourself. There is no particular color associated with Spirit – perception is all-important. If you choose to represent Spirit on the altar, you may do so however you wish. You are free to use your intuition, but you must have a very strong awareness of your reason for choosing that particular symbol and your connection with it.

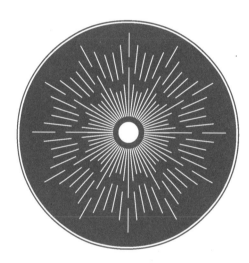

DIFFERENT TYPES OF SPELL-WORKING

ELEMENTAL

In this particular type of magic, the Elements of Fire, Earth, Air and Water are given their own directional focus to create added power and give extra energy to your spells. You will no doubt find that you tend to favour one particular direction but should be able to use all of them.

COLOR

Perhaps the simplest form of magic is that which involves color. This method of working is also used in conjunction with various other forms of magic.

Color can enhance, alter and completely change moods and emotions and therefore can be used to represent our chosen goal. At its simplest it can be used alone and can be used in dressing an altar. We give some color correspondences on pages 48-49.

HERBAL

Herbal magic is often used alongside many other forms of magic. Used as talismans and amulets – for example in a pouch or bag – herbs become protective; the oil from herbs can also be used in candle magic. There are many different types of herbs available for use in this way. Each herb has its own specific use, but frequently is used along with many other herbs and oils to produce a desired result.

CANDLE

In candle magic, humans discovered the ability to control light and this is one of the oldest forms of magic as well as one of the most simple. Using candles to symbolize ourselves and our beliefs means that we have access to a power beyond ourselves. Candle magic also forms an effective back-up for most other forms of magical working.

CRYSTAL

Every stone or gem has its own attributes which can be used in magic. Crystals are used extensively in healing because of the vibrational impact they can have. Because of this, they lend themselves to the enhancement of any spell-making or magical

working. Even ordinary stones have their own power and can be used as repositories for all sorts of energies and powers.

KNOT

Knot magic works partly with the principle of binding, which is a type of bidding spell and also with that of weaving, which was traditionally a female intuitive occupation. It utilizes ribbon, rope, string, yarn, or anything that can be knotted or plaited to signify our aspiration. It is a type of representational magic, and is used in conjunction with many of the other forms. The techniques of color, form and use of energies are all used here.

REPRESENTATIONAL

Representational magic involves using an object that represents something or someone for whom you are working the spell. It helps in concentrating the energy and visualizing the desire and the end result. Representational objects should never be used for negative purposes.

SYMBOLIC

In this system different symbols, rather than objects, are used to represent various ideas, people or goals. These symbols can be personal to you or such things as Tarot cards, Runes, Hebrew letters or numerology. You will often use symbolic magic in your magical workings and will soon develop your own preferred symbols.

TALISMANS, AMULETS AND CHARMS

These devices use all the other forms of magic in their formation, but principally representational and symbolic magic. They are "charged" (given power) magically and usually are worn or carried on the person for protection or good luck. Many are worn around the neck, perhaps as jewellery, or carried in a pouch and incorporate crystals, herbs or other magical objects.

There are many types of each of these objects and you will gradually learn to differentiate between them.

CANDLES

Candles should be chosen carefully with regard to type, and color, depending on the purpose of the spell. It is often better to use your intuition when choosing the type of candle, although for ease of reference, below is a list of the principal types. There are other types available, but these are the most suitable for magical working.

Table

The most readily available candle, they are ideal for many of the spells in this book. They usually burn for six to eight hours and need to be properly seated in suitable candlesticks. All colors can be used, but they should not be dipped, except in exceptional circumstances, and should be of the best quality possible.

It is sensible to keep a ready supply of these at hand.

Pillar

This is a free-standing candle. It is usually in the form of a simple pillar, although it can sometimes be made in other shapes which can be used as part of the spell, for example heart shapes for love spells. This type of candle is best burned on a flat holder since it usually takes some time to burn out.

Taper

These candles are tall and thin and need a particularly stable candle-holder. They are either made in a mould, or by the traditional method of dipping a length of wick into hot molten white or colored wax. For magical purposes they should be colored all the way through. They can often be used when a quick result is required. Because they are quite fragile, you need to be careful not to break them when anointing them.

Tea lights

These small candles are excellent for use when a candle must be left to burn out, but are less easy to anoint with essential oils. Poured in small metal pots like small votives, they are normally used in oil burners or specially-made tea-light holders. Depending on their size, they usually burn for approximately four hours.

Votive

This type of candle is specially designed as an offering, to carry prayers to whichever deity you honour. As the wax melts, the holder, which is made of glass, can become hot so some care must be taken when using them. They are designed to be long-burning, usually between one and seven days.

CHOOSING YOUR CANDLES

There are several things you need to remember when choosing a candle:

1. Choose your candle type as above.

2. Candles used for magic should always be virgin (unused) at the start of the working, unless you have deliberately cleared them of past influences. Using candles that have been previously lit can have a detrimental effect on your spell. They may have picked up influences from previous use.

3. Charge your candle before using it. This can be done by anointing it with oils associated with the magic you intend on performing, or by simply touching it and filling it with your own energy.

4. The oils used in the anointing of your candle should, where possible, always be natural fragrances. While charging the candle, smooth from top to bottom when drawing energy toward you, bottom to top

when sending energy outwards. Particularly when anointing candles for altar use, anoint from the middle to the top and from the middle to the bottom to signify the union of spiritual and physical realms.

5. If you enjoy craftwork, it is a very good idea to make your own candles for magical use. It is a whole art in itself – you infuse your candles with your own energy and thus increase the magical potency of the candle many times over. It is relatively easy to make your own candles: simply heat the wax until it is liquid and pour into a mould which is threaded with a wick. The wax should now be left to cool, after which the mould can be removed. Oils and colors can be added for extra potency.

DRESSING AND CHARGING CANDLES

Dressing (anointing) and charging candles are perhaps candle magic in its simplest form. Dressing a candle performs two functions. By anointing it with oil you ensure that it burns safely and you also have the opportunity to infuse it with the required vibration for your working. Charging a candle ensures you fix the intent of your magical working and also dedicates the candle to its purpose.

DRESSING CANDLES

Any oil can be used for dressing a candle but initially it is best to use either your favourite essential oil, such as frankincense, or perhaps an oil infused with a suitable herb appropriate to the task in hand. A list of oils suitable for various purposes is given on pages 104–6.

There are various ways to dress a candle but what is important is the direction in which you anoint it. If you remember that working from the top down draws in power from spiritual sources, and working from the bottom up draws in energy from the earth, it is very easy to work correctly for your purpose. Never rub the candle with a back and forth movement, as you will end up with a confusion of energies – not to say a sputtering candle.

You will need
- Candle
- Oil

Method
Sit quietly and, holding the candle, think carefully about your intent. If you have learned to meditate, then enter a meditative state and allow the energies to build up within you.

To bring something to you, rub oil on the candle in a downward motion from the top to the middle and then from the bottom to the middle.

To send something away from you, you rub the oil from the middle of the candle out to the ends.

Continue with either movement until you have a sense that you have done enough. If you have any oil left on your hands either rub your hands together until the oil is absorbed or dab the remaining oil from your fingers onto the centre of your forehead, which is the Third Eye and the seat of vision. Then say the following or something similar:

I cleanse and consecrate this candle
(in the name of your chosen deity of you
choose to use one).

May it burn with strength in the service
of the Greater Good.

Your candle is now ready for use.

Charging Candles

This is a quick, uncomplicated method of more fully charging a candle. This method can be used without having to set up your altar completely. It can equally be used to charge your altar candles.

You will need

- A candle or candles of the appropriate color (if preferred, mark them with appropriate symbols)
- A candle holder
- Matches rather than a lighter

Method

Hold the candle in your "power hand" (the hand you consider you give out energy with).

Open the other hand and turn that palm towards the sky.

Breathe deeply and visualize your goal.

Now perceive whatever you think of as Universal Energy flowing through the palm that is turned skyward, filling your body.

Visualise that Universal Energy mixing within you with the energy of your intention.

Now allow that mixed energy to flow into the candle.

Be conscious of the energy as it builds up.

Feel the energy streaming into the candle.

Fill it from bottom to top as though the candle were an empty vessel.

If you are comfortable with doing so, speak your intention out loud.

As you place the candle in its holder, stabilize the thought within the candle so that it will be converted into pure clear intent.

Strike a match above the candle.

Draw down the flame toward the candle, lighting the wick.

Extinguish the match flame, but do not blow it out in case you blow out the candle.

Stay with the candle for a few moments visualizing your intention, feeling its energy moving into the universe.

Leave the area and let the candle burn right down as it does its work.

Candle color and the symbols inscribed on them create additional power. As you become more proficient, you will find yourself using

certain colors and symbols more often. Try not to be too rigid, and always be open to widening your focus.

CANDLE COLORS

Many different colors are used in candle magic and below are listed the most common ones, along with their key associations and purposes. You may not wish to use black candles because of their pop-cultural association with Satanic magic. If so, dark grey is a good substitute. White candles can be used as a substitute if your chosen color is not available.

White
- The Goddess
- Higher Self
- Purity
- Peace

Black
- Binding
- Shape shifting
- Protection
- Repels negativity

Brown
- Special favours
- To influence friendships
- Healing earth energies

Orange
- General success

- Property deals
- Legal matters
- Justice
- Selling

Purple
- Third eye
- Psychic ability
- Hidden knowledge
- To influence people in high places
- Spiritual power

Blue
- The Element of Water
- Wisdom
- Protection
- Calm
- Good fortune
- Opening communication
- Spiritual inspiration

Pink
- Affection
- Romance
- Caring
- Nurturing
- Care for the planet Earth

Green
- The Element of Earth
- Physical healing
- Monetary success
- Mother Earth
- Tree and plant magic

- Growth
- Personal goals

Red
- The Element of Fire
- Passion
- Strength
- Fast action
- Career goals
- Lust
- Driving force
- Survival

Silver
- The Moon Goddess
- Astral energy
- Female power
- Telepathy
- Clairvoyance
- Intuition
- Dreams

Copper
- Professional growth
- Business productivity
- Career manoeuvres
- Passion
- Money goals

Gold
- The Sun God
- Promote winning
- Male power
- Happiness

Yellow
- The Element of Air
- Intelligence
- The Sun
- Memory
- Imagination supported by logic
- Accelerating learning
- Clearing mental blocks

SIGNS FROM CANDLE-BURNING

Not every magical practitioner takes heed of the manner in which spell-casting or ritual candles burn; there is often a great deal to be learnt from understanding a little bit more about how to interpret the way a candle burns.

It is worth remembering that some candles are simply poorly made and will burn badly no matter what you do with them. If the wick is the wrong size, for instance, the candle may be of no use for magical work. It is nice to make one's own candles, although there is quite an art to it and the novice may end up feeling rather frustrated, if the intention behind the candle is not quite right.

External factors can also play a huge part in how candles burn. The way the candle is placed in the holder, the temperature in the surrounding area, an open window causing a draught, and other such things can all make a difference. Equally, the candle can be affected by your own mood and really until you have learned how to meditate using a

candle flame you need not worry too much to begin with. All that having been said, here are some of the things to watch for when burning candles.

THE CANDLE GIVES A CLEAN, EVEN BURN This might be called a successful burn and suggests the spell will most likely achieve the right result. If a glass-encased candle burns and leaves no marks on the glass that is best. If a free-standing candle leaves little or no residue, this is by far the best result.

THE FLAME FLARES, DIPS, GUTTERS, REPEATEDLY Check first for draughts and then decide intuitively whether there is a pattern to the flaring and guttering. If you are performing the spell with someone in mind, you may feel the recipient of your spell is trying to block your efforts. Sit quietly for a while until you feel you have grasped the significance of the pattern, which may be because the spell itself is not right for the time. In this case simply be prepared to try again another time.

A FREE-STANDING CANDLE RUNS AND MELTS A LOT WHILE BURNING This gives you an opportunity to observe the flow of wax for signs. Quickly melting wax shows there is a good deal of positivity available. If one side burns quicker than the other, a balance can sometimes be achieved by

turning the candle round and it is useful to note how many times you do this, since this can indicate the number of adjustments the person may have to make to ensure success. Other people prefer to let nature take its course and to watch the wax run for signs, without interfering in its movements.

A FREE-STANDING CANDLE BURNS DOWN TO A PUDDLE OF WAX OR SETS IN RUNS DOWN THE SIDE OF THE CANDLE When this happens, most workers will examine the shape of the wax for a sign. For instance, a heart-shaped wax puddle is a good sign if you are burning a red candle for a love spell. You may see something of importance there, for the shape of the run may suggest an outcome regarding the matter at hand. Wax puddles come in all kinds of shapes; most candle-workers look for symbols in the wax, or sometimes use numerology or other divination techniques similar to teacup reading, to discover the meaning of a shape.

A GLASS-ENCASED CANDLE BURNS CLEAN TO BEGIN WITH BUT "DIRTY" WITH A GREAT DEAL OF SMOKE LATER This indicates that things will go well to begin with, but there are other conditions that have not yet revealed themselves and will need to be resolved. Someone may be working against the required outcome, so the correct timing and correspondences of further spells are crucial. Information on

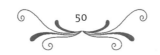

timings and correspondences can be found on pages 140-5.

A FREE-STANDING CANDLE LETS OUT A LOT OF SMOKE BUT BURNS CLEAN AT THE END Difficult conditions need to be dealt with first of all but eventually conditions improve.

THERE IS A DIRTY, BLACK BURN (ESPECIALLY ONE THAT DEPOSITS SOOT ON A GLASS-ENCASED CANDLE) This means things are not going to go well – the spell may not work, the blessing may fail, the person is in deeper stress or trouble than you first thought. There is a great deal of negativity around. Sometimes it is good to change the focus of the candle and ask that it be used to burn off the negativity, which will enable you to get a handle on the situation.

THE CANDLE GOES OUT BEFORE COMPLETELY BURNING This can mean that the spell you are using is not the most appropriate one and you need to use stronger means than you first employed. It can also mean that someone is actively working against you. In this case it is wise to go back to the beginning and start your spell over.

THE CANDLE TIPS OVER AND FLAMES UP INTO A POTENTIAL FIRE HAZARD Provided that you know you have placed the candles properly, this indicates there is

danger about for you or the person you are casting for. You should clear your sacred space and cleanse it by whatever means you prefer. It is probably wise to wait a while before retrying the spell and remember to take a ritual bath (see page 106) before you do.

THE CANDLE BURNS TOO QUICKLY Generally a fast burn is good, but an overly fast burn means that, although the work will go well, its effect will not last long. Again, you might wait before retrying the spell, though sometimes a fast result is required. You should use your own judgement.

Disposal of candle wax

In European-American traditions, many people bury candle wax and other remains after a spell is cast. Burial toward the appropriate quarter of the compass is considered a thoughtful way to go about this. Some Neo-Pagans dispose of ritual or spell remains in a bonfire or fireplace.

CRYSTALS

There are many crystals that can be used in magical workings and as you become more practised in spell-making, and more interested in their various attributes, you will discover for yourself that certain crystals resonate for you more than others.

Crystals are such a fundamental part of spell-working, with so many levels of awareness inherent in them, that it is well worth taking the time to learn as much as you can about them, in order that you can use them in whatever way is appropriate for you. You might, for instance, like to place a large crystal of, say, rock quartz on your altar as representative of the Earth Element and all its power and goodness. On the other hand, you may wish to wear a "charged" crystal (a crystal that has had extra energy added to it) to protect you.

Using techniques for "finding" crystals and being open to them "finding" you, are the best ways of obtaining the crystals you need. Because our lives are so busy, many of us will come into contact with crystals only as gifts or in a commercial environment. You may acquire them by various methods, for example buying them, receiving them as gifts, or very occasionally unearthing them.

One relatively common way of "finding" the best crystal for you is by using the "first recognition" method.
• Stand in front of a group of crystals.

• Close your eyes.
• Open your eyes quickly and pick up the first crystal you see or the one that attracts you in any way.
• When holding a particular crystal or running your hand over it, you may find that your hands tingle or you have some other physical reaction. This usually means it is for you.
• At other times you may feel drawn to a particular crystal without knowing why. The crystal may not necessarily be for you, and could be for somebody else or a purpose not yet specified.
If you are choosing a crystal for a specific purpose (meditation, healing, and so forth), hold that purpose in mind as you choose. Usually you will sense an energy "reaction" from a particular crystal, perhaps in the form of a tingling sensation, heat or a flash of light.

Cleansing a crystal

When you acquire a new crystal, you should first of all cleanse it and then dedicate it for the purpose intended. This can be done simply by holding the crystal while consciously thinking that it will be used only for good, or during a meditation. You could also call upon your deities, if you wish, using your own ritual.

There are many different ways of cleansing crystals. Below are several of the more practical approaches.

• Take the crystal to the sea, clean it thoroughly in the sea water, and allow the water to wash over it for several minutes. The crystal should then be left in the sun or in moonlight, whichever pleases you most, where it can "energize".

• If you cannot use sea water, soak the crystal in salt water for anything from one to seven days – you will know instinctively how long is needed. Use the proportions of approximately three tablespoons of salt to a cup of water (the water must fully cover the stones), put the salt water in a glass container with the crystals and leave in a sunny or moonlit place.

• Bury the crystal in commercial sea salt for at least seven and up to 24 hours (overnight is good), then rinse it with pure water and "energize" it in the sun as before. *Note:* Salt or abrasive substances may impair the surface of your crystal; this will not affect the properties of the crystal, but is aesthetically not very pleasing.

• If you have a sacred space out in the open, bury the crystals for 24 hours, and as you bury them ask that they may be cleansed ready for your work. Don't forget to mark the spot where they are buried – it is very easy to lose them!

• Smudge the crystal thoroughly with, for example, a sage smudge stick or favourite incense. That is, allow the crystal to be engulfed in the smoke until such time as it feels clear.

• Clean the crystal in flowing spring, lake, river or tap water and then energize it by leaving it in the sun. It is important to think of the crystal being cleansed by the movement of the water.

Programming a crystal

Crystals are prepared for programming by charging them. Programming a crystal aligns the energy of the crystal to the intent. Using a carefully thought-out affirmation and directing this to the centre of the crystal is sufficient to programme it. Below are three of the most common ways of programming.

• Place the crystal on a large crystal cluster dedicated to the specific purpose for which it is required.

• Place the crystal in the centre of a circle of other crystals whose ends are pointing towards the centre and the new crystal.

• Put the crystal in sun and/or moonlight, stating the specific intent connected with the crystal. Many people believe that the days relating to the summer and winter solstices, the Full and the New Moon, and the vernal and autumnal equinox are more heavily charged than other days.

Magical crystals and stones

To get you started in your use of crystals and gemstones, there is a list below of those that you are most likely to use in your workings. To make it easy, they are categorized according to their planetary

influence. The correspondences here are for the seven planets used by the Ancients. This astrological classification has the idea of crystals being captured light or energy, and the knowledge that the power of the planets can be harnessed by this method, is a powerful aid in spell-making.

The Sun

The Sun is generally associated with strength, determination, vitality and self-expression. It also relates to the arts, banking, corporate bodies, fame, fatherhood, government office, health, honour and esteem, influence, leadership, nobility, organization, public acclaim, rulership and teaching.

AVENTURINE promotes health, vigour and cheerfulness; it promises emotional moral support in new commercial undertakings; gets rid of doubt, diminishes anxiety and eases bodily aches and pains; strengthens resolve against hardship.

CITRINE is linked with boldness, courage, mastery; it promises victory over sporting, business or romantic rivalry; wards off infections and any unwanted attention; prevents accident or injury, especially on journeys; draws wealth and prosperity.

DIAMOND heightens awareness, encourages enterprise and strengthens resolve; it brings personal progression and acclaim;

affords relief from mental or emotional stress, confounds enmity and protects from physical dangers.

HELIODOR gives the advantage to speculators, gamblers and sportsmen; promotes prosperity and happiness; prevents deception and disillusionment; lifts depression and helps the body recover and recuperate.

TOPAZ bestows courage, determination, desire, confidence and judgment; promises health and joy and prosperity; improves physical fitness and raises the spirits; overcomes envy and malice.

TOURMALINE brightens up the imagination and sharpens the intellect; promotes harmony and brings financial reward; defends the home from theft; improves vision, relieves tension and anxiety; lifts depression.

ZIRCON energizes the body and will; heightens awareness and sharpens the intellect; brings rich rewards; overcomes obstacles and opposition; strengthens the constitution; safeguards and protects travellers and property.

The Moon

The Moon generally rules over domesticity, emotional responses, fluidity, inspiration,

instinct and sensitivity. It also rules over feeling and rhythm. It relates to antiques, commitment, inevitability, introspection, isolation, karma, maturity, mining, morality, property management, social welfare and tenacity in life.

CHALCEDONY attracts public favour, recognition and financial reward; increases popularity, enthusiasm and fitness; dispels gloom, despondency, envy or anger; affords protection to travellers and helps support nursing mothers.

FELDSPAR (also felspar) strengthens bonds of affection and promotes marital happiness; it is associated with fertility; mitigates quarrels and poor situations; protects from sunstrokes, headaches and nosebleeds.

FLINT expands consciousness and prompts prophetic dreams; improves memory and heightens intellectual capacity. It also helps ward off physical danger, dispels melancholy and aids union between children and parents.

GYPSUM signifies hope and youthfulness, and benefits children and adults wanting to "go it alone". It reduces swellings and aids digestion; averts the envy of others; and brings peace of mind.

LABRADORITE brings prophetic visions and expands consciousness; promotes harmonious relationships; dispels anxiety, enmity and strife; gives relief from various nervous disorders.

MAGNESITE clarifies vision, both literally and figuratively; improves profitability and wins admiration and respect; provides freedom from adversity; aids digestion and releases emotional stress.

MOONSTONE affords vitality and fertility; awards success to artistic and creative efforts and new commercial projects; heals relationship rifts; protects crops; aids digestion and concentration.

MORGANITE induces love, devotion and friendship; promises career advancement or improved financial viability; reconciles difference of opinion and dispels anger; offers safety to travellers in any dimension.

PEARL rewards charitable deeds and selfless actions with love and respect; promotes harmony and understanding; protects those traveling over water; eases muscular tension and lifts depression.

PUMICE is linked with purity, vision, truth and development. It helps sociability and personal gain; bestows success on long-term ventures; guards against illusion and delusion; brings comfort to a troubled mind or spirit.

ROCK CRYSTAL represents purity, hope and chastity; expands conscious awareness and prophetic visions; brings trust and harmony; dispels bad dreams, delusion and illusion; safeguards the very young and astral travellers from harm.

Mercury

Mercury rules communication, healing, hyperactivity, the intellect, shrewdness and versatility. It relates to accountancy, curiosity, impressionism, invention, land or air travel, language, learning, mathematics, the media, public speaking, publishing of all types, vehicles and wit.

AGATE promotes good health and fortune; increases physical stamina and brings benefits through wills or legacies; repels anger, mistrust and enmity; affords protection against rumour and gossip.

CHRYSOPRASE brings joy to the wearer; sharpens the intellect, opens up new areas and rewards initiative; gets rid of envy, jealousy and complacency; dispels anxiety, lifts depression and helps insomnia.

ONYX looks after business shrewdness; vitalizes the imagination and increases stamina; dispels nightmares and eases tension; brings emotional and mental relief.

SARDONYX inspires love, romance and vitality; helps confidence and fitness; ensures a result in contractual difficulties; wards off infectious disease; improves vision; heals fragile relationships.

SERPENTINE attracts respect and admiration; sharpens the intellect; rewards innovation and creativity; offers the wearer protection from hostility, jealousy or rivalry; improves the effect of medicine.

TIGER'S EYE defeats the opponent and ensures victory in any competitive situation; commands love and loyalty; offers protection from treachery and deception; strengthens the body's immune system.

Venus

Venus correlates to harmony, growth and development as well as love and marriage. It also extends to aesthetics, the affections, dance and music, fashion, femininity, materialism, personal finances, pleasure, relationships, sexuality and union.

ALMANDINE is linked with achievement, improvement, self-confidence and determination. It enhances psychic ability; makes clear existing problems or difficulties; overcomes rivalry and obstacles in the form of human behaviour.

AQUAMARINE encourages hope, and promotes youthfulness and physical fitness.

It is a powerful token of love and friendship; eases digestive or nervous disorders and mental distress; renews confidence and energy; relaxes fear.

AZURITE commands social success and friendship as well as constancy in love; improves vision, both physically and psychically; protects from deceit and disillusion; affords help to those faced with generative difficulties.

BERYL represents hope, friendship, and domestic harmony; sharpens the intellect and favours new commercial projects; clarifies and resolves problems; reduces susceptibility to deception or disillusionment.

CAT'S EYE encourages success in speculative ventures or competitive sport; strengthens ties of love or affection; protects the home from danger; brings relief to those with respiratory problems.

CORAL helps vitality, good humour and harmonious relationships; expands horizons and helps encourage development; prevents damage to crops and property; protects travellers, mariners and small children.

EMERALD favours love and lovers, promising constancy and fidelity; inspires confidence and emotional fulfillment; strongly protective, especially against deceit or delusions; ensures safety of travellers and expectant mothers.

JADE promotes good health and good situations; favours artistic and musical endeavours; dulls pain and helps soundness of sleep; also improves a poor memory; and is strongly protective.

LAPIS LAZULI inspires confidence, courage and friendship. It helps the wearer to succeed, anywhere; averts danger and preserves travellers and expectant mothers from harm; eases circulation problems.

MALACHITE wins favourable judgements in lawsuits or actions; enhances social standing and increases prosperity; lifts depression, induces sound sleep and serenity; affords protection against infection.

OPAL signifies fidelity and friendship; highlights psychic and prophetic talents; stimulates memory and intellect; and improves vision, digestion and resistance to stress. It also safeguards property against intruders and theft.

ROSE QUARTZ enhances psychic awareness and creative talents; sharpens intellect; preserves the home and family; heals rifts; brings peace of mind and understanding.

TURQUOISE inspires health, wealth and

happiness; affords a successful conclusion to any constructive enterprise; counteracts negative influences; wards off harmful psychic or physical harm.

Mars

Mars symbolizes competition and confrontation, determination, focus and masculinity. It is also related to an adventurous spirit, the armed forces, courage, engineering, the fire service, forcefulness, male sexuality, metalwork, speed of reactions and sports.

BAUXITE enlivens the personality and strengthens the will to succeed; it encourages wise investment and fruitful speculation; lifts flagging spirits and speeds recovery from illness; negates strife and reconciles parted lovers.

BLOODSTONE promotes eloquence, trust, loyalty, and devotion; boosts courage, vitality and the ability to earn money; heals discord; relieves digestive orders or stress and strengthens recuperative powers.

CARBUNCLE increases energy, determination and confidence; boosts income and social standing; maintains physical fitness and fights infection; reconciles differences between friends.

HAEMATITE promotes successful legal action and official contracts; increases sexual drive and fitness; helps overcome anxiety and irritability; improves circulation.

JASPER helps in psychic development; inspires confidence, friendship and loyalty; defends home and family; inhibits pregnancy.

MAGNETITE prompts respect of others, loyalty and devotion; increases stamina and virility; promises success and happiness; brings relief from stressful situations; helps speed recovery from illness or depression.

RUBY highlights vitality and virility, bringing pleasure and prosperity; it is good for property development; protects crops and offers security to descendants; dispels strife and dissent.

Jupiter

Jupiter covers charity, majesty, mental and physical searching, might and wisdom. It also covers friendships, good judgement, knowledge and understanding, legal matters, philosophy, theosophy, traveling abroad and any other long journeys.

ALEXANDRITE refreshes the body and mind, and brings hidden talents to the fore. It is strongly protective especially against deceit or treachery; it awards relief from imaginary fears or phobias.

BLUE JOHN attracts honours, wealth,

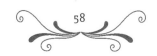

prestige and social success; improves business and personal relationships; guards the wearer against injury or accident while traveling; mitigates the envy of others.

CALOMINE favours visionary and human undertakings; affords success to joint ventures, especially overseas; deflates skin and fever irritation; dispels parental anxiety and helps with uneasy consciences.

CARNELIAN helps with peace, pleasure and prosperity; brings joy to those going on a long journey or moving house; offers protection to travellers, speakers and expectant mothers; assuages strife, anger and disappointment.

OBSIDIAN encourages boldness, determination and vigour; overwhelms opposition and promotes personal achievement; is strongly protective against psychic attack, accident or injury; and strengthens weakened spirits or tiredness of the body.

SAPPHIRE affords good health, strength and efficiency; heightens perception and rewards commercial and social efforts; is strongly protective against antagonism and malice; effects reconciliation between lovers.

SPINEL enhances speculative powers and creativity. It rewards efforts made towards financial prosperity and social prestige;

guards against psychic attack, mental stress and emotional blackmail; ensures safety and protection for travellers.

Saturn

Saturn signifies concentration, conversation, destiny, experience and perseverance. It relates to agriculture, antiques, career status, economy, karma, isolation, tenacity, maturity, mining, morality and social welfare.

ALABASTER brings success in litigation, official and contractual disputes, and wins respect, recognition and reward. It heals rifts; offers protection against loss of status; and inhibits disease.

ALUNITE attracts good fortune, health and happiness; helps understanding and domestic harmony; speeds recovery from illness; protects home and property against physical and psychic danger.

BORAX inspires confidence, perseverance and determination; it helps to make bad situations good; overcomes fear, hesitation and self doubt; improves circulation and offers relief from migraine, indigestion and/or gout.

GARNET helps with devotion, humour and loyalty; increases drive and determination and physical fitness; wards off thunder and lightning and protects travellers from injury or contagious disease.

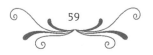

GRANITE wins friendship and fortune; helps with confidence, particularly in the area of examination sitting or employment; eases depression; resolves conflict and helps find practical solutions to current problems.

JET strengthens determination and focus; affords success to those heading into business; eases childbirth and dispels fever; offers protection against gossip and other harmful actions.

MARBLE improves financial position and status in the community; commands respect and admiration; relieves headaches, and stress; preserves home and property from fire, flood and storms.

MEERSCHAUM benefits philanthropic ventures and investment; favours those working in big organizations; clarifies problems and provides practical solutions; relieves anxiety, depression and nervousness.

SCHEELITE highlights diplomacy, business acumen and self-assurance; promises commercial and domestic happiness; alleviates strife and envy; is handy for nervous disorders and nursing mothers.

SULPHUR highlights clear expression and physical fitness; rewards professional acumen with public acclaim; is powerful against malice; purifies the blood and relieves menstrual tension.

Crystals can have many uses and the spell below uses their power to enhance a healing technique. When you eventually know your planetary correspondences well, you can use the above crystals for many purposes.

A Crystal Healing Spell

This spell is used in this instance to charge (energize) water for healing. You can drink the water or juice, or use the former in your bath. By using planetary significances, you can see how many aspects of your magical working might be enhanced.

You will need

• A crystal appropriate for your needs (in this case it would be for healing, although if you use the crystal for another purpose, you would obviously choose an appropriate crystal for that use)
• A glass of water or fruit juice

Method

Place the crystal in the glass of water or juice overnight, or for 24 hours if you want a balance of solar and lunar energies. After removing the crystal, drink the water or juice and visualize its energy flowing through you. You can use the crystal again for the same purpose at another time.

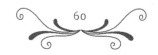

I dedicate this bath to the healing of [state difficulty]

Since in this case the crystal has been used in liquid, you may need to recharge it, in which case bury it in earth in a safe place until you need it again. This technique uses the power of the crystal, but in returning it to the earth you are acknowledging the power of Mother Earth, as well as the Elements.

One way of using crystals is to keep an assortment of small ones in a special talisman bag. The simplest method of use is to shake the bag, and while focusing on the question to be asked, take out the first two or three that you touch. See if the answer comes spontaneously to mind, before you consult the lists above for correspondences.

You can also cast your crystals into a specially drawn circle, the first crystal drawn being the crystal of Self, the second the crystal of others and the third being the crystal of happiness to come. Boards on to which crystals are thrown are available from specialist shops and have proved useful for many people. More complex questions can be answered and guidance for the future gained by using crystals with any suitable Tarot spread.

The associations of some of the more common crystals are shown on the table over the page.

Agate	Success in worldly matters
Amethyst	Shifts in consciousness and life changes
Black agate	Prosperity and courage
Red agate	Longevity and good health
Aventurine	Growth and expansion
Blue lace agate	A need for healing
Citrine	Wisdom in celestial matters
Diamond	Permanence
Emerald	Fertility
Jade	Immortality and perfection
Red jasper	Worldly affairs
Lapis lazuli	Favoured by the divine
Clear quartz	Self-healing and love
Ruby	Passion and power
Sapphire	Chastity and truth
Snowflake obsidian	Closure of a challenging time
Tiger's eye	The need to look beneath the surface
White quartz	Change of a profound nature
Unakite	Integration and composure

Enhancing your magic

Crystals and stones are gifts from nature and as mentioned above can also be used to enhance your rituals and magic. They can become sacred, magical tools in their own right. When consecrating a circle, creating your sacred space or making a shrine, you may like to search out stones which can represent the Elements, so here are a few suggestions:

Air

When looking for stones to represent Air, you need to think of crystal-clear stones or yellowish-tinged ones. A quartz crystal point can often be picked up quite cheaply and, of course, it does not matter if it is flawed because, with a little imagination, these flaws can often look like clouds. Quartz pebbles are often found on the seashore, weathered by the water.

Fire

Stones to represent Fire should be red or orange or sometimes black. Any stone which has the feeling of passion or fiery emotion will do very well – carnelian or red jasper work particularly well. Volcanic rocks, or other very hard ones, often signify Fire since they are the outcome of fire from the earth.

Water

Blue or blue-green stones are good if you wish to represent Water and if you are near

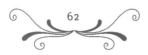

the sea you might find a piece of salt or sand-blasted glass, which is ideal. Although glass is man-made, nature has done its work. White or greyish pebble stones actually found in water are also very useful, while a piece of stone with seaweed attached is also good. Some agates are very pretty and can echo wave patterns.

Earth

The colors for Earth are green and brown, and many of the stones associated with Earth are green as well. All stones are the product of Earth so almost any stone will do, particularly if you have got to know it as suggested above. Use it wisely and it will always repay you. Remember that you do not need polished stones for this – the more natural they are the better.

Spirit

Most clear crystals can be used to represent the fifth Element of aether, or Spirit, as can the purple-hued ones. Amethyst is particularly good, as it is both a transmitter and a receiver of psychic and spiritual energy. Mostly, those stones which are capable of representing spirit will "speak" to you and if you choose more than one you will have to use your intuition so that you choose the right one for your purpose.

Preparing a crystal circle

If you wish to use stones and crystals when laying out your circle or sacred space, you can use a mixture of both. You might mark each quarter with a large stone, particularly if you are outside, and then place other appropriate stones on top. Even if you use candles to mark the four quarters of the circle, you could surround or circle each candle with any or all of the following gems, either rough or polished:

North:	moss agate, emerald, jet, olivine, salt, black tourmaline
East:	imperial topaz, citrine, mica, pumice
South:	amber, obsidian, rhodochrosite, ruby, lava, garnet
West:	aquamarine, chalcedony, jade, lapis lazuli, moonstone, sugilite

Over time, gather a number of appropriate stones together. Beginning and ending in the north, lay out 7, 9, 21 or 40 stones of any size to define your circle. (These are magical numbers and will enhance the power, so always bear in mind the purpose of your circle.) If you normally use ribbon or cord to mark out your circle, your stones can be placed either inside the cord or ribbon or in place of it.

If the magical working to be conducted within the circle is sending the power outwards, place any crystal with definite points facing outward. If the magic is of a

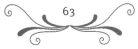

protective nature, place them with points facing inward. Use your good sense when constructing your circle. If it is outdoors, somewhere you use often and think of as your sacred space, you may wish to leave the larger stones in position and carry the smaller gems with you. This way, no matter where you are, you can mark out a circle with the small stones and have available the power and energy of the larger space available to you.

HERBS

Most magical practices make use of herbs in various ways, usually in rituals and other magical workings. Often, they are used as incense, when they are crushed and powdered, or as oils. Their properties mean that they create a type of force field that intensifies the vibration needed. Additionally, when the practitioner calls upon the power of the gods and spirits, the herbs can become even more effective.

Simply having particular herbs in your sacred space or having them about your person is sufficient to begin the process of enhancing the area or your personal vibration. You can use them in incense and dedicate them to the appropriate Elements and deities. Many of the herbs mentioned can be obtained from a good herbalist, though for those of you who are truly interested it would be worthwhile creating a small herb garden.

The uses of herbs
Protection

Such herbs guard against physical and psychic attacks, injury, accidents and such things as wicked spirits. They usually offer protection in a general sort of way.

Love

The vibration of these herbs is such that they can help you to meet new people, to overcome shyness and let others know that you are open to new relationships. They put out a particular vibration so that those who are interested will answer the call. The safest way to use them is to accept that several people may be attracted to you and you will then be able to make an informed choice.

Fidelity

Some herbs and plants can by tradition be used to ensure fidelity. You do have to have a firm belief that you have a right to another's devotion before imposing your will on them. Using a spell for fidelity amounts to a binding spell and you must make allowances for the person's own integrity. It should always be remembered that it is unwise, and sometimes unhelpful, to both parties to hold anyone in a relationship against their will.

Healing

Many herbs have healing properties, which can help from both a physical and a magical viewpoint. A practitioner working from

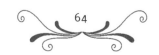

both points of view can be of tremendous help in managing illness. However, always remember to advise anyone you work with in this way to seek qualified medical assistance. Never allow yourself to be drawn into being a substitute for medical help.

Health

Not only the smell of herbs and plants but also their vibration can help to prevent illness and restore good health. So, if you are prone to illness, carry health herbs with you and make sure they are always as fresh as possible.

Luck

Luck is the knack of being in the right place at the right time and being able to act on instinct. Luck herbs help you create your own good fortune. Once you have such a foundation, you can build upon it.

Money

It is sometimes easier to visualize the outcome of having money – that is, what you are going to spend the money on – than visualizing actual money coming to you. Certain herbs create an environment in which things can happen. They enable the creation of the means to fulfil your needs – perhaps a gift, a pay rise or some such thing.

The A–Z of Magical Plants

ALOE is feminine and ruled by the Moon.

Its Element is Water. Its magical properties are protection, success and peace. Aloe has always been known for its healing qualities, for treating wounds and maintaining healthy skin. It also helps to combat a variety of bacteria that can commonly cause infections in skin wounds.

AMARANTH (cockscomb) is feminine and ruled by Saturn. Its Element is Fire. When used magically, it is said to repair a broken heart, so therefore would be useful in certain love spells and rituals. Formerly it was reputed to bestow invisibility.

ANGELICA is a masculine plant ruled by Venus. Its Element is Fire. It is particularly useful when dealing with protection and exorcism; the root can be carried as an amulet with the dried leaves being burnt during exorcism rituals.

ANISE is masculine and ruled by the Moon or Jupiter. Its Element is Air. Its magical properties are useful in protection and purification spells. It brings awareness and joy.

APPLE is feminine and ruled by Venus. Its Element is Water. It is used most effectively in the making of magical wands, in love spells and good luck charms.

ASH is masculine and ruled by the Sun. Its Element is Water. Its uses are protective and

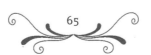

it is often chosen as a material for making brooms for cleansing and wands for healing. If the leaves are put underneath a pillow, they will help to induce intuitive dreams. The leaves also bring luck and good fortune when carried in a pocket or bag worn around the neck.

BALM OF GILEAD is feminine and ruled by Saturn. Its Element is Water. The buds are carried to ease a broken heart and can be added to love and protection charms and spells.

BASIL, one of the most masculine of plants, is ruled by Mars and has Fire as its Element. It is protective, good for love and is said to promote wealth and business success. It is also useful for healing relationships and for assuring genuineness in a partner.

BAY LAUREL is a masculine plant ruled by the Sun and the Element of Fire. It promotes wisdom and is also a protector, bringing to the fore the ability to develop psychic powers. It finds and forces out negative energy.

BENZOIN is a masculine plant that the Sun rules, along with the Element of Air. A good purifier and preservative, it is used widely in purification incenses.

BETONY is masculine and is ruled by Jupiter and the Element of Fire. Its

magical properties are protection and purification. It can be added to incense for this purpose or stuffed in a pillow to prevent nightmares.

CARAWAY is a masculine plant ruled by the planet of Mercury. Its Element is Air. Its magical properties are protection and passion. When added to love sachets and charms, it attracts a lover in the physical aspect.

CARNATION is masculine and is ruled by the Sun. Its Element is Fire. Traditionally, it was worn by witches for protection during times of persecution. It adds energy and power when used as an incense during a spell or ritual.

CATNIP is feminine and is ruled by Venus. Its Element is Water. Its magical properties are connected with cat magic, familiars, joy, friendship and love. As an incense it may be used to consecrate magical tools.

CAMOMILE is masculine, and is ruled by the Sun or Venus. Its Element is Water. Its magical properties show that it is good as a meditation incense, for centring and creating an atmosphere of peace. Sprinkle it in your home for protection, healing and money. Plant camomile in your garden to be the guardian of the land, and you will assure yourself of certain success. It is an excellent calming herb.

CELANDINE is masculine and is ruled by the Sun. Its Element is Fire. When worn as an amulet it helps the wearer to escape unfair imprisonment and entrapment. It can also alleviate depression.

CINQUEFOIL is masculine and is ruled by Jupiter. Its Element is Earth. Hang it around your doors and windows to protect you from evil. It is used in spells and charms for prosperity, purification and protection.

CINNAMON is masculine and is ruled by the Sun. Its Element is Fire. Its magical properties are used to help in spiritual quests, augmenting power, love, success, psychic work, healing and cleansing. It is used in incense for healing, clairvoyance and high spiritual vibrations; it is also reputed to be a male aphrodisiac. Use it in prosperity charms. It is an excellent aromatic and makes a good anointing oil for any magical working.

CLOVE is masculine and is ruled by the Sun. Its Element is Fire. Wear it in an amulet or charm to dispel negativity and bind those who speak ill of you. Cloves strung on a red thread can be worn as a protective charm. It helps with money matters, visions, cleansing and purification.

CLOVER is masculine and is ruled by Mercury; it is also associated with the Triple Goddess. Its Element is Air. Use it in

rituals for beauty, youth, healing injuries, and helping alleviate mental difficulties. A four-leaved clover is said to enable one to see fairies and is considered a general good-luck charm.

COMFREY is a feminine plant and is ruled by Saturn. Its Element is Water. It is useful for travel, casting spells for money and healing. It also honours the Crone aspect of the Goddess.

CORIANDER is masculine and is ruled by Mars and the Element Fire. It is a protector of the home and is useful in the promotion of peace. It encourages longevity and is helpful in love spells.

COWSLIP is feminine, ruled by Venus with its Element Water. Said to bring luck in love, it also induces contact with departed loved ones during dreams. A woman who washes her face with milk infused with cowslip will draw her beloved closer to her.

CYPRESS is masculine and is ruled by Saturn and its Element Earth. It is connected with death. Often used to consecrate ritual tools, cypress also has preservative qualities.

DAISY is feminine and is ruled by Venus and the Element Water. If you decorate your house with it on Midsummer's Eve, it will bring happiness into the home. Daisies

are also worn at Midsummer for luck and blessings. Long ago, young maidens would weave daisy chains and wear them in their hair to attract their beloved.

DANDELION is masculine plant and is ruled by Jupiter and the Element Air. It is useful for divination and communication.

DILL is masculine and is ruled by Mercury. Its Element is Fire. It is useful in love charms. Dill may also be hung in children's rooms to protect them against evil spirits or bad dreams.

DRAGON'S BLOOD is masculine, and is ruled by Mars with the Element Fire. A type of palm, it is widely included in love, protection and purification spells, usually in the form of a resin. It is carried for good luck; a piece of the plant kept under the bed is said to cure impotency. Dragon's blood increases the potency of other incense.

ELDER is a feminine plant ruled by Venus and the Element Air. Its branches are widely used for magical wands and it is considered bad luck to burn elder wood. Leaves hung around the doors and windows are said to ward off evil.

ELECAMPANE is a masculine plant ruled by Mercury and the Element Earth. It is a good aid in meditation and for requesting the presence of spirits.

EUCALYPTUS is feminine and is ruled by the Moon and the Element Air. It is used in healing rituals and in charms and amulets. If the leaves are put around a blue candle and burnt in a room, this is good for increasing healing energies.

EYEBRIGHT is masculine and is ruled by the Sun. Its Element is Air. This plant is said to induce clairvoyant visions and dreams if you anoint the eyelids daily with an infusion of leaves.

FENNEL is masculine and is ruled by Mercury. Its Element is Fire. Including the seeds in money charms is said to bring prosperity and ward off evil spirits. The plant itself is used for purification and protection.

FERN is feminine and is ruled by the planet Saturn and the Element Earth. This plant is a powerful protector and if grown near your home will ward off negativity.

FRANKINCENSE is a masculine herb under the rulership of the Sun and therefore the Element of Fire. A purifier of ritual spaces, it is probably the most powerful aid to meditation there is.

GARDENIA is feminine and is ruled by the Moon with its Element Water. Used extensively in Moon incenses, it attracts good spirits to rituals and enhances love vibrations.

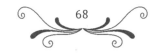

GARLIC is a masculine herb ruled by the planet Mars and consequently the Element of Fire. It protects and is a useful healer and promoter of courage.

GINGER is a masculine herb ruled by Mars and Fire. It encourages power and success, especially in love and financial dealings. It is also a good base for spells because it enhances the vibration.

GINSENG is masculine, ruled by the Sun with the Element of Fire. It aids love and lust and is useful in enhancing beauty. It is also a good reliever of stress.

HAWTHORN is masculine, ruled by Mars and the Element of Fire. It is used in protective sachets. It can enforce celibacy and chastity and is said to promote happiness in marriage or other relationships.

HAZEL is masculine and ruled by the Sun and the Element of Air. It is a very good wood for magical wands and is the only wood that should be used for divining. It also promotes good luck, particularly when it is bound by red and gold thread.

HEARTSEASE is feminine, ruled by Saturn and the Element of Water. It is actually a wild pansy and demonstrates its power by its name. If you can find any then it can be used with other herbs to ease heartache.

HOLLY is masculine and is ruled by Mars and its Element of Fire. When planted around the home it protects against evil. Holly water is said to protect babies, and when thrown at wild animals it calms them down. The leaves and berries can be carried as an amulet by a man to heighten his masculinity and virility, enabling him to attract a lover.

HONEYSUCKLE is feminine and is ruled by Jupiter and its Element Earth. Planted outside the home it brings good luck. It is also used in prosperity spells and love charms, and to heighten psychic ability.

HOPS, a masculine plant ruled by Mars and the Element of Water, is best used in healing and for aiding sleep.

HYSSOP is masculine. Its ruler is Jupiter and its Element is Fire. The plant was widely used during the Middle Ages for purification, cleansing and consecration rituals. Use it in purification baths, and for protective and banishing spells. Hyssop works best in the form of an essential oil in incense.

IVY is a masculine plant, ruled by Saturn and its Element is Water. It protects the houses it grows on from evil and harm. In the old traditions, ivy and holly were given to newly-weds as good-luck charms.

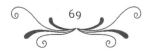

JASMINE is feminine and is ruled by Jupiter and the Element Earth. It attracts men and has been used throughout history by women for this purpose.

JUNIPER is a masculine plant, ruled by the Sun and its Element Fire. It gives protection against accidents, harm and theft. Once they have been dried and worn as a charm, the berries are used to attract lovers. Juniper also breaks hexes and curses.

LAVENDER is a masculine plant ruled by Mercury and the Element of Air. It is one of the most useful herbs and can be used for healing, promoting good wishes and sleep; it can also be used to attract men.

LEMON BALM is feminine and is ruled by the Moon or Neptune. Its Element is Water. It is a strong aphrodisiac, promotes fertility but is also an anti-depressant that is especially useful at the end of a relationship.

LEMON VERBENA is feminine, ruled by Venus and the Element Air. It is used in love charms to promote youth, beauty and attractiveness to the opposite sex. Wear it around your neck or place it under a pillow to prevent bad dreams. It helps to heal wounds.

LILAC is a feminine plant that is ruled by the planet Venus. Its Element is Air. It is a good protector that also banishes evil.

LINDEN is feminine, ruled by Jupiter and its Element is Water. It is said to be the tree of immortality and is associated with conjugal love or attraction and longevity. It is supposed to help in preventing intoxication.

LOVAGE is masculine, ruled by the Sun. Its Element is Water. The dried and powdered root should be added to cleansing and purification baths to release negativity. Carry it to attract love and the attention of the opposite sex. Also carry it when meeting new people.

MANDRAKE is a masculine plant ruled by Mercury and the Element Earth. It is very useful in incense for increasing the sex drive (both male and female) and is best used prior to the Full Moon.

MARIGOLD is masculine and ruled by the Sun. Its Element is Fire. Prophecy, legal matters, the psyche, seeing magical creatures, love, divination dreams, business or legal affairs and renewing personal energy are all assisted by marigold. It is good for finding someone who has done you wrong. It is sometimes added to love sachets. It should be gathered at noon.

MARJORAM is masculine and is ruled by Mercury with the Element Air. It protects against evil and aids love and healing; it is also helpful for those who are grieving.

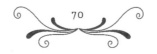

MEADOWSWEET is feminine, its planet is Jupiter and it is ruled by Water. It is a sacred herb of the Druids and gives protection against evil influences; it also promotes love, balance and harmony. Place meadowsweet on your altar when making love charms and conducting love spells to increase their potency. It can be worn at Lammas to join with the Goddess.

MINT (spearmint and peppermint) is a masculine plant that is ruled by Mercury or Venus and has the Element Air. It promotes healing, the ability to gain money and is useful for successful travel. Known to be a digestive, it also calms the emotions.

MUGWORT is a feminine plant that is ruled by Venus and the Element of Air. It is probably the most widely used herb by witches and promotes psychic ability and gives prophetic dreams. It is very good for astral projection.

MULLEIN is a masculine plant, ruled by Saturn and has the Element of Fire. This is used for courage and protection from wild animals and also from evil spirits. It is also used for cleansing and purifying ritual tools and altars and the cleansing of psychic places and sacred spaces before and after working. It guards against nightmares and can be substituted for graveyard dust.

MYRRH is a feminine plant that is ruled by the Moon or Jupiter and Water. It is purifying and protective and is especially useful when used with frankincense.

MYRTLE is feminine, ruled by Venus, and its Element is Water. Myrtle was sacred to the Greek goddess Venus and has been used in love charms and spells throughout history. It should be grown indoors for good luck. Carry or wear myrtle leaves to attract love; charms made of the wood have special magical properties. Wear fresh myrtle leaves while making love charms, potions or during rituals for love and include it in them. Myrtle tea drunk every three days helps maintains one's youthfulness.

NETTLE is a masculine plant ruled by Mars and its Element is Fire. It is a guard against danger and promotes courage.

NUTMEG is feminine, ruled by Jupiter, and its Element is Air. It helps to develop clairvoyance and psychic powers. When used with green candles it aids prosperity. It is also said to help teething.

OAK is masculine and is ruled by the Sun and the Element of Fire. It is often used by witches and used in power wands. It also protects against evil spirits and can also be used to promote a better sex life.

ORANGE is a feminine plant ruled by Jupiter and the Element of Water. It can be used as a love charm, while in the East it is used for good luck.

ORRIS ROOT is a feminine plant, is ruled by Venus and has the Element of Water. The powder is used as a love-drawing herb and to increase sexual appeal. Used in charms, amulets, sachets, incenses and baths it will also protect you. Hung on a cord it can act as a pendulum.

PARSLEY is a masculine herb that is ruled by Mercury and Air. It wards off evil and is a useful aid to those who drink too much. Parsley may be used in purification baths and as a way to stop misfortune.

PATCHOULI is a feminine plant which is ruled by Saturn. Its Element is Earth. This plant is aphrodisiac and an attractant of lovers for either sex. It is sometimes used in fertility talismans and can be substituted for graveyard dust. Use it with green candles to ensure prosperity. Sprinkle it on money to spread your wealth.

PENNYROYAL is a masculine plant ruled by Mars; its Element is Fire. It is used for protection, and, because it prevents weariness during long journeys, it is often carried on ships. Pennyroyal is also an insect deterrent. It should be avoided while pregnant.

PEPPER (black) is a masculine plant which is ruled by Mars with its Element of Fire; it can be used in protective charms against the evil eye. Mixed with salt it dispels evil, which may be why it is used on food.

PIMPERNEL is a masculine plant which is ruled by Mercury and has the Element of Air. You should wear it to keep people from deceiving you. It wards off illness and stops accidents. The juice is used to purify and empower ritual weapons.

PINE is masculine and ruled by Mars; it has the Element of Air. It aids you to focus and if burnt it will help to cleanse the atmosphere where it is burnt. Its sawdust is often used as a base for incense, particularly in those associated with money.

POPPY is feminine, ruled by the Moon, and has the Element of Water. It is said that you can eat poppy seeds as a fertility charm; they can also be used in love sachets. You should carry the seeds or dried seed-pod as a prosperity charm.

ROSE is a feminine plant that is ruled by Venus and the Element of Water. It is perhaps the most widely used plant in love and good-luck workings. Roses are also added to "fast luck" mixtures designed to make things happen quickly. It is also a good calmer when situations become difficult.

ROSEMARY is a masculine plant that is ruled by the Sun and the Element of Fire. It improves memory and sleep; it is an excellent purifier. It should be used to cleanse your hands before performing magic or rituals. You can hang it in doorways to prevent thieves entering.

ROWAN is a masculine plant which is ruled by the Sun and the Element of Fire. Rowan wood is used for divining rods and wands; its leaves and bark are used in divination rituals. It is also used for protection, good luck and healing. When two twigs are tied together to form a cross it is a protective device.

RUE is masculine, ruled by the Sun and the Element of Fire. Protective when hung at a door, it can break hexes by sending the negativity back from whence it came. It is good for clarity of mind, clearing the mind of emotional clutter and purification of ritual spaces and tools.

SAFFRON is masculine, ruled by the Sun and the Element of Fire. It was used in rituals to honour the Goddess of the Moon, Ashtoreth. It dispels melancholy and restores sexual prowess in men. It is used to cleanse the hands in healing processes and is also used in prosperity incenses.

SAGE is masculine, ruled by either Jupiter or Venus and the Element of Air. It promotes financial gain and good wishes; it is also a good healer and protector.

ST JOHN'S WORT is a masculine plant that is ruled by the Sun and the Element of Fire. This protects a person against bad dreams and encourages the willpower to do something difficult.

SANDALWOOD is feminine, ruled by the Moon, and its Element is Air. It has high spiritual vibrations so should be mixed with frankincense and burned at the time of the Full Moon. Anything visualized at this time is said to come true. It also clears negativity, so is good for purification, protection and healing workings.

SUNFLOWER is masculine and is ruled by the Sun and the Element of Fire. It is extremely useful, for the seeds aid fertility while the plant allows you to discover the truth, if you sleep with it under your bed. It is said to guard the garden against marauders and pests.

THYME is a feminine herb that is ruled by the planet Venus and the Element of Water. It is a good guardian against negative energy and an extremely good cleanser if combined with marjoram. It helps to develop your psychic powers and it is said to make women irresistible.

VALERIAN is feminine and is ruled by Venus and the Element of Water. One of the best sleep enhancers available, it also promotes love and rids your house of evil. It is said to protect against lightning.

VANILLA is feminine, ruled by Venus, and its Element is Water. The bean is used in love charms, while the oil is worn as an aphrodisiac. Mix it with sugar to make infusions for love.

VERVAIN is feminine and is ruled by Venus with the Element of Earth. Good for the ritual cleansing of sacred space, magical cleansing baths and purification incenses, it should be hung over the bed to prevent nightmares. Vervain is also excellent for use in prosperity charms and spells as it brings good luck and inspiration. It should be picked before sunrise. While it is said to control sexual urges (supposedly for seven years), it is also used in love and protection charms, presumably to ensure fidelity.

VIOLET is feminine, ruled by Venus, and its Element is Water. It brings changes in luck or fortune. Mix with lavender for a powerful love charm. A violet and lavender compress will help in eliminating headaches. The flowers are carried as a good-luck charm. The scent will soothe, clear the mind and relax the wearer.

WALNUT is masculine, ruled by the Sun, and the Element is Fire. Carry the nut as a charm to promote fertility and strengthen the heart. It attracts lightning.

WILLOW is feminine and ruled by the Moon. The Element is Water. Willow wands can be used for healing and are at their strongest when used at the New Moon. Willow guards against evil and this is where the expression "knock on wood" comes from.

WITCH HAZEL is masculine, ruled by the Sun, with the Element of Fire. The wood is used to make divining rods. Witch hazel gives protection and promotes chastity, healing the heart. It cools all the passions.

WORMWOOD is masculine, ruled by Mars, with the Element of Air. Wormwood is poisonous but is sometimes burned in smudge sticks to gain protection from wandering spirits. It is said that it enables the dead to be released from this plane so they may find peace. It is also used in divinatory and clairvoyance incenses, initiation rites and tests of courage. Mixed with sandalwood, it summons spirits.

YARROW is feminine and ruled by Venus. Its Element is Water. There is evidence that yarrow was often a component in incense used for incantations. It is a powerful incense additive for divination and love spells, too.

It exorcises evil, dispelling negativity, yet also enhances psychic ability and divination. Yarrow tea drunk prior to divination will enhance powers of perception; a touch of peppermint enhances the action of this brew and always helps it to work better. The plant is also traditionally used in courage, love and marriage charms.

YUCCA is masculine, and ruled by Mars. Its Element is Fire. Yucca is said to help with shape-shifting. If a strand of a leaf is tied around one's head and then an animal is visualized the wearer becomes (takes on the qualities of) that animal. Yucca is used to purify the body before performing magic. To get rid of illness, bathe at least twice using suds from the boiled plant juices. A cross formed from yucca leaves is said to protect the hearth, the centre of the home.

Making a Herb Bundle

The first thing to remember when you are making your herb bundle is that, as with any spiritual intent, be sure to wash and cleanse yourself – deliberately getting rid of any negative energy in the process – before you begin. There are also a few other guidelines you'll need to follow.

• Before picking the plant matter, honour the plant and ask its permission to take a branch or stem for your spiritual intent.

Respect the plant and let it continue to give of its life.

• When picking stems, make sure they are long enough to be bound together.

• Use any of the herbs mentioned above or use pine or cypress, if your location allows. You do not have to use plants and herbs that are there in your immediate vicinity – though, if you have grown the plants yourself, this will give you tremendous satisfaction.

• If you want to, add essential oils, but use them sparingly and try to choose one that will enhance the purpose of, or add an extra quality to, your bundle.

You will need
• Selection of leaves and stems
• Elastic band
• Thick cotton twine
• Small bowl

Method
Arrange a small handful of leaves and stems fairly symmetrically into a bundle – don't use too many.

Put the stems in the elastic band to keep the pieces together while you tie the bundle, removing it when you have finished.

Take a long piece of thick cotton twine and place the bundle top (the thicker end) in the middle of it.

Using the two ends of the twine, bind the bundle together tightly in a criss-cross

fashion, starting at the top and finishing at the bottom part of the stems. (Take your time over this – the more secure you make the bundle the better it will burn. Some leaves or twigs may protrude, so you need a receptacle to catch falling ashes.)

Bind the end of your bundle securely with the twine and perhaps make a dedication to your purpose.

You will now have a cone-shaped bundle. Let it dry out thoroughly before burning it, because it won't burn properly if it is at all damp or green.

To use the herb bundle, light the thicker top end and then blow the flame out so it smoulders. Some bits may drop out of the bundle so remember to have a bowl or receptacle handy to catch them.

Herb bundles are moved to where the fragrant smoke is needed. In rituals, you would use the cardinal points. Walk around slowly, wafting the smoke into the corners of the room as you do so. (You may have to keep blowing on the lit end to keep it burning.) As you blow, remember that you are using the principle of Air. You can also direct the smoke with either of your hands, the small branch of a plant, or even a special crystal or stone. Amber can also be used – especially appropriate as it is a resin from a plant. This action should get rid of any negative vibrations at the same time as energizing the protective frequencies.

If you want to cleanse the energy of a friend (or yourself), waft the smoke all around the body, starting at the head and gradually moving down to the feet. Move in a clockwise direction because this creates positivity. You can direct the smoke with your hand or a feather or whatever feels good for you. A seashell is a good idea since it represents the Goddess. You can also chant or sing at this time. Whatever you do, do it with a pure mind and spirit. When you have finished, keep the bundle safe until it has extinguished itself and then open a window to clear the space.

Decorative bundles

If you don't intend to burn the bundle then there are many other possibilities open to you. Bundles can be bound with color, feeling and meaning. Oils will add energy and aroma. You can use spices, fruits, fragrant wood, minerals, crystals, resins or flowers like rose, marigold or lavender. Depending on how you plan to display the bundle, you can use pretty much anything that has meaning and fragrance.

INCENSE

As well as making use of herbs as plants, decorations and for healing, their most important use in magic was – and still is – in incense. Incense symbolizes the Element Air and the spiritual realms and has been part of ritual use by magical workers and priests alike for thousands of years. Granular incense, with its basis of resins and gums, is

nowadays usually preferred for magical workings or ritual worship. It has a magic all of its own. For this reason a good incense burner will be one of your most important tools. You should choose this carefully and not just for its aesthetic sense, because it is vital that the incense is allowed to burn properly.

Since time immemorial, people have burned sweet-smelling woods, herbs and resins to perfume, cleanse and clarify the atmosphere in which they exist. During outdoor rituals special woods and herbs with magical qualities would be thrown onto bonfires or into altar cauldrons. In the home, open-hearth fires could be used to give off perfumed smoke which sweetened or freshened the air. The word "perfume" means "through smoke".

Initially, resins and gums were used most successfully, so in areas where resinous trees grew, incenses were used to honour the gods. Egypt became especially renowned for its high standard of blending and the use of ritual incense. There was a particular class of incense – which is still available today – called Khyphi. It required magical techniques and the finest ingredients for its manufacture.

Kyphi Incense
- 1 part myrrh resin
- 1 part frankincense resin
- 1 part gum arabic
- 1 part Balm of Gilead buds
- 1 part cassia or cinnamon

- Few drops of lotus oil
- Few drops of musk oil

Nowadays incense is most often encountered in the form of joss sticks, which were introduced to the West in the 1960s by travellers to India who brought them back with them. For short rituals these work very well, though they are not to everyone's taste. Dhoop, or incense cones, as they are known, are another way of using the same material.

The best method of using incense is to burn the granular type on a charcoal disc. By this method the charcoal disc is lit and placed in a fireproof receptacle. The incense is then piled onto the concave surface and allowed to do its work. After use, the charcoal discs remain very hot. You should dispose of them very carefully, dousing them with water and ensuring they are no longer "alive" and thus potentially harmful. You might like to bury what remains of the incense as an offering to the earth.

Making and using incenses
Many of the herbs already discussed are suitable for incense, if you wish to make your own. You should choose your correspondences carefully, according to your spell or ritual, and may like to make incense in tune with the cycles of life and planetary correspondences. You will soon find out what works for you. You can also use essential oils as part of your incense-making.

The use of incense in magical workings can be quite a personal act of worship; the various blends can sometimes either appeal to your senses or smell absolutely foul, often depending on your mood. For this reason, a number of blends from numerous sources are given here. Experiment until you settle on your own particular favourites and then work from there.

There does need to be some clarification of the lists of ingredients, however. A "part" indicates one measure or a proportion, which may be a teaspoon, a cup and so forth. Fractions indicate portions of a part. Personal experience shows that making small quantities is best as the incense then stays fresher and is often more cost-effective. If you plan on making quantities of several types of incense, collect a number of individual portion jars in which jams and honeys are packed. Such an amount is ideal for your immediate use.

Unless otherwise specified, use dried herbs, flowers, roots and resins, since these are often both easier to get hold of than fresh and are packed in suitable quantities and compositions for incense-making. The more unusual herbs, oils and resins can usually be obtained from any good herbalist, and there are now also several suppliers who can deliver by mail order and will often blend their own mixtures.

Initial purchase of the various ingredients is quite expensive, so if you work with other people you may wish to share the cost in some way. Start off with the first ingredient, grind it small and then add each subsequent ingredient in small quantities until it smells and feels right.

Incense Preparation

This is an accepted way of making incense, but you do need to be patient. The art of blending is highly skilled and your own experiments will show you the best methods for you. If you know your correspondences, you can call on the various deities to help you in your task, or just simply bear in mind the ultimate purpose of your incense. Most oils and binders such as the gums are added last.

You will need

• Pestle and mortar (Your pestle and mortar can be of any material, though one that does not pick up the perfumes of the ingredients is obviously best. If you do not have a pestle and mortar, a chopping board and rolling pin will suffice, though it is messier this way.)
• Set of measuring spoons
• Large bowl in which to blend your mixture thoroughly
• Your chosen herbs, resins, oils etc.
• Small containers with lids
• Labels
• Charcoal blocks for burning the incense

Method

Make sure that you grind each quantity of the herbs and resins as small as possible.

When each ingredient is ground, place it in your large bowl, reserving a small quantity in the right proportions of each ingredient with which to do a test run.

Mix in each ingredient thoroughly as you add it to the bowl. Mixing by hand is probably most successful, since this allows you to introduce your own personal vibration. You could also use a wand of sacred wood reserved specifically for the purpose if you so wish.

As you mix, say:

May this herb [resin/oil] enhance the power
of this offering for the spirits of Air

Add any oil last and make sure that this is thoroughly mixed in and not left in one place in the mixture.

When all ingredients are combined, spend some time thinking about your purpose and gently mixing and remixing your incense.

Remember that if you are making incense for a particular purpose, the herbs and resins used should correspond to that purpose, therefore your incense may not necessarily smell as pleasant as you would like.

If wished, ask for a blessing or consecration for the incense, as follows:

May this the work of my two hands
Be blessed for the purpose of [state your
purpose clearly]

Now test your sample by lighting a charcoal block, placing the incense on it then burning it carefully in a safe place.

Your incense is now ready, though it is best not to use it for at least 24 hours to enable the perfumes and qualities to blend properly. Many incenses blend, change and strengthen when stored correctly and incense often improves with keeping, so your sample may not smell the same as your stored incense. If it is to your liking and you feel it is suitable for your purpose, fill the containers, secure them tightly and label them clearly. They should be stored in a cool, dark place.

Incense Blends
Banishing, Exorcism and Purification

All the following incenses work on the principle that certain energies need to be banished in order for the practitioner to work effectively. The creation of peace, purification of the area and, of course, exorcism of unwanted spirits all come under this heading. More prosiac banishings such as those of an unwanted ex or a bad situation are also covered. Do think very carefully about what you wish to achieve before deciding which incense is right for your purpose. Suggestions are given here or

the purpose is clearly indicated in the title.

It is always possible to make substitutions in the ingredients. They can all be mixed and matched ad infinitum, though you may have to experiment with the quantities until the incense "feels" right (or until it smells right).

Banishing and Exorcism
Banishing Incense
- 1 part bay leaves
- 2 parts cinnamon
- 1 part rose petals
- 2 parts myrrh resin
- pinch of salt

Clearing Incense
- 1 part frankincense resin
- 1 part copal resin
- 1 part myrrh resin
- ½ part sandalwood

Burn this with the windows open.

Exorcism Incense
- 3 parts frankincense resin
- 1 part rosemary
- 1 part bay leaves
- 1 part avens
- 1 part mugwort
- 1 part St John's Wort
- 1 part angelica
- 1 part basil

Burn this incense with the windows open to drive out very heavy spiritual negativity from your surroundings.

Ending Negativity Incense
- 1 part marjoram
- 1 part thyme
- ½ part oregano
- ¼ part bay leaves
- ¼ part cloves

Jinx-removing Incense
- 2 parts clove
- 1 part deerstongue
- Few drops of rose geranium oil

This incense can be used when you think someone is against you.

Uncrossing Incense
- 2 parts lavender
- 1 part rose
- 2 parts bay
- 1 part verbena

Use this incense when you feel you or your home has been "cursed" or that you are under attack in some way.

Purification
Purification Incense 1
- 2 parts sandalwood
- 1 part cinnamon
- 2 parts bay
- 1 part vervain
- pinch of salt

Burn this incense with the windows open to clear a disturbed home after an argument.

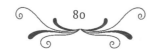

Purification Incense 2

• 2 parts sandalwood
• 1 part cinnamon

Leave the windows open to clear an atmosphere quickly.

Purification Incense 3

• 3 parts frankincense resin
• 2 parts dragon's blood resin
• 1 part myrrh resin
• 1 part sandalwood
• 1 part wood betony
• ½ part dill seed
• Few drops of rose geranium oil

This is good for clearing your new home of old energies.

Domestic Tranquility Incense

• ¾ part sage
• ¼ part rue
• ½ part ground ivy
• Few drops of bayberry oil
• ¼ part bayberry
• 1¼ parts linden (lime)

Hearth and Home Incense

• 2 parts dragon's blood resin
• ½ part juniper
• ½ part sassafrass
• ½ part orange flowers
• 2 parts myrrh resin
• ½ part rose petals

This incense should be burnt when you wish to create a safe, warm, loving home.

Protection

There are many ways of protecting both yourself and your own space by the use of incense. If you simply wish to protect against the intrusion of negative energies, it is probably best to use those incenses that are based mainly on the resinous substances. This is for two reasons. First, most resins are relatively slow-burning, high-vibrational energy substances, so their effect is long-lasting; secondly, you have more opportunity when grinding them to introduce specific intents into the incense. Perhaps, for instance, you might wish to protect yourself against the jealousy of a former lover or against financial loss. Using substances that have a high vibration helps to build a "wall" of protection, which means that neither the bad thought nor the subtle energies activated on a more spiritual level can harm you.

Some of the incenses below are specifically to protect against not just negativity on a purely physical plane, but also malign energy deliberately directed at you and your loved ones. Incense such as the ones for psychic protection will give you the security you need to know that you can combat such intrusion.

Other incenses mean that you can react quickly to outside influences should you need to do so. There are many alternatives in this, as in other sections, so that you can decide for yourself which ones work best for you. A lot will depend on what is local to you, and so far as protection incenses

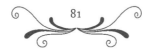

are concerned, the sensitivities can change depending on the environment surrounding the individual. Where the incense is for a specific purpose, that information is given.

Once again, it is always possible when making these incenses to substitute the ingredients. They can all be mixed and matched ad infinitum, though you may have to experiment until they "feel" right.

Peace and Protection Incense
- 4 parts lavender
- 3 parts thyme
- 2 parts vervain
- 3 parts basil
- 1 part frankincense resin
- Pinch of rue
- Pinch of benzoin resin
- Few drops of bergamot oil
- Few drops of jasmine oil

This can be used in both peace and protection spells and rituals.

Protection Incense 1
- ½ part bay leaves
- ½ part cloves
- ¾ part oregano
- ¾ part sandalwood

Protection Incense 2
- *4 parts verbena*
- *1 part galangal root (ground)*
- *1 part peppermint1 part cinnamon*
- *½ part rue*

Protection Incense 3
- ¼ part basil
- ½ part cinnamon
- ½ part rosemary
- 1½ parts thyme
- ½ part sage
- ½ part star anise

Total Protection Incense
- 2 parts frankincense resin
- 1 part dragon's blood resin
- ½ part wood betony

This incense creates quite a high vibration and protects on all levels of existence.

Iron Protection Incense
- ¼ part iron filings
- 1 part galangal root (powdered)
- Few drops of citronella oil

This incense uses the ancient idea that iron will change a negative vibration.

New Orleans Protection Incense
- 2 parts myrrh resin
- ½ part bay leaves
- 1 part cloves
- 1 part cinnamon

This is an incense that is often used in Hoodoo work.

Sandalwood Protection Incense
- 3 parts sandalwood
- 2 parts juniper
- 1 part vetivert

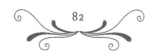

Pennyroyal Protection Incense
- 2 parts verbena or vetivert
- 1 part galangal
- 1 part pennyroyal
- ¼ part rue
- ½ part cinnamon

Rosemary Protection Incense
- 2 parts rosemary
- ½ part orris root (ground)
- 1 part basil
- 1 part frankincense resin

10 Herb Protection Incense
- *2 parts frankincense resin*
- *2 parts myrrh resin*
- 1 part juniper berries
- ½ part rosemary
- ¼ part avens
- ¼ part mugwort
- ¼ part yarrow
- ¼ part St John's Wort
- ½ part angelica
- 1 part basil

5 Resins Protection Incense
- 2 parts frankincense resin
- 1 part copal resin
- 1 part myrrh resin
- ½ part dragon's blood resin
- ½ part gum arabic

Home Protection Incense
- ½ part frankincense resin
- ¾ part sage
- ½ part basil
- ½ part mistletoe
- ¼ part garlic (mix of dried and ground)
- ¾ part rosemary
- ¼ part rue
- 1 part sandalwood
- ½ part myrrh resin
- ½ part orris root
- ½ part yarrow

Note: The next two incenses can be used if you wish to protect your surroundings against theft and burglary.

Prevent Theft Incense
- 1 part ground ivy
- ½ part juniper
- 1½ parts rosemary

Stop Theft Incense
- ½ part dogwood
- ¼ part caraway
- ½ part rosemary
- ¼ part tarragon
- 1 part willow
- Few drops honeysuckle oil

Note: The next four incenses deal specifically with protection on a psychic level, while the two following deal with the effects of an unwanted spiritual visitation. They could be considered to belong to the banishing and exorcism categories.

Psychic Protection Incense 1
- ½ part elder
- 1 part cinquefoil
- ½ part bay leaves
- ⅛ part valerian

Psychic Protection Incense 2
- ¼ part broom
- ½ part agrimony
- ½ part basil
- ¼ part cranesbill
- *1 part vetivert*
- ½ part oregano

Psychic Protection Incense 3
- ¼ part frankincense resin
- ½ part oregano
- ¼ part lovage
- ½ part cloves
- ¼ part ginger root (ground)
- ½ part sandalwood
- ¼ part star anise

Psychic Protection Incense 4
- ½ part benzoin resin
- ¼ part dragon's blood resin
- ½ part frankincense resin
- ¼ part camphor gum
- ½ part cassia
- ¼ part patchouli
- *2 parts sandalwood*

Each ingredient in this incense is a resin.

Note: These next two incenses help to keep your home clear of spirit interference unless you have specifically asked for spirit to be present.

Spirits Depart Incense
- 2 parts fennel seed
- 2 parts dill seed
- ½ part rue

Spirit Portal Incense
- ½ part cinnamon
- ½ part lavender
- pinch of wormwood

Note: The next five protection incenses all have as their main ingredients resins, particularly frankincense. If you dislike the perfume of frankincense, experiment with the proportions of your other resins.

Protection Incense 1
- *4 parts frankincense resin*
- *3 parts myrrh resin*
- *2 parts juniper berries*
- *1 part rosemary*
- ½ part avens
- ½ part mugwort
- ½ part yarrow
- ½ part St. John's Wort
- ½ part angelica
- ½ part basil

This incense is so all-enveloping that it will protect against almost everything.

Protection Incense 2
- 2 parts frankincense resin
- 1 part dragon's blood powder or resin
- ½ part betony

This incense is particularly potent when attempting to visualize and identify the source of your problem.

Protection Incense 3
- 2 parts frankincense resin
- 1 part sandalwood
- ½ part rosemary

Protection Incense 4
- 1 part frankincense resin
- 1 part myrrh resin
- ½ part clove

Protection Incense 5
- 2 parts frankincense resin
- 1 part copal resin
- 1 part dragon's blood powder or resin

LUST, LOVE AND RELATIONSHIPS
The idea of trying to influence someone else directly goes against the ethics of many magical practitioners. One must be very careful because incense prepared with the intention of trying to make someone do that which they do not want to, or which goes against their natural inclination, can possibly misfire and cause you a good deal of difficulty.

Love incense really should only be used with the intent that the occurrence will only be in accordance with the Greater Good, whether it be the beginning or the ending. That is, that you are helping something to happen, not forcing it. Apart from that, many of these incenses have a beautiful perfume and can help to create a loving atmosphere.

It is always possible when preparing incense to make substitutions in the ingredients. They can all be mixed and matched ad infinitum, though you may have to experiment with the quantities until they "feel" right.

There are many different aspects to relationships. In this section the individual titles of each recipe are self-explanatory.

Loving Friends Incense
- ½ part acacia
- 1 part rosemary
- ¼ part elder
- ½ part frankincense resin
- 1 part dogwood

Attract a Lover Incense
- 1 part lovage
- ½ part orris root (ground)
- 1 part lemon verbena
- ¼ part patchouli
- Few drops of lemon verbena oil

Attract Love Incense
- ½ part cloves
- 1 part rose
- ¼ part saw palmetto

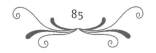

- ½ part juniper
- Few drops of musk oil
- Few drops of rose oil
- ½ part red sandalwood

Draw and Strengthen Love Incense
- 2 parts sandalwood
- ½ part basil
- ½ part bergamot
- Few drops of rose oil
- Few drops of lavender oil

Love Incense 1
- 1 part orris root (ground)
- Few drops musk oil
- 1 part sandalwood
- 1 part violet
- Few drops of gardenia oil

Love Incense 2
- 2 parts dragon's blood resin
- 1 part orris root (ground)
- ½ part cinnamon
- ½ part rose petals
- Few drops of musk oil
- Few drops of patchouli oil

Love Incense 3
- 1 part patchouli
- Few drops of musk oil
- Few drops of civet oil
- Few drops of ambergris oil

This incense makes the opposite sex more aware of you.

Love Incense 4
- 1 part violets
- 1 part rose petals
- ½ part olive leaves

Love Incense 5
- 2 parts sandalwood
- 2 parts benzoin resin
- 1 part rosebuds
- Few drops of patchouli oil
- Few drops of rose oil

Love Incense 6
- 2 parts sandalwood
- ½ part basil
- ½ part bergamot
- Few drops of rose oil
- Few drops of lavender oil

Burn this incense to attract love, to strengthen the love you have and also to expand your ability to give and receive love.

Increase Love Incense
- ½ part benzoin
- ¼ part jasmine
- 1 part rose
- ¼ part patchouli
- ½ part musk root
- ½ part sandalwood
- Few drops of musk oil
- Few drops of civet oil
- Few drops of rose oil
- Few drops of jasmine oil

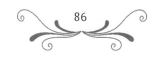

This incense can be used in love rituals when you wish to strengthen the bonds that already exist between you.

Note: The next three incenses are all thought to have an effect on the libido.

Fiery Passion Incense
- ¾ part yohimbe
- ½ part cinnamon
- ¼ part ginger root
- 2½ parts damiana
- Few drops of ambergris oil

Passion Incense
- ½ part cranesbill
- 1¼ parts cascara
- ½ part savory
- Few drops of civet oil
- ½ part musk root

Physical Love Incense
- ¾ part damiana
- ½ part yohimbe
- ½ part musk root
- ¾ part cascara
- Few drops of bergamot oil
- Few drops of ambergris oil

Fidelity Incense
- ¼ part basil
- ¼ part dragon's blood resin
- 1 part red sandalwood
- ½ part rosemary

- 1 part dogwood
- Few drops of honeysuckle oil

Marital Bliss Incense
- 1 part vanilla bean (ground)
- 2 parts wintergreen
- 1 part khus khus
- 1 part narcissus
- Few drops of wintergreen oil

Burn this incense at night, just before you go to bed.

Note: The following five incenses should be used carefully because it is not wise to try to influence someone against their will. Your choice of words when performing the ritual is important.

Stay at Home Incense
- ½ part clove
- ½ part allspice
- ½ part deerstongue
- *1 part mullein*
- *1 part sage*

Divorce Incense
- ½ part frankincense resin
- ½ part rue
- ½ part allspice
- ¼ part marjoram
- ¾ part pennyroyal
- ½ part yarrow
- ⅛ part camphor resin
- ½ part sandalwood

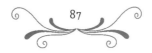

End an Affair Incense
- ¼ part menthol
- 1½ parts willow
- 1½ parts lavender

Love Breaker Incense
- ½ part vetivert
- 1 part patchouli
- 1 part lemongrass
- ½ part mullein

This incense can be used to aid the smooth break-up of a relationship.

Release and Ending Incense
- ½ part bay
- ½ part lemon balm
- ¼ part yarrow
- ½ part pennyroyal
- 1 part willow
- Few drops of lemon balm oil
- Few drops of peppermint oil

BUSINESS, MONEY, PROSPERITY AND SUCCESS

After love incense, incense that can be used to bring about success in business affairs and finance are the ones that intrigue people most. On the quiet, many business people who use incense would concede that they have received assistance, but they would hate to admit it publicly. These incenses are especially appropriate for those who value secrecy, because they can be used without fuss to create circumstances where the desired effect becomes inevitable. Using these incenses might be considered by some to be employing thaumaturgy – magic that is designed to have an effect specifically on the mundane world. Wherever possible, keep your intent as altruistic and as clearly in mind as you can when using incense. The "higher" the intent, the more likely it is to happen because it can be said to be in accord with the Greater Good. It is suggested that any prosperity, money or success you receive as a consequence is tithed; that is, a portion is dedicated to good causes – in old-style belief, 10 per cent.

It is always possible when preparing incense to make substitutions in the ingredients. They can all be mixed and matched ad infinitum, though you may have to experiment with the quantities until they "feel" right (or until they smell right).

Business
These first ten incenses are burnt when you wish to increase your personal portfolio and business acumen. Burning the confidence incenses, for instance, will help you to gain confidence, but only if you have something to build on in the first place.

Business Incense
- 2 parts benzoin resin
- 1 part cinnamon
- 1 part basil

Confidence Incense 1
- I part rosemary
- ¼ part garlic
- ½ part camomile
- I part musk root
-

Confidence Incense 2
- I part St John's Wort
- I part thyme
- ½ part oak
- ¼ part sweet woodruff

Recognition Incense
- 2 parts benzoin resin
- I part rue
- I part sandalwood

This incense can be used when you feel your efforts should be recognized and rewarded. *Note:* These next three incenses should be used when you require a little extra "oomph" to carry you along a chosen path.

Determination Incense 1
- ½ part althea
- ½ part camomile
- I part thyme
- ¼ part garlic

Determination Incense 2
- I part rosemary
- I part willow
- I part musk root
- Few drops of musk oil

Determination Incense 3
- ½ part allspice
- I¼ parts St John's Wort
- ½ part southernwood
- ¾ part willow

Note: These following three incenses can be used when you wish to encourage the flow of money towards you.

Financial Gain Incense 1
- I part lovage
- I part bay
- ¼ part cinnamon
- ½ part meadowsweet

Financial Gain Incense 2
- ½ part star anise
- ¼ part poppy seed
- ½ part mistletoe
- ½ part juniper
- I part cherry

Financial Increase Incense
- ¼ part cucumber
- ¾ part allspice
- I part sunflower
- ¼ part saw palmetto
- ½ part marigold

This incense can be used when you are deliberately wishing to increase what you already have; that is, make a profit, rather than simply gain money.

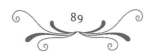

Note: These following two incenses may be used when additional information or insight is needed either in specific circumstances or on a day-to-day basis. They are good incenses to burn in a training situation.

Gain Knowledge and Wisdom Incense 1

- ¼ part angelica
- ¼ part vervain
- I part sage
- ½ part Solomon's Seal

Knowledge and Wisdom Incense 2

- I part Solomon's Seal
- ¼ part benzoin resin
- ½ part vervain
- ½ part cloves
- ½ part bay

Money Incense 1

- I part basil
- I part cinquefoil
- ½ part hyssop
- ½ part galangal

Money Incense 2

- I¼ parts lavender
- ¼ part camomile
- ¼ part comfrey
- I part red clover
- ¼ part acacia

More Money Incense

- ¾ part cinnamon
- ½ part dragon's blood resin
- I¼ parts cascara

Note: These next five incenses are good for accruing more than your immediate needs. The last two enable you to call in, and give, favours when necessary.

Prosperity Incense

- I part frankincense resin
- ½ part cinnamon
- ¼ part nutmeg
- ½ part balm

Wealth Incense

- I part nutmeg
- ½ – I part pepperwort
- I pinch saffron

Increased Wealth Incense

- 2 parts frankincense resin
- I part cinnamon
- I part nutmeg
- ½ part clove
- ½ part ginger
- ½ part mace

Riches and Favours Incense 1

- 2 parts benzoin resin
- ½ part clove
- ½ part pepperwort

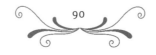

Riches and Favours Incense 2
- 2 parts benzoin resin
- 1 part wood aloe
- ½ part peppermint
- ½ part clove

Note: These next three incenses are used to pull success towards you, whatever you may perceive that to be.

Success Incense 1
- ½ part basil
- ½ part bay
- 1 part cedar
- ½ part oak

Success Incense 2
- ¼ part mistletoe
- ½ part marigold
- ½ part sunflower
- ¼ part onion
- 1 part sandalwood

Success Incense 3
- ¼ part frankincense resin
- ½ part sweet woodruff
- 1½ parts vetivert
- ¼ part angelica
- 1 part sandalwood

Note: This following incense can be used when you wish to build on success you have already had.

Greater Success Incense
- 1½ parts sandalwood
- ½ part sarsaparilla
- ½ part motherwort
- ½ part quassia
- Few drops of jasmine oil

Luck
These next four incenses are all designed to bring good fortune. Your intent is very important when you use a first-rate luck incense. The incenses open the way to you winning, rather than actually winning for you.

Good Luck in Life Incense
- ½ part musk root
- 1½ part rose
- ½ parts red clover
- ½ part galangal root
- Few drops of rose oil

Good Luck Incense
- ½ part dragon's blood resin
- ½ part mistletoe
- 1 part cascara
- 1 part linden

Improve Luck Incense
- 1 part rosemary
- ½ part dragon's blood resin
- ½ part musk root
- ½ part sandalwood
- Few drops of rose oil
- Few drops of musk oil

Games of Chance Incense

- ½ part dragon's blood resin
- 2 parts gum mastic resin
- 1 part frankincense resin

This incense could be used, for example, when you wish to try your luck and place a bet.

Physical and Emotional Health and Healing

Any incense used for the purpose of health and healing should only be used as an adjunct to other methods. If you are prepared to use incense in this way, you will probably have an awareness of alternative healing methods anyway, but they cannot – and should never – be used as substitutes for proper medical advice.

Many of the herbs given here are those which have been used for centuries to alleviate certain conditions, but bearing in mind modern laws and thought, you must make your own decisions as to their effective use. Seek the help of your herbalist or medical practitioner as to the nature of the ingredients and what form they should take (root, powder, and so forth).

It is always possible when preparing incense to make substitutions in the ingredients. They can all be mixed and matched ad infinitum, though you may have to experiment with the quantities until they "feel" right (or until they smell right).

PHYSICAL HEALTH

Cold-healing Incense

- 1¼ parts pine
- ½ part cedar
- ⅛ part camphor
- ⅛ part menthol
- ½ part spruce
- Few drops of pine oil

Resins have always had their part to play in incense. This particular incense will help ease the symptoms of a cold – you can see from its ingredients it is as much medicinal as magical.

Healing Incense 1

- 2 parts myrrh resin
- 1 part cinnamon
- 1 pinch saffron

Healing Incense 2

- 1 part rose
- 1 part eucalyptus
- 1 part pine
- 1 pinch saffron

Healing Incense 3

- 1 part rosemary
- 1 part juniper

When used in oil form – that is, on a tissue placed on a radiator or in a burner – this incense is easily used in a hospital environment.

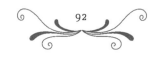

Regain Health Incense
- 3 parts myrrh resin
- 2 parts nutmeg
- I part cedar
- I part clove
- ½ part balm
- ½ part poppy seeds
- Few drops of pine oil
- Few drops of sweet almond oil

This incense acts as a good "pick-me-up".

EMOTIONAL HEALTH

All of these incenses help to alter the state of mind and increase the ability of a person to think positively.

Courage Incense
- 2 parts dragon's blood powder or resin
- I part frankincense resin
- I part rose geranium
- ¼ part tonka beans
- Few drops of musk oil

Ease Emotional Pain Incense
- 3 parts bay
- ¾ part allspice
- ¼ part dragon's blood powder
- ¾ part frankincense resin or gum arabic

End Negativity and Give Hope Incense 1
- I part thyme
- ½ part rue
- ½ part sweet woodruff
- ½ part cloves

End Negativity and Give Hope Incense 2
- I part dittany
- ½ part camomile
- ¼ part patchouli

Happiness Incense 1
- ½ part myrrh resin
- ¼ part marjoram
- I part dittany
- ¾ part sandalwood
- ¾ part oregano
- Few drops of spearmint oil

Happiness Incense 2
- I part oregano
- I part rosemary
- I part marigold

"Poor Me" Incense
- ½ part cloves
- ¼ part juniper
- 2 parts willow
- ⅛ part menthol
- Few drops of eucalyptus oil
- Few drops of wintergreen oil

This incense can be used for when you feel the whole world is against you.

Tranquility Incense

- 1 part sage
- 1½ parts rose
- ¼ part benzoin resin
- ½ part meadowsweet
- Few drops of rose oil

This incense induces a sense of tranquility which allows you to rebalance and recharge your batteries.

Note: These next two incenses give strength and integrity in a chosen task.

Strength Incense 1

- ½ part dragon's blood powder or resin
- ½ part musk root
- 1½ parts vetivert
- ½ part cinquefoil
- Few drops of musk oil
- Few drops of Ambergris oil
-

Strength Incense 2

- ½ part cinnamon
- ¼ part dragon's blood powder or resin
- ¼ part frankincense resin
- ½ part musk root
- ¼ part patchouli
- 1 part vetivert
- ¼ part yarrow
- Few drops of musk oil

Study Incense

- 2 parts gum mastic
- 1 part rosemary

Burn this incense to strengthen the conscious mind for study, to develop concentration and to improve your memory.

PSYCHIC POWERS, DIVINATION AND PROPHETIC DREAMS

Remembering that the use of mind-altering substances should be very carefully considered, this section sets about indicating substances that alter your sensitive vibrational rate. Each one of us consists of at least a physical body, an astral body and a spiritual aspect. These subtle energies can be successfully adjusted to connect us with other subtle vibrations – it is a little like logging on to a computer and connecting with a particular programme.

The incenses below help us to do this and enable us to work without interference from other less manageable energies. They put us in touch with those inner powers that we use to penetrate other dimensions and help us to develop them without disquiet. Their specific purpose is, by and large, stated in the name of the incense.

It is always possible when preparing incense to make substitutions in the ingredients. They can all be mixed and matched ad infinitum, though, as always, you may find that you have to experiment with the quantities until they "feel" right (or until they smell right).

DIVINATION

The following incenses can be used in divinatory rituals.

Divination Incense 1
- I part St John's Wort
- ¾ part wormwood
- ¾ part bay
- ½ part frankincense resin

Divination Incense 2
- ¾ part cinquefoil
- ⅛ part valerian
- ½ part deerstongue
- ½ part frankincense resin
- I part sandalwood

Divination Incense 3
- ½ part cinnamon
- ½ part chickweed
- I part thyme
- I part sandalwood

Divination Incense 4
- I part yarrow
- I part St John's Wort
- ¼ part frankincense resin
- ½ part bay

Divination Incense 5
- I part lavender
- I part rose
- ½ part star anise

Divination Incense 6
- 2 parts sandalwood
- I part orange peel
- ½ part mace
- ½ part cinnamon

PSYCHIC POWERS

These next four incenses are particularly good for enhancing the psychic powers during magical rituals.

Psychic Power Incense
- I part frankincense resin
- ¼ part bistort

Psychic Incense 1
- 2 parts sandalwood
- I part gum arabic

Psychic Incense 2
- 2 parts sandalwood
- I part gum acacia (or arabic)

Psychic Incense 3
- I part frankincense resin
- I part sandalwood
- I part cinnamon
- I part nutmeg
- Few drops of orange oil
- Few drops of clove oil

PAST LIVES

These next two incenses can be used when you wish to find out about past lives.

Recall Past Lives Incense

- 1½ parts sandalwood
- ½ part water lily
- ½ part holly
- ½ part frankincense resin
- Few drops of lilac oil

Remember Past Lives Incense

- 1 part sandalwood
- ½ part cinnamon
- ½ part myrrh resin
- Few drops of myrrh oil
- Few drops of cinnamon oil
- Few drops of cucumber oil
- Spirit Presence

These next three incenses are for inviting positive energies to be present during rituals.

Spirit Incense 1

- 1 part sandalwood
- 1 part lavender

Burn on your altar or in your sacred space.

Spirit Incense 2

- 2 parts sandalwood
- 1 part willow bark

This incense is a good one to use (particularly outdoors) when performing rituals during the waxing Moon.

Open Eyes To Spirit World

- 1 part gum mastic
- 1 part amaranth
- 1 part yarrow
- Visions

The next four incenses can all be used as part of rituals where you wish to make a connection with other realms.

Psychic Vision Incense

- 3 parts frankincense resin
- 1 part bay
- ½ part damiana

Second Sight Incense

- 1 part parsley
- ½ part hemp seeds
- ½ part frankincense resin

Sight Incense

- 2 parts gum mastic
- 2 parts juniper
- 1 part sandalwood
- 1 part cinnamon
- 1 part calamus
- Few drops of patchouli oil
- Few drops of ambergris oil

Vision Incense

- 3 parts cinquefoil
- 3 Parts chicory root
- 1 part clove

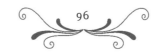

Celestial Influences

This section is probably for those of you who have chosen to travel a little further on your voyage of discovery. The incenses again are used to make a link or to enhance a specific purpose. It will depend on your own personal belief whether, for instance, you wish to use a specific incense to link with planetary energy or to use a specific incense at the times of the various Sabbats and Moon phases. Planetary influences and correspondences are explained more fully in the Spells Preparation section.

Accepted use has meant that certain woods and herbs are associated with days of the week, seasons of the year and lunar cycles. What follows is an easy-to-consult listing to enable you to get the best out of your rituals. There is nothing to stop you from mixing and matching as you so wish. You may find certain aromas more pleasurable than others.

DAYS OF THE WEEK

The incenses and oils in the table below may be used alone or combined for your daily rituals to have maximum effect. They have been recommended according to the planetary ruler of each day of the week.

Day of the Week	Planetary Influence	Aroma
Monday	Moon	Jasmine, lemon, sandalwood, Stephanotis
Tuesday	Mars	Basil, coriander, ginger, nasturtium
Wednesday	Mercury	Benzoin, cary sage, eucalyptus, lavender
Thursday	Jupiter	Clove, lemon balm, melissa, oakmoss, star anise
Friday	Venus	Cardamon, palma rosa, rose, yarrow
Saturday	Saturn	Cypress, mimosa, myrrh, patchouli
Sunday	Sun	Cedar, frankincense, neroli, rosemary

THE SEASONS

The following fragrances, either as plants or – where appropriate – essential oils, can be used to welcome each new season in your personal rituals.

Spring:	All sweet scents, particularly daffodil, jasmine and rose.
Summer:	All spicy scents, particularly carnation, clove and ginger.
Autumn:	All earthly scents, particularly oak moss, patchouli and vetiver.
Winter:	All resinous and woody scents, particularly frankincense, pine and rosemary.

The following seven incenses are suitable for the various seasons and can be used either to honour the turning of the year or the ideas inherent in seasonal worship.

Spring Incense
- ¼ part primrose
- I part cherry
- I part rose
- ½ part sandalwood
- Few drops of lilac oil
- Few drops of rose oil
- Few drops of strawberry oil

Summer Incense 1
- I½ parts lavender
- I part St John's Wort
- ½ part mistletoe

Summer Incense 2
- I part cedar
- ½ part juniper
- I part sandalwood

Autumn Incense
- ¼ part oak
- ½ part pine
- ¼ part frankincense resin
- ¼ cinnamon
- ¼ part cloves
- ½ part rosemary
- ¼ part sage
- ½ part pomegranate

Winter Incense
- I¼ parts lavender
- ½ part cloves
- ½ part cinnamon
- ¼ part benzoin resin
- ¼ part patchouli
- ¼ part mistletoe
- ¼ part orris root
- Few drops of bergamot oil

Winter Incense 2
- ½ part mistletoe
- ¼ part holly
- ½ part bay

- ½ part oak
- I part pine
- ½ part cedar
- Few drops of pine oil
- Few drops of cedar oil
- The Lunar Cycle

Incense and perfumes can be utilized during the phases of the Moon to put you in touch with lunar energy.

SANDALWOOD is particularly appropriate for the first quarter when the Moon's waxing enhances spirituality.

JASMINE has the full-blown energies of the Full Moon.

LEMON, which is more ethereal, is symbolic of the lessening of the Moon's influence as it wanes in the last quarter.

CAMPHOR signifies the cold New Moon.

THE ELEMENTS

Tradition dictates that you honour the four "directions" and their appropriate Elements. The following four incenses are suitable for honouring the four directions or cardinal points before moving onto the ritual proper. You can then use any of the other incenses for their appropriate purpose.

Air Incense
- 2 parts benzoin resin
- I part gum mastic
- ½ part lavender
- ¼ part wormwood
- I pinch mistletoe

Earth Incense
- I part pine
- I part thyme
- Few drops patchouli oil

Fire Incense
- 2 parts frankincense resin
- I part dragon's blood resin
- I part red sandalwood
- I pinch saffron

Water Incense
- 2 parts benzoin resin
- I part myrrh resin
- I part sandalwood
- Few drops of lotus oil
- Planetary

These incenses can be used when you wish to call particularly on the power of the planets in your rituals. Incenses suitable for use with Neptune, Uranus and Pluto are not included, as here you might like to use your own intuition. You will find the significances of the planets in the astrological section on page 142.

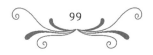

Sun Incense 1
- 3 parts frankincense resin
- 2 parts myrrh resin
- 1 part wood aloe
- ½ part Balm of Gilead
- ½ part bay
- ½ part carnation
- Few drops of ambergris oil
- Few drops of musk oil
- Few drops of olive oil

Burn this incense to draw on the influences of the Sun and for spells involving promotions, friendships, healing, energy work and magical power.

Sun Incense 2
- 3 parts frankincense resin
- 2 parts sandalwood
- 1 part bay
- 1 pinch saffron
- Few drops of orange oil

Sun Incense 3
- 3 parts frankincense resin
- 2 parts galangal root
- 2 parts bay
- ¼ part mistletoe
- Few drops of red wine
- Few drops of honey

Egyptian Solar Incense
- 3 parts frankincense resin
- 1 part clove
- ½ part red sandalwood

- ½ part sandalwood
- ¼ part orange flowers
- 3 pinches of orris root

Moon Incense 1
- 2 parts juniper
- 1 part calamus
- ½ part orris root
- ¼ part camphor
- Few drops of lotus oil

Moon Incense 2
- 4 parts sandalwood
- 2 parts wood aloe
- 1 part eucalyptus
- 1 part crushed cucumber seeds
- 1 part mugwort
- ½ part ranuculus blossoms
- 1 part selenetrope (you can substitute gardenia or jasmine if you cannot find selenetrope easily)
- Few drops of ambergris oil

Moon Incense 3
- 2 parts juniper berries
- 1 part orris root
- 1 part calamus
- Few drops of spirits of camphor or camphor
- tincture or ¼ part genuine camphor
- Few drops of lotus bouquet oil

Moon Incense 4
- 2 parts myrrh resin

- 2 parts gardenia petals
- 1 part rose petals
- 1 part lemon peel
- ½ part camphor
- Few drops of jasmine oil

Moonfire Incense 5

- 1 part rose
- 1 part orris root
- 1 part bay
- 1 part juniper
- 1 part dragon's blood powder or resin
- ½ part potassium nitrate (saltpetre)

Burn this incense when you wish to call on the power of the Moon while performing divination and love rituals. The potassium nitrate (saltpetre) is included to make the incense sparkle and glow. Do not add too much though, and add it gradually – it will explode otherwise.

Earth Incense

- 2 parts pine
- 1 part patchouli
- 1 part cypress
- 1 pinch salt

Mercury Incense 1

- 2 parts benzoin resin
- 1 part mace
- ½ part marjoram
- Few drops of lavender oil

Burn this incense to invoke Mercury's powers and qualities when performing

rituals for such things as intelligence, travel, communication and divination.

Mercury Incense 2

- 2 parts sandalwood
- 1 part mace
- 1 part marjoram
- 1 part mint or a few drops of mint oil

Venus Incense 1

- 2 parts sandalwood
- 1 part benzoin resin
- 1 part rose petals
- Few drops of rose oil
- Few drops of patchouli oil

Venus Incense 2

- 3 parts wood aloe
- 1 part red rose petals
- Few drops of olive oil
- Few drops of musk oil
- Few drops of ambergris oil

You may find it easier to mix the oils together first. Burn this for help from Venus in spells for love, healing and rituals involving women and beauty.

Mars Incense 1

- 2 parts galangal root
- 1 part coriander
- 1 part cloves
- ½ part basil
- Pinch of black pepper

Mars Incense 2

- 2 parts dragon's blood powder or resin
- 1 part cardamom
- 1 part clove
- 1 part Grains of Paradise

This is a good incense to use if you need the assertive qualities of Mars.

Mars Incense 3

- 4 parts benzoin resin
- 1 part pine needles or resin
- Scant pinch of black pepper

Burn this incense to utilize the powers and attributes of Mars or during spells involving lust, competition of any sort and anything to do with the masculine.

Jupiter Incense

- 1 part clove
- 1 part nutmeg
- 1 part cinnamon
- ½ part balm
- ½ part lemon peel

Remember that Jupiter is the planet and god of expansion, so you need to be very specific in your intent when calling upon Jupiter.

Saturn Incense 1

- 2 parts sandalwood resin
- 2 parts myrrh resin
- 1 part Dittany of Crete
- Few drops of cypress oil
- Few drops of patchouli oil

This is the recommended Saturn incense formula. Remember that Saturn does put blocks in the way, but then also encourages from behind.

Saturn Incense 2

- 2 parts cypress
- 1 part myrrh resin
- 1 part dittany
- Few drops of patchouli oil

Ceremonial and Consecrational

Here we have put together some of the older types of incense. Some are suitable for consecrating your altar, your tools, your circle and other artefacts, while others will help strengthen the magic in the ritual itself.

Altar Incense

- 1 part frankincense resin
- ½ part myrrh resin
- ¼ part cinnamon

Consecration Incense

- 1 part mace
- ½ part frankincense resin
- 1 part benzoin resin
- 1 part gum arabic

This incense can be used for consecrating your sacred space as well as any ritual tools.

Ceremonial Magic Incense

- 1 part frankincense resin
- ½ part gum mastic
- ¼ part sandalwood

Ritual Magic Incense
- 2 parts frankincense resin
- 1 part wood aloe
- Few drops of musk oil
- Few drops of ambergris oil

Circle Incense
- 2 parts frankincense resin
- 1 part myrrh resin
- 1 part benzoin resin
- ½ part sandalwood
- ¼ part cinnamon
- ½ part rose
- ½ part bay
- ¼ part vervain
- ¼ part rosemary

Sacred Space Incense
- ½ part bay
- ½ part camphor
- ½ part lavender
- ½ part broom
- ½ part linden
- ½ part ground ivy

Crystal Purification Incense
- 2 parts frankincense resin
- 2 parts copal resin
- 1 part sandalwood
- 1 part rosemary

This incense is used when consecrating your crystals so that they work magically for you. It "wipes" all other vibrations and aligns the crystal with your purpose.

Offertory Incense
- 2 parts frankincense resin
- 1 part myrrh resin
- 1 part cinnamon
- ½ part rose petals
- ½ part vervain

Burn this incense while honouring the goddesses and gods and also as an offering during rituals.

Talisman and Amulet Consecration Incense
- 2 parts frankincense resin
- 1 part cypress
- 1 part tobacco
- ½ part ash

Talisman Consecration
- 2 parts frankincense resin
- 1 part cypress
- 1 part ash leaves
- 1 part tobacco
- 1 pinch valerian
- 1 pinch alum
- 1 pinch of asafoetida powder (smells horrible)

Temple Incense
- 3 parts frankincense resin
- 2 parts myrrh resin
- Few drops of lavender oil
- Few drops of sandalwood oil

Burn this incense in your sacred space or grove. This is a good general incense.

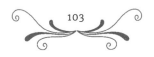

Universal Incense
- 3 parts frankincense resin
- 2 parts benzoin resin
- 1 part myrrh resin
- 1 part sandalwood
- 1 part rosemary

Burn this incense for all positive magical purposes. If used for negative magical goals, it will cancel out the spell or ritual.

The use of incense becomes such a part of everyday life that you will often find yourself feeling quite bereft when you are not within your own personally enhanced environment. Given below is a way of being able to enhance your environment wherever you are.

OILS

At various points in the book, you will read of the many oils that can be utilized as adjuncts to the various types of magic. They are an easy way of using plants in magical workings, particularly when space is at a premium.

Below are some oils that should be part of every magical practitioner's way of working. For your reference their Latin names are also given. All of them are simple to acquire and even though the initial expense may seem to be prohibitive, if they are stored according to directions, they will last for some time.

CINNAMON (*Cinnamomum zeylanicum*), with its warm vibration, brings into our hearts love from higher realms, if only we allow it. The warm glow of cinnamon exudes right through space and time, transforming sadness into happiness. Cinnamon was used in China in 2700BCE, and was known to the Egyptians by 1500BCE.

CLARY SAGE (*Salvia sclarea*) has benefits for both the physical and mental aspects of mankind, teaching us to be content with what we have. It brings prosperity of the spirit, and the realization that most problems arise in our imagination. This herb lifts the spirit and links with eternal wisdom.

FRANKINCENSE (*Boswellia carterii*) holds some of the wisdom of the universe, both spiritual and meditative. Able to cleanse the most negative of influences, it operates as a spiritual prop in a wide range of circumstances. It works far beyond the auric field, affecting the very subtle realms of energy and adapting the spiritual state. Frankincense is sometimes called olibanum.

GERANIUM (*Pelargonium graveolens*) resonates with Mother Earth and all that is feminine. It typifies the archetypal energy of Goddess culture. Its energy is transformational and as such it must always be used with respect. It comforts, opens our hearts and heals pain.

JASMINE (*Jasminum officinale*) provides us with our personal sanctuary and allows

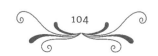

us access to a greater understanding of the spirit. It is said that jasmine brings the angelic kingdom within our reach, thus allowing us to be the best we can. It gives understanding and acceptance of the true meaning of spirituality.

LAVENDER (*Lavendula augustifolia*) is caring and nurturing. By allowing the heavenly energies close to the physical, it brings about healing and thus signifies the protective love of Mother Earth. Gentle and relaxing, it changes the perception to enable one to make progress. Lavender will not allow negative emotion to remain present within the aura for long.

MYRRH (*Commiphora myrrha*) signifies the pathway of the soul, allowing us to let go when the time is right. Wounds of body, mind and spirit are healed by myrrh and it brings realization that we no longer need to carry our burdens, releasing them from deep within. When combined with other oils, it enhances – and is enhanced by – them.

NEROLI (*Citrus aurantium*) is one of the most precious essential oils, its vibration being one of the highest. It is pure spirit and is loving and peaceful. It brings self-recognition and respite because it allows development of a new perspective, allowing us to cast off the bonds of old ways of relating and to develop unconditional love.

In magical working it allows one to be a pure channel.

NUTMEG (*Myristica fragrans*) helps us to reconnect with the higher realms of spirit and to experience again a sense of spiritual wonderment. When the spirit is affected by disappointment, spiritual pain and displacement, nutmeg works to bring hopes, dreams and prayers back into focus. At one time, nutmeg was given to people who were thought to be possessed by spirits.

ROSE ABSOLUT (*Rosa centifolia*) In India the "Great Mother" was known as the "Holy Rose" and this personification reveals just how profound the effects of this perfume are when used magically. Said to be the perfume of the guardians or messengers who guide us in times of need, it is a soul fragrance which allows us to access the divine mysteries. It is associated with the true needs of the heart.

ROSEMARY (*Rosmarinus officinalis*) reminds us of our purpose and of our own spiritual journey. It opens the human spirit to understanding and wisdom, and encourages confidence and clarity of purpose. It cleanses the aura and enables us to assist others in their search for spirituality.

SANDALWOOD (*Santalum album*) acts as a bridge between heaven and earth and allows us to make contact with divine beings. It

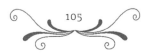

enables us to be calm enough to hear the music of the spheres and beings us into balance with the cosmos. It clarifies our strength of conviction.

YLANG YLANG (*Cananga odorata)* gives a new appreciation of the sensual side of our being. It balances the spirit so that we can be open to pleasures of the physical realm while still appreciating spiritual passions. It brings a sense of completion to the tasks that belong to the physical realm. Used magically, it achieves a balanced manifestation.

Ritual Bathing

One way in which essential oils can be used is in preparation for ritual and spell-making. Magical practitioners know that ritual bathing is an intrinsic part of any working and that they should come to their work as pure and unsullied as possible. Purification baths are not about personal cleanliness, but are part of acknowledging that the power and energy will flow more freely through a cleansed "vessel". There is a method for a ritual bath here, as well as a way of preparing bath salts.

Essential oils have within them all four of the Elements, a fact that many people like to acknowledge. They are products of the Earth, having been distilled, they flow (Water), they will burn (Fire) and they release perfume (Air). When the water and salt –

which also has a cleansing effect – of a ritual bath are combined, we have a perfect vehicle for cleansing our subtle energies.

Below are some ideas for you to try as blends for use in your ritual bath. The particular blends do have different effects, depending on the individual, so experiment until you find the one that suits you best. Make sure the oils are well blended.

Ritual Bath Oil Blends
- Neroli 3 drops
- Orange 1 drop
- Petitgrain 2 drops
- Myrtle 3 drops
- Clary sage 1 drop
- Lemon 1 drop
- Rosemary 2 drops
- Eucalyptus 1 drop
- Lavender 3 drops
- Chamomile 3 drops
- Mandarin 3 drops
- Frankincense 4 drops
- Lemon 2 drops
- Rose 3 drops
- Neroli 3 drops
- Essential oil blends

Essential oils can be used in spells to generate a higher vibration. The following blends can be used for anointing candles and for blessing objects as well as for personal use. Ideally, when you combine oils, they

should be well shaken together and left for at least an hour so that the synergy begins to work. Synergy takes place when the subtle vibrations of the oils blend to create a further vibration, therefore enhancing their energy.

If you are intending on using essential oils as massage oils, remember to use a carrier oil such as almond or grapeseed. Neat essential oils should, as a rule, never be used directly on the skin or ingested.

Romance Magnet Oil
- 2 drops ylang ylang oil
- 2 drops sandalwood oil
- 2 drops clary sage oil

To attract love, rub romance magnet oil onto a pink candle and then burn it for three hours a day, every day, until the person makes an advance. The candle should be snuffed rather than blown out.

Lover's Oil
- 5 drops rosewood oil
- 5 drops rosemary oil
- 3 drops tangerine oil
- 3 drops lemon oil

Lover's oil may be used to enhance a relationship in all sorts of ways. Consecrate a candle with lover's oil and light it half an hour before your date arrives.

Marriage Oil
- 2 drops frankincense oil
- 3 drops cypress oil
- 2 drops sandalwood oil

This combination of oils is used to reinforce a marriage relationship, whether the union is good or not. It may also be used to help steer a relationship towards marriage or further commitment. Simply burn a pink or lilac-colored candle anointed with marriage oil when you and your partner are together.

Desire Oil
- 3 drops lavender oil
- 3 drops orange oil
- 1 drop lemon oil

Desire oil is meant to entice another person to want you. If someone already does, but needs a little pushing, a red, orange, pink, blue, or white candle should be anointed and lit when the two of you are together. If you love someone and they are showing no response, speak their name as you light a candle blessed with desire oil. Allow the candles to burn for two hours before you snuff them out. Repeat each night, until the person reacts.

Dream Potion
- 10 drops jasmine oil
- 10 drops nutmeg oil
- 3 drops clary sage

This oil can be used to enhance the atmosphere of the bedroom before sleep. It is best burnt in an aromatherapy lamp rather being used as a body oil.

To Strengthen an Existing Relationship

- 10 drops rose oil
- 10 drops sandalwood oil
- 5 drops lavender oil

This oil can be used as a perfume or to scent the atmosphere.

Aphrodisiac Oils

Use the following two potent mixtures as a perfume or added to 50 ml (2 fl oz) of unscented massage oil (such as grapeseed or almond oil) and have fun!

- 10 drops ylang ylang
- 2 drops cinnamon
- 5 drops sweet orange
- 3 drops jasmine oil
- 10 drops patchouli
- 10 drops sandalwood
- 10 drops ylang ylang
- Oils for Ritual Work

The following oil blends can all be used in ritual work.

Sacred Space Blend

- 20 drops juniper berry oil
- 10 drops frankincense oil
- 10 drops sandalwood oil
- 5 drops rosemary oil
- 2 drops nutmeg oil

This is a good blend to use when you need to create a sacred space or magical circle.

Prosperity Blend

- Equal parts of patchouli and basil oil

This combination creates the right vibration for prosperity of all sorts (not necessarily financial).

Altar Oil Blend

- 4 parts frankincense
- 3 parts myrrh
- 1 part galangal
- 1 part vervain
- 1 part lavender

This blend is one that can be used to anoint your altar, if you use one, or to diffuse around your sacred space at regular intervals, before you undertake any ritual, to purify and empower the space.

Goddess Oil Blend

- 10 drops neroli oil
- 5 drops nutmeg oil
- 10 drops sandalwood oil
- 10 drops jasmine oil

When you invoke the Goddess, this oil is wonderful for allowing your vibration to meet with hers at any time of the year.

Protection Blend

- 10 drops juniper oil
- 5 drops vetiver oil
- 5 drops basil oil
- 2 drops clove oil

Should you feel that you are in need of protection, this oil can be burnt in an

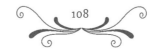

aromatherapy burner or sprinkled on a tissue and placed on a warm radiator.

Using Essential Oils in the Auric Field

As they begin working magically, almost all practitioners will find that they become more sensitive to the vibrations of the ordinary, everyday world. A crowded train, for instance, when you are bombarded by the various vibrations of your fellow travellers, can be very difficult to handle. This difficulty arises because your own particular "force field," called the aura – which you carry with you always – begins to vibrate at a different level than the one to which you are accustomed and do not notice on an everyday level.

If you begin to do a great deal of magical work, you must learn to protect yourself, perhaps from onslaughts of negativity or subtle vibrations over which others have no control. Always remember that you have at your disposal the means for control and it should become a regular part of your routine to enhance your own aura and to protect that of others. Essential oils can help you to do this.

Methods of Using Oils for Protective Purposes

Method 1

Put just one drop of your chosen pure essential oil in the centre of your palm and rub your hands together. In this instance the oil is used neat. Holding your hands about 10 cm (4 in) away from your body, smooth around the outside of this space, starting from the top of your head down to your feet and then back up again. Make sure you have covered every part that you can reach of this very subtle body. This is also known as protecting your aura.

Method 2

Use your chosen oils in a spray or diffuser, spraying around your body and over the top of your head again, ensuring that you cover the whole area. Prepare your oils in advance, combining them as necessary. Leave them for a week in a quiet, dark place away from electrical equipment. On the eighth day use a new fragrance sprayer, preferably a glass bottle, add about 25 ml (1 fl oz) of the purest water available and the essential oils and shake the sprayer vigorously. This can also be used to protect your sacred space or immediate environment.

Energizing Oils

The following are energizing oils and will give a real lift to your power (the proportions used can be to your own personal preference): Basil, Coriander, Eucalyptus, Fir, Lemon, Peppermint, Spruce.

Harmonizing Oils

The oils in this next group are used for establishing harmony, both in person who uses them and in the atmosphere: Clary sage, Fennel, Geranium, Ginger,

Juniper, Lavender, Mandarin, Orange, Petitgrain.

Following is a selection of recipes based on all these oils:

Cleansing blend
- Pine 4 drops
- Lemon 3 drops
- Basil 3 drops
- Fir needle 5 drops
- Spruce 5 drops

This blend cleanses the aura, as suggested above, and gives an idea of the correct proportions to use.

Aura harmonization
- Geranium 4 drops
- Juniper 2 drops
- Orange 6 drops

- Fennel 1 drop
- Petitgrain 6 drops

This blend is particularly useful when you wish to cleanse and harmonize your aura.

Connecting with the Essential
The oils below help you to make a connection with your spiritual self, the essential you: Frankincense, Rose, Neroli, Linden blossom, Jasmine.

Linking blend
- Galbanum 1 drop
- Frankincense 4 drops
- Jasmine 2 drops
- Neroli 7 drops
- Rose 7 drops

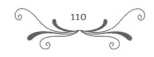

DEITIES AND THEIR WORSHIP

The more accustomed you become to making spells, the more you will begin to appreciate the power of the various deities and how that power was used by our forebears. While many of us probably subscribe to the belief that there is one God, we cannot help but marvel at the complexity of the energies and powers that go into making up that entity. For this reason it is sometimes more comforting to be able to approach that complexity in the way our forefathers did – with reverence for a particular aspect. We do this when we call upon the various deities.

In a book such as this, where the perspective is as wide as possible, it would be remiss not to give some information on the deities associated with the major religions, particularly when those religions are of such antiquity. Unfortunately, it is possible only to give information on a basic level, but it will enable you to begin exploring for yourself the myriad energies available to you.

Most religions pay due attention to the masculine and feminine polarities and energies. When you choose to personalize

those energies, you find yourself in a new relationship with them. In many ways the personalization of energy is one of the most important aspects of working with the deities. It allows us to feel close to something that is otherwise intangible; to feel that we are in touch with another dimension of being that is considerably wiser and more powerful than we are.

For many people, perceiving the masculine as Lord and the feminine as Lady is enough. Others need something more mundane and down to earth, and will attribute the masculine to the Sun and the feminine to the Moon, and thus allow themselves access to the rich symbolism there is in doing so. Many others will want to break down aspects of the masculine and feminine into various qualities and find it easier to work with representations of those qualities. Universal power in its entirety is often difficult for the beginner to understand or work with, yet ultimately we have to recognize its potency. You may find that a dualistic way of working with energy is not

for you and that is also completely fine. Use your intuition to understand the divine in the universe and what that means to you.

By placing representations of the deities on your altar or in calling on them to assist in your spells, you are accessing an energy which perhaps would not be otherwise be available to you. At all times you must be comfortable with this and will therefore use the entities that most appeal to you. Only use a deity from a belief system other than your own if you feel it is right.

Included here is a comprehensive selection from a number of belief systems, mostly major deities, but also some rather intriguing minor ones. There are some spells, rituals and incenses to give you some idea of how to call upon the gods or to use their energies. You may like to research further, both to find gods and goddesses appropriate for your own workings and also for spells which satisfy your creativity.

CELTIC GODS AND GODDESSES

Gaulish Gods

BELENUS (also Bel) is the God of light and the Sun, also known as the Shining One. The most extensively worshipped Celtic god, he has particular authority for the welfare of sheep and cattle. The Feast of Beltane means "Fire of Bel".

CERNUNNOS is a god of fertility, life, animals, wealth and the underworld. Usually shown with a stag's antlers, he carries a purse filled with coins. The horned god, he is born at the winter solstice, marries the Goddess of the Moon at Beltane, and dies at the summer solstice. Worshipped all over Gaul, he is identified as Herne the Hunter in Britain. With the Goddess of the Moon, he jointly rules over the cycle of life, death and reincarnation.

OGMIOS is the God of scholars and eloquence. Known in Ireland as Ogma, he is a hero god who invented the runic language of the Druids, the Ogham Staves. Sometimes associated with the Greek hero Heracles, he is shown as a bald old man, dressed in a lion's skin.

SUCELLUS is the guardian of forests and the God of agriculture; he also ferries the dead to the afterlife. He is often portrayed with a huge hammer and a dog by his side. In this aspect he links with the Norse Thor and the Egyptian Anubis.

TARANIS, whose name means "the thunderer," has as his symbols the wheel, representing the Wheel of Life and the lightning flash. He is sometimes identified with the Roman God Jupiter and the Norse God Thor.

TEUTATES is a god of war, fertility and wealth; his name means "the god of the tribe". He was greatly worshipped at a time

when human sacrifices were made. He was the counterpart of the Roman god Mars and was also known as Alborix, King of the World.

Gaulish Goddesses

BELISAMA is goddess of light and fire, forging and craft; she is the wife of Belenus. She relates to the Roman goddess Minerva, and to the Greek goddess Athena. Her name means "most brilliant".

EPONA is the goddess of horses, mules and cavalrymen. She is usually shown lying on a horse, sitting sidesaddle or standing surrounded by many horses. Her other symbol is that of the cornucopia – the horn of plenty – which suggests that she may also have been a fertility or corn Goddess.

ROSMERTA is a goddess of fertility and wealth. Her stick with two snakes links her to Mercury, messenger of the Roman gods. The cornucopia – another of her symbols – identifies her as a fertility goddess and thus connects her with Epona.

Irish Gods

BRES is the god of fertility and agriculture. He is the son of Elatha, a prince of the Fomorians, and Eriu, a queen of the Tuatha De Danann.

BILE corresponds with the Gaulish God Belenus and shares his attributes.

DAGDA (also Dagde, DaGodevas) is God of the Earth and Father-God, that is, the masculine principle. A formidable warrior and skilled craftsman, he has a club that can restore life as well as kill. His symbols are a bottomless cauldron of plenty and a harp with which he rules the seasons.

DIAN CECHT (also Dianchcht) is a god of healing. He rules the waters that restore life to the old and dying gods. When Nuada (king of the Tuatha De Danann) lost his hand in battle, Dian Cecht made him a silver one.

LUGH was worshipped during the thirty-day midsummer feast in Ireland. Magical sexual rites undertaken in his name ensured ripening of the crops and a prosperous harvest. He is linked with Rosmerta in Gaul and also corresponds to the Roman god Mercury. His animal totems are the raven and the lynx, representing deviousness. He is known as Lleu in Wales.

NODENS was a god of healing. His magic hounds were believed to be able to cure the sick.

Irish Goddesses

AIRMID is a healing goddess and has responsibility for medicinal plants. She is the keeper of the spring that brings the dead back to life.

BOANN is a goddess of bounty and fertility, whose totem is the sacred white cow. She

was the wife of Nechtan, a water deity. One story is that the father of her son was Dagda.

BRIGHID (also Bridget, Brigit, Brighid, Brigindo) is the goddess of healing and fertility, patroness of smiths, poets and doctors. Often symbolized by a white swan or a cow with red horns, she was thought to be the daughter of Dagda. Her festival is that of Imbolc, observed on 2 February. She shares attributes with the ancient Greek Triple Goddess Hecate.

DANU (also Don in Welsh) probably existed earlier as Anu, the Universal Mother. She is said to be to be the mother of Dagda, God of the Tuatha De Danaan.

MORRIGAN is the goddess of war and death. Married to Dagda, she is linked with negative femininity and the more fearsome characteristics of the Triple Goddess. She could transform into a crow or raven.

TUATHA De Danann ("People of the Goddess Danu") are the members of an ancient race who inhabited Ireland before Danu made Dagda, her son, their God. They perfected the use of magic and are credited with the possession of magical powers and great wisdom. The plough, the hazel and the Sun were sacred to them.

Welsh Gods

AMAETHON is the Welsh god of agriculture.

BRAN is a hero god and also the god of poetry and the underworld. His name means "raven".

BELATU-CADROS is a god of war and of the destruction of enemies. His name means "fair shining one". The Romans linked him with Mars.

DEWI is a dragon god, represented by the Great Red Serpent. The official emblem of Wales is derived from this representation.

DYLAN is a sea god, brother of Lleu. He is said to have slipped into the sea at birth, possibly in order to avoid the curses their mother Arianrhod placed upon them.

GWYDION is a warrior and a magician god. He was brother to Arianrhod. There are various stories about him – the most well-known suggesting that he fathered Lleu and Dylan or that he raised and passed on his knowledge to Lleu.

LLEU (also Lleu Llaw Gyffes) is god of arts and crafts, also a solar and hero god. His name translates as "the fair one has a skilful hand". Brother of Dylan, he was denied a name by his mother Arianrhod (see below). Overcoming these problems, he became one of the most revered of Welsh gods.

MATH is an eminent magician and lord of North Wales, brother of Don, the Welsh mother-Goddess. Returning from battle he discovered that his foot-holder, who had to be a virgin, had been raped by his nephews (see Arianrhod). Furious, he turned them first of all into a stag and a hind, then a boar and a sow, and then a wolf and a she-wolf.

Welsh Goddesses

ARIANRHOD is a Moon goddess. Her name means "silver wheel". She is the daughter of Don, sister of Gwydion. Given the position of foot-holder to Math, and therefore supposedly a virgin, she nevertheless gave birth to Dylan and Lleu, cursing the latter, thus taking her revenge on all men. She is an aspect of the Triple Goddess.

BRANWEN is the goddess of love and beauty. She is linked with the Greek goddess Aphrodite and the Roman goddess Venus.

CERIDWEN is best known in her aspect of the "Dark Goddess". She was the keeper of the Cauldron of Inspiration and Knowledge. She causes things to be reborn (changed, by having been given her protection) and at the same time is in charge of the actual process of generation. She has the power of knowing what is needed, whatever the circumstances.

RHIANNON is believed to be the Welsh counterpart of the Gaulish horse goddess Epona and the Irish goddess Macha.

Egyptian Gods

AMUN (also Ammon, Amon Ra) was a supreme god of the ancient Egyptians. His worship spread to Greece, where he was identified with Zeus, and to Rome where he was known as Jupiter Ammon.

ANUBIS is the god of mummification and protector of tombs and is often represented as having a jackal's head. He is said to have weighed the souls of the dead against a feather.

ATUM was known as "the complete one". He is a great creator-god thought to have been the oldest worshipped at Heliopolis. He is usually shown as a man wearing a double crown.

APIS, a God depicted as a bull, symbolized fertility and strength in war. Apis was worshipped especially at Memphis.

BES is a protector of women during pregnancy and childbirth. Fond of parties and sensual music, he is also credited with being able to dispel evil spirits.

GEB (also Kebu, Seb, Sibu, Sivu) is a God of the earth, earthquakes and fertility. His sister Nut was his counterpart as the Sky Goddess.

HORUS, a sky god whose symbol is the hawk, is usually depicted as a falcon-headed man. He was regarded as the protector of the

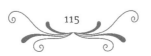

monarchy and his name was often added to royal titles. He assumed various aspects and was known to the Greeks as Harpocrates (Horus the Child).

KHEPHRA (also Khephera, Khopri) is said to have been self-created and God of the Dawn Sun. His symbol is the scarab beetle, which stands for health, strength and virility. Wear a scarab amulet if you wish to invoke Khephra's protection.

KHONSU, whose name means "he who crosses," was a Moon god worshipped especially at Thebes and was the divine son of Amun and Mut.

OSIRIS, a god originally associated with fertility, was the husband of Isis and father of Horus. He is known chiefly through the story of his death at the hand of his brother Seth and his subsequent restoration by his wife Isis to a new life as ruler of the Afterlife.

PTAH was an ancient deity of Memphis, creator of the universe, god of artisans and husband of Sekhmet. He became one of the chief deities of Egypt and was identified by the Greeks with Hephaestus.

RA, the supreme Egyptian Sun God, was worshipped as the creator of all life and often portrayed with a falcon's head bearing the solar disc. He appears traveling in his ship with other gods, crossing the sky by day and journeying through the underworld at the dead of night.

SETH, as one of the oldest of the Egyptian deities, is the god of chaos and evil. He is shown as a man with the head of a monster.

THOTH is the God of knowledge, law, wisdom, writing and the Moon. He is also the measurer of time and depicted either as an ibis, a man with the head of an ibis, or as a baboon.

Egyptian Goddesses

BAST (also Bastet) is a goddess who is usually shown as a woman with the head of a cat and wearing one gold earring and carrying a sistrum in her right hand. She is the goddess of pleasure, dancing, music and joy. Cats were considered to be her sacred animal and were therefore protected from harm.

HATHOR is a sky goddess, the patron of love and joy, represented variously as a cow, with a cow's head or ears or with a solar disk between the cow's horns. Her name means "House of Horus".

ISIS is first a nature Goddess, wife of Osiris and mother of Horus. Her worship spread to Western Asia, Greece and Rome, where she was identified with various local goddesses. When Seth killed Osiris she sought his scattered body in order that she could give birth to Horus, a sky god.

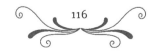

MAAT is the goddess of truth, justice and cosmic order and was the daughter of Ra. She is depicted as a young and beautiful woman, seated or standing, with a feather on her head.

MUT is the queen of all the gods and regarded as the wife of all living things. She was also the wife of Amon and mother of Khonsu. She is usually depicted with the head of a vulture. Her name means "the mother".

NUT, the Sky Goddess, was thought to swallow the Sun at night and give birth to it in the morning. She is usually shown as a naked woman with her body arched above the earth, which she touches with her feet and hands.

SEKHMET is a fierce lion goddess, counterpart of the gentler cat goddess Bast and wife of Ptah at Memphis. Her messengers were abominable creatures who could bring about diseases and other curses on mankind.

Greek Gods

APOLLO, son of Zeus and Leto, and brother of Artemis, is presented as the ideal type of manly beauty. He is associated with the Sun and linked especially with music, poetic inspiration, archery, medicine and pastoral life.

ASCLEPIUS, as god of healing and the son of Apollo, is often represented wearing a staff with a serpent coiled round it. He sometimes bears a scroll or tablet thought to represent medical learning.

CHAOS is the first created being, from which came the primeval deities Gaia, Tartarus, Erebus and Nyx.

CRONUS (also Kronos) is the leader of the Titans and the ruler of time. He married his sister Rhea, who bore him several children who became Gods, including Zeus, who eventually overthrew him.

DIONYSUS was called Bacchus by the Romans and was originally a god of the fertility of nature. Associated with wild and ecstatic religious rites, in later traditions he is a god of wine who loosens inhibitions and inspires creativity in music and poetry.

EREBUS is the primeval god of darkness, son of Chaos.

HADES is the God of the Underworld who received as his weapon the helmet of invisibility. He captured Persephone as his consort, causing chaos in the upper world when Demeter went searching for Persephone.

HELIOS is the Sun personified as a god. He is generally represented as a charioteer driving daily from east to west across the sky.

HEPHAESTUS is the god of fire (especially the smithy fire) and was identified with Vulcan by Romans. He is also the god of craftsmen of all kinds – metalworkers, blacksmiths, leatherworkers, weavers, potters, and painters.

HERMES is the messenger of the gods and the god of merchants, thieves and public speaking. Usually pictured as a herald equipped for traveling with broad-brimmed hat, winged shoes and a winged rod, he was identified by the Romans with Mercury.

HYPNOS, the god of sleep, was the son of Nyx (night).

PAN, as a god of flocks and herds, is usually represented with the horns, ears and legs of a goat on a man's body. He was thought of as loving mountains, caves and lonely places as well as playing on the pan-pipes. He is also a god of Nature.

POSEIDON is the god of the sea, water, earthquakes and horses. When angered, he was perceived as needing to be pacified. He is often portrayed with a trident in his hand and is identified with the Roman god Neptune.

PROTEUS is a minor sea god with the power of prophecy but who would assume different shapes to avoid answering questions.

SILENUS, an ancient woodland deity, was entrusted with the education of Dionysus. He is shown either as stately, inspired and tuneful or as a drunken old man.

URANUS is a personification of heaven or the sky, the most ancient of the Greek gods and the first ruler of the universe.

ZEUS is the supreme god. He was the protector and ruler of humankind, the dispenser of good and evil and the god of weather. He was identified with Jupiter by the Romans.

Greek Goddesses
ACHLYS is the Greek Mother – the first being to exist, according to myth. She gave birth to Chaos.

AMPHITRITE is a sea goddess, wife of Poseidon and mother of Triton.

APHRODITE is the goddess of beauty, fertility and sexual love, identified by the Romans with Venus. She is portrayed both as the daughter of Zeus and Dione, or as being born of the sea foam.

ARACHNE is a spider Goddess. Originally a mortal, she was a talented weaver who challenged Athene to compete with her. Athene was greatly displeased by Arachne's subject matter and in retribution turned her into a spider.

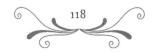

ARTEMIS, a huntress goddess, is often depicted with a bow and arrows and is associated with birth, fertility and abundance. She was identified with the Roman goddess Diana and with Selene.

ATHENE is identified with the Roman Minerva and often symbolized as an epitome of wisdom and strategy; she is also called Pallas. Statues show her as female and fully armed; the owl is regularly associated with her.

CYBELE is a goddess of caverns and of the primitive earth. Also known as a bee goddess, she ruled over wild beasts.

DEMETER is a corn and barley goddess, and also goddess of the earth in its productive state. She is mother of Persephone. She is identified with Ceres and also Cybele; her symbol is often an ear of corn.

HECATE is the goddess of dark places, often associated with ghosts and sorcery and worshipped with offerings at crossroads. Identified as Queen of the Witches in the modern day, she is frequently identified with Artemis and Selene.

HERA was worshipped as the queen of heaven and a marriage goddess. The Romans identified her with Juno.

HESTIA is a goddess of hearth and fire, much like Brigid. She was believed to preside at all sacrificial altar fires and prayers were offered to her before and after meals. In Rome, Hestia was worshipped as Vesta.

NEMESIS is a goddess usually portrayed as the agent of divine punishment for wrongdoing or presumption. She is often little more than the personification of retribution.

NIKE is the goddess of victory, who challenged her suitors to outrun her.

PERSEPHONE was called Proserpina by the Romans. From a magical perspective her story symbolizes the return of fertility to the earth. Hades, king of the underworld, wanted her as his wife, carrying her off and making her queen of the underworld. Demeter, her mother, unable to find her, began to pine and famine began to spread around the world. Eventually it was agreed that she would spend six months on earth and six months in the underworld.

SELENE, the Goddess of the Moon, is identified with Artemis.

THEMIS is the daughter of Uranus (Heaven) and Gaia (Earth). She is the personification of order and justice, who convenes the assembly of the gods.

Roman Gods

CUPID is the god of love and was identified by the Romans with Eros. He is often pictured as a beautiful naked boy with wings, carrying a bow and arrow, with which he pierces his victims.

JANUS is an ancient Italian deity. He is guardian of doorways, gates and beginnings and protector of the state in times of war. He is usually represented with two faces, so that he looks both forwards and backwards.

JUPITER is the chief god of the Roman state, giver of victory, and is identified with Zeus. Also called Jove, he was originally a sky god associated with lightning and the thunderbolt. His wife was Juno.

MARS is the god of war and the most important god after Jupiter. He is identified by the Greek with Ares and was probably originally an agricultural god. The month of March is named after him.

MERCURY is the god of eloquence, skill, trading and thieving. He was a herald and messenger of the gods, who was identified with Hermes.

NEPTUNE is the god of water, originally fresh water and latterly of the sea. He is also the god of horse-racing, and is also identified with the Greek Poseidon.

PLUTO is the God of the Underworld and of transformation. He has responsibility for precious metals and was sometimes known as the Rich One.

SATURN is an ancient god identified with the Greek Cronus, often regarded as a god of agriculture. His festival in December, Saturnalia, eventually became one of the elements in the traditional celebrations of Christmas.

SILVANUS is an Italian woodland deity identified with Pan. He is also worshipped in the Celtic religion.

Roman Goddesses

ANGERONA is the goddess of secrecy and is portrayed with her mouth bound and sealed, her finger raised to her mouth in a gesture of warning.

BONA Dea is an earth goddess of fertility who was worshipped by women only – no men were allowed present during her rites. The Romans would even cover up statues of the male gods when her rite was performed.

CERES, the corn goddess, is commonly identified by the Romans with Demeter.

DIANA is an early goddess identified with Artemis and associated with hunting, virginity and the Moon.

JUNO is an ancient mother goddess and became the most important goddess of the Roman state. She was the wife of Jupiter.

MINERVA is the goddess of handicrafts, commonly worshipped and associated with Athene. Because of this association, she came to be regarded as the goddess of war.

MUSES (Roman and Greek) are the goddesses who presided over the arts and sciences. Customarily nine in number (Calliope, Clio, Eurterpe, Terpsichore, Erato, Melpomene, Thalia, Polyhymnia and Urania), their functions and even their names differ widely between the various sources.

VENUS, the supreme goddess of beauty, is identified with Aphrodite and was honoured as the mother of the Roman people. In earlier times, she was a spirit of kitchen gardens.

VESTA, the goddess of the hearth and household, was considered important enough to have her own handmaidens, the vestal virgins.

Norse Gods and Goddesses

Deities in Scandinavia were originally of two sorts – Aesir and Vanir. These latter were largely nature deities rather than fertility gods and goddesses, and were incorporated into the former after warring with them. The Scandinavian creation myth is that the gods Odin, Vili and Ve, three brothers, were walking by the sea when they found two trees out of which they fashioned the parents of the human race, giving them spirit, life, wit, feeling, form and the five senses. They then retired to Asgard where they dwelt in a great house or hall called Gladsheim. Valhall in Gladsheim was Odin's place of the warriors, while Yggdrasil, the "World Tree" – a universal column sustaining everything – was one version of the Tree of Life. It is sometimes thought to be the sacred ash tree.

Gods

There are many Scandinavian deities. Some of the most important ones to appeal to in spell-making are:

BALDER, whose name means bright, was the son of Odin and Frigg. The wisest of the gods, his judgements were final. He was killed by Loki, who gave him mistletoe, the only plant that had not agreed to protect him.

FREY is the God of Yule, traditionally born on the winter solstice, usually 21 December. He is a god of peace and plenty who brings fertility and prosperity. His effigy was paraded by the people on a wagon throughout the land, in the dead of winter.

LOKI is the personification of malicious mischief. Probably initially a fire god, he is supposed to bring the gods great hardship

but also to be able to relieve this. He is somewhat capricious and not to be trusted. He is known as The Trickster.

NJORD rules the winds and quietens both the sea and fire. He is appealed to when undertaking a journey, and when hunting. He is worshipped by seafarers. Also the god of wealth, he is often coupled in toasts with his son, Frey.

ODIN (also Woden) is a magician and wise one. He learned the secrets of the runes by hanging himself from the ash tree Yggdrasil for nine nights. He was a shape-shifter and was known as Father of the Gods. Wednesday (Odin's Day) was named after him.

THOR is the Thunderer, who wields his divine hammer – he was the strongest of the Gods. His chariot racing across the sky is said to generate thunder, though other stories suggest this is done when he blows into his beard. He is also a fertility god. Thursday (Thor's Day) was named after him.

TYR is the god of battle, identified with Mars, after whom Tuesday is named.

Goddesses

FREYA, the daughter of Njord, is the goddess of love, beauty and sexuality. She is said to choose the souls of those who have fallen in battle to take them to Valhalla (Odin's heaven). She is particularly skilled in magic.

FRIGG is Odin's wife and the foremost of the Asyngur (Goddesses). She is the patroness of the household and of married women. She was, and is, invoked by the childless. Also the mother of the Aesir, she gives her name to Friday. She was inadvertently instrumental in Balder's death – all things took oaths not to hurt him, except mistletoe, which was considered by Frigg to be too young.

IDUNN possessed the apples of immortality, which rejuvenated the gods when they grew old. Because Scandinavian gods were not immortal, they therefore depended upon her and her good will for the continuation of life.

NORNS are the three virgin goddesses of destiny (Urd or Urder, Verdandi and Skuld). They sit by the Well of Fate at the base of the ash tree Yggdrasil and spin the Web of Fate.

OSTARA'S symbols are the egg and the hare. While not strictly Nordic, she is a Germanic goddess of fertility who is celebrated at the time of the spring equinox. She was allegedly known by the Saxons as Eostre, the goddess of spring, from whom we have derived the word Easter, though modern-day research tends to disprove this.

SKADI was the consort of Njord and is said to have preferred to live in the mountains rather than by the sea. She is the Goddess of death, independence and hunting.

South American Gods

BACABS (Mayan) are the gods of the four points of the compass, who hold up the sky. They are also lords of the seasons.

CHAC (Aztec and Mayan) is a rain and vegetation god. He is also the lord of thunder, lightning, wind and fertility and revered particularly by farmers.

CUPARA (Jivaro) and his wife are the parents of the Sun, for whom they created the Moon from mud to be his mate. The children of the Sun and Moon are the animals.

HUNAB KU (also known as Kinebahan) is the chief god of the Mayan pantheon, the Great God without Form, existing only in spirit.

HUEHUETEOTL (Aztec), a fire god, is also patron of warriors and kings. Associated with creation, he is often depicted as a crouched old man with a bowl of burning incense on his head.

HURAKAN (Mayan) is god of thunderstorms and the whirlwind. His name gave us the word "hurricane". At the behest of his friend Gucumatz, son of the Sun and the Moon, Hurakan created the world, the animals, men and fire.

IMAYMANA VIRACOCHA AND **TOCAPO VIRACOCHA** (Inca) are the sons of the creator god Viracocha. They gave names to all the trees, flowers, fruits and herbs and supervised the people, telling them which of these could be eaten, which could cure, and which could kill.

INTI (Inca) is a Sun god. His image is a golden disk with a human face surrounded by bright rays. Every day Inti soars across the sky to the western horizon, plunges into the sea and swims under the earth back to the east. His sons, Viracocha, Manco Capac and Pachamac, are all creator gods.

ITZAMNA (Maya) is a sky god and healer and son of Hunab Ku. God of drawing and letters, patron of learning and the sciences, Itzamna is said to be able to bring the dead back to life.

KINICH AHAU (also Ah Xoc Kin) (Mayan), the Sun god, is usually shown with jaguar features, wearing the symbol of Kin (the Mayan day). As Ah Xoc Kin, he was associated with music and poetry.

KUKULCAN (Mayan) is a serpent god and has similarities to Quetzalcoatl of the Aztecs.

NGURVILU (Araucanian, Chile) is god of lakes and seas.

PILLAN (Araucanian, Chile) is god of fire, thunder, and war, chief of all the gods. Aided by brigades of evil spirits, he causes

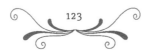

earthquakes and volcanic eruptions, blights crops, creates storms and sends war.

QUETZALCOATL (Aztec) is an ancient deity and greatly revered; he is also believed to have been the creator god and is identified with the planet Venus. He is also identified with breath, wind, rain and sea breezes. The incense below is a powerful one, that is suitable for use in spells and rituals which appeal to Quetzalcoatl or any of the major Aztec gods and goddesses.

TEZCATLIPOCA (Aztec) is an all-powerful god who can see everything that happens in the world as it is reflected in his mirror. He is associated with night, the jaguar, sorcery, natural forces, human strength, weakness, wealth, happiness and sorrow.

TUPAN (Tupinamba, Brazil) is god of thunder and lightening. When Tupan visits his mother, the passage of his boat causes storms. The Tupinamba respect, but do not worship, Tupan.

VIRACOCHA (Inca) means, literally, sea foam. The creator and teacher of the world, Virococha made new people out of clay after the Great Flood. On each figure he painted the features, clothes and hairstyles of the many nations, and gave to them their languages, songs and the seeds they were to plant. Bringing them to life, Viracocha ordered them to travel underground and emerge at different places on the earth. Then Viracocha made the Sun, Moon and stars, and assigned them to their places in the sky.

South American Goddesses

AUCHIMALGEN (Araucanian, Chile) as Moon goddess and wife of the Sun wards off evil.

EVAKI (Bakairi) is goddess of night. She is said to place the Sun in a pot every night and move it back to its starting point in the east every day.

IX CHEL (Maya) is consort of Itzamna and goddess of the Moon, weaving and medicine. Except for Hunab Ku, all the other gods are the progeny of Ix Chel and Itzamna.

MAMA QUILLA (Inca) is goddess of the Moon and protector of married women. Her image is a silver disc with a human face.

TONANTZIN (Aztec) is a goddess of fertility.

XOCHIQUETZAL (Aztec), originally a Moon goddess of the earth, flowers, plants, games and dance, is principally a goddess of love. Also beloved of artisans, prostitutes, pregnant women and birth, she is the most charming of the Aztec pantheon. She is responsible for butterflies, symbolic of love, death and rebirth, transformation, hope, freedom, and spiritual awakening, and birds.

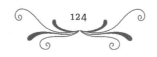

Sumerian, Assyrian and Babylonian Gods and Goddesses

Many of the gods and goddesses shown below are well-known through myth and other stories handed down through time. Only true scholars of the period are able to differentiate between the cultures. The creation stories however give us access to some very primeval, raw energies. These entities release a great deal of energy for use in magic and spell making, so only use them if you feel confident that you have learnt to understand them.

Gods

ANSHAR is father of all the gods. Anshar is the male principle, Kishu, his sister, the female. Anshar is the sky, Kishu the earth. He led the gods in the war against Tiamat.

ANU is the god of the sky and one of four Sumerian creator gods. Lord of all, the fountainhead of order in both the natural and supernatural worlds, Anu dwells exclusively in the celestial heaven.

APSU is the Abyss, the waters upon which the earth floats. When the gods were first created, their noise disturbed Apsu, who complained to the great dragon Tiamat (see below).

EA (also Enki) is the god of water, particularly fresh. He is the supreme god of magic and wisdom, patron of the arts and consulted as an oracle. Mating with Ninhursag, he created plants and gave men agriculture. In Sumerian belief he is the son of Nintu.

ENLIL is the god of earth and wind and the master of men's fates. One of four Sumerian creating gods, he is the god who dries up the flood waters, yet who brings rain, fills the sails of ships and boats; and fertilizes the palm blossoms. He is the god who struggles against the suffering of the world and is the active principle which drives the earth.

GILGAMESH was, like Hercules, a hero-god, two parts divine and one part human. Gilgamesh, having fought and tamed the wild man Enkiddu, set out with him on a quest. Enkiddu's death drove Gilgamesh to seek immortality, and eventually with his wife, he was granted eternal life by the gods.

KINGU is consort of Tiamat and keeper of the tablets of destiny, which hold the divine plan for all the cosmos. Ninhursag used Kingu's blood to make the first man, and from this comes the rebellious aspect of human nature.

MARDUK is the counterpart of the Sumerian Anu and Enlil. Chief god of Babylon, he became the lord of the gods of heaven and earth after conquering Tiamat, the monster of primeval chaos, thus bringing order and life to the world.

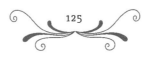

NEBO (also Nabu) is god of writing and speech, speaker for the gods. Nebo maintains records of men's deeds and produces them for judgment after death. His symbol is the stylus.

NERGAL is god of the underworld, consort of Ereshkigal.

SHAMASH (also Babbar) is the son of Sin, brother and husband to Ishtar. The enemy of darkness and all the evil darkness brings, in Sumeria he is a god of divination. He requires justice of earthly kings and champions their subjects, especially the poor.

SIN is the Moon god who flies through the sky in his sailing boat every night. Wise and secretive, the enemy of all evil spirits, he is the counterpart of the Sumerian Nanna.

TAMMUZ (also Dumuzi) is an agricultural god. The god who dies and rises again, he became the personification of the seasonal death and rebirth of crops. He corresponds to the Greek Adonis and to the Green Man.

Goddesses

ASTARTE (Phoenician) is a goddess of fertility and sexual love; she later became identified with the Egyptian goddess Isis and the Greek Aphrodite, among others.

DAMKINA is the Earth Mother goddess, wife of Ea and mother of Marduk.

ERESHKIGAL is goddess of the underworld, consort of Nergal. Some consider her a dark side, aspect or sister of Ishtar. When Ishtar descended into the underworld, Ereshkigal tricked her into leaving part of her clothing or insignias at each of the underworld's seven gates as she passed through them. Standing naked at the seventh gate, Ishtar threw herself on Ereshkigal's mercy. Ereshkigal confined Ishtar in the underworld until Ea contrived her release with a trick.

ISHTAR (also Inanna) is a goddess whose name and functions correspond to those of Astarte. A great goddess, the goddess of love and war, Ishtar's worship involved phallic symbols, sacred whores and painted priests in women's clothing.

NINHURSAG is an Earth Mother, corresponding to Egyptian Ma'at.

NINTU (also Ki) is a great Sumerian goddess, wife of Anu and mother of all gods. She created humans from clay.

TIAMAT is the representation of primeval chaos. Angered by the gods, she fought against them and was slain by Marduk. Being split in two, one half became the Heavens and the other the Earth. She is sometimes known as the Great Serpent and gave rise to the concept of the original Leviathan – the primeval monster of the deep.

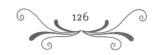

African Gods and Goddesses

In African religions, many beliefs go back some 6,000 years and there are numerous deities and traditions associated with them. Only a few are included here and, as always, your own personal research will give you much satisfaction, should you choose to appeal to these gods and goddesses.

ANANSI (various tribes) is a creator god. He is also a trickster and corresponds to Loki. Viewed as something of a scoundrel, he is well liked and many amusing and fanciful stories are told of him. He is often used to frighten children.

ANYIEWO (Ewe) is the Great Serpent who comes out to graze after the rain. The rainbow is his reflection.

BUKU (various West African peoples) is a sky god sometimes worshipped as a goddess. Buku created everything, even the other gods.

DANH (also Dan Ayido Hwedo) (Dahomey) is a snake god; the Haitians know him as Dan Petro. Danh is often portrayed with his tail in his mouth as a symbol of unity and wholeness, similar to the ouroboros. As the rainbow, he is a spiral around the earth and holds it together. He is known in Vodou as Damballa.

DXUI (Bushman; to the Hottentots, Tsui; to the Xhosa and Ponda, Thixo) is a creator god. He took the form of a different flower or plant every day, becoming himself at night, until he had created all the plants and flowers that exist.

ESHU (Yoruba) is a trickster and shape-shifter who can change his form at will. He also knows all human tongues, and acts as a go-between for mortals and the gods.

GUNAB (Hottentot) is the enemy of Tsui-Goab (see below). He kept overpowering him but the latter grew stronger after each battle. He is considered responsible for all misfortune, disease and death.

GUA (Ga tribe of West Africa) is the god of thunder, blacksmiths and farmers. He corresponds to Thor. Gua's temples are often found at blacksmith's forges.

LEZA (Central Africa) is known to a number of peoples. He is the supreme god who rules the sky and sends wind and rain.

MAWU-LISA (Ewe) are the great god and goddess of the Sun and Moon. Lisa is the Sun and Mawu is the Moon.

MULUNGU (East Africa) is God, the Supreme Being. The concept of a supreme being and creator is nearly universal in Africa and is known by many names. Mulungu is said to speak through thunder, but is considered to be somewhat remote.

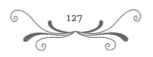

NGAI (Masai) is a creator god. Ngai gives each man at birth a guardian spirit to ward off danger and carry him away at the moment of death. The evil are carried off to a desert, while the good go to a land of rich pastures and many cattle.

NYAME (Ashanti) is the Supreme God of Heaven, both the sun god and the Moon goddess. Nyame created the three realms: the sky, the earth and the underworld. Before being born, souls are taken to Nyame and washed in a golden bath. He gives the soul its destiny and places some of the water of life in the soul's mouth. The soul is then fit to be born.

NYASAYE (Maragoli, Kenya) is the chief god of the Maragoli. Spirits aid the Maragolis' work, and they are represented by round stones circling a pole, which represents the god, thus echoing the universal concept of the World Tree.

TSUI GOAB (Hottentot) is a rain god who lives in the clouds, a great chief and magician. Tsui Goab made the first man and woman from rocks. He fought consistently with Gunab.

UNKULUNKULU (Zulu) is both the first man and the creator. He showed men how to live together and gave them knowledge of the world in which they lived.

YO (Dahomey) is a trickster, neither god nor human, Yo's greed constantly gets him in trouble.

Oceanic Gods and Goddesses

There are many gods and goddesses indigenous to the Oceanic region, and the few discussed here show the similarities between creation myths. It has proved difficult to narrow down the Australian gods and goddesses into their Aboriginal tribes.

AGUNUA (Solomon Islands) is a serpent god. All other gods are only an aspect of him. The first coconut from each tree is sacred to Agunua.

BUNJIL (Australian) is a sky god. He made men out of clay while his brother, Bat, made women out of water. To mankind Bunjil gave tools, weapons and religious ceremony.

DARAMULUN (Australian) is a sky god, a hero. There are many tales of his adventures. Daramulun is usually portrayed with a mouth full of quartz and a huge phallus, carrying a stone axe.

DREAM TIME (Australian) is the period of creation when the gods brought the world and all living creatures into being.

GIDJA (Australian) is a Moon god. In the Dream Time, Gidja created women by castrating Yalungur, for which he was

punished by Kallin Kallin. Gidja floated out to sea and ended up in the sky, where he became the Moon.

GREAT RAINBOW SNAKE (Australian) is also known by many other names. The great giver of life, he lives in a deep pool. He stretches across the sky and shines with water drops, quartz and mother of pearl, whose iridescence holds his life force. In the Dream Time, the Great Rainbow Snake created all waterways – which must not be contaminated with blood – and all living creatures.

IO (New Zealand) is the Supreme Being of the Maori, master of all the other gods, known only to the priesthood.

KALLIN KALLIN (Australia) punished Gidja for castrating his brother Yalungur, the Eaglehawk. Kallin Kallin then took Yalungur as his wife and so established the custom among Australian aborigines of taking wives from different communities.

MARRUNI (Melanesia) is the god of earthquakes. Marruni's tail terrified his wives, so he cut it into pieces and made animals and human beings from them.

MAUI (Polynesia) is a trickster and a hero god. He lived when the world was still being created, and fought on the side of humankind, constantly struggling to get them a better deal. Maui raised the sky and snared the sun. His death at the hands of Hina brought death into the world.

NAREAU (Micronesia) as Old Spider created the world from a seashell, but the heavens and the earth were not properly separated, so Young Spider enlisted the aid of Riiki, the eel, to fix the problem. They then created the sun, Moon and stars, and a great tree from which came the race of men.

PELE (Polynesia) is goddess of volcanic fire and sorcery. She lives on Mount Kilauea in Hawaii. Altars to her are built beside lava streams, though strictly only her descendants worship her.

QAT (Polynesia) is a creator god. Qat was born when his mother, a stone, suddenly exploded. He made the first three pairs of men and women by carving them from wood and playing drums to make them dance. He stopped night from going on forever by cutting it with a hard red stone, which is the dawn. Qat sailed away in a canoe filled with all manner of wonderful things, leaving behind the legend that he would one day return. When the Europeans first arrived in Polynesia, many believed that he had finally returned.

TAWHAKI (Polynesia) is the god of thunder and lightning. He is said to be noble and handsome.

TU (Polynesia) is a god of war and one of the most widely worshipped gods of Polynesia.

WONDJINA (Australia) are the primordial beings of the Dream Time, who created the world. They give both rain and children, and the paintings depicting them are refreshed every year so that they will continue to bring rain at the end of the dry season.

YALUNGUR (Australia) defeated the terrible ogress Kunapipi, was castrated by Gunja and thus became the first woman.

THE ARCHANGELS

The four archangels can be found in a variety of protective incantations and invocations. Their purpose is to guard the four quarters or cardinal points. They are an almost universal symbol that can turn up in many different aspects, from nursery rhymes to the guardians of the dead.

For our purposes, they might be thought of as extra help in living our lives successfully. Think of yourself making a connection to Michael for love, so that you can love more fully; Gabriel for strength, to fill you with power for the next day; Uriel for suffusing you with the light of the mind or understanding; and Raphael for healing all your ills. When you are having a hard time, you can send a brief prayer or request to whichever one is most appropriate.

Generally there are, in fact, considered to be seven archangels and it will depend on your own teaching as to which school of thought you choose to follow in naming them. Because the teachings were initially by word of mouth, there are many different lists of archangels deputed to help the world upon its way. The four archangels considered here are the ones that appear consistently in most lists and are therefore the best known

universally. They are the ones most often called upon in magical workings. The only problem is that sometimes Michael and Uriel appear to swap places in some traditions, which can be confusing. If the attributions given here do not feel right, try the ritual the other way about and change the words accordingly. Do ensure that you still call upon all four archangels, however.

MICHAEL, which means "Who is as God" in Hebrew, is one of the seven archangels and also chief of the four closest to God. The Roman Catholic Church regards Michael in much the same light as does the Church of England, with his festival, Michaelmas, being held on 29 September. He is known in mythology as the one who attempted to bring Lucifer back to God. In Ezekiel's vision of the cherubim, or the four sacred animals, he is the angel with the face of the lion. Michael is often visualized as a masculine archangel dressed in robes or armour of red and green. He stands in the attitude of a warrior amid flames. Bearing either a sword or a spear, Michael is the guardian against evil and the protector of humanity. He is stationed in the south.

RAPHAEL is one of four archangels stationed about the throne of God; his task is to heal the earth. Initially he was pictured with the face of a dragon, but this was changed in later imagery to the face of a man. He is often visualized as a tall, fair figure standing upon the clouds in robes of yellow and violet, sometimes holding the Caduceus of Hermes as a symbol of his healing powers. He is God's builder or composer and has the task of building or rebuilding the earth, which the fallen angels have defiled. Raphael's name in Hebrew means "Healer of God" or "God has Healed". Raphael Ruachel ("Raphael of Air") is stationed in the east.

In Hebrew, GABRIEL means "Strong One of God". He is one of the four archangels who stand in the presence of God, and was sent to announce to Mary the birth of Jesus. In Ezekiel's vision of the four sacred animals, he has the face of the eagle. Gabriel is often visualized as a feminine archangel holding a cup, standing upon the waters of the sea, and wearing robes of blue and orange. Gabriel is also at one with the higher ego or inner divinity. Gabriel Maimel ("Gabriel of Water") is stationed in the west.

URIEL (or Auriel's) name in Hebrew means "Light of God". Specifically, he is the angel or divinity of light – not simply of physical light, but of spiritual illumination. Also referred to as "The Angel of Repentance," he is the angel of terror, prophecy and mystery. He was sometimes ranked as an archangel with Michael, Gabriel, and Raphael and believed to be the angel who holds the keys to the gates of Hell. He is also often identified as the angel who drove Adam and Eve from the Garden of Eden and was thought to be the messenger sent to warn Noah of the forthcoming floods. As "Uriel Aretziel" ("Uriel of Earth") he is stationed in the north. He is often seen rising up from the vegetation of the earth holding stems of ripened wheat and wearing robes of citrine, russet, olive and black.

ARCHANGELS AND THE ELEMENTALS

Each archangel of the Elements has as his servant one of the kings of the Elemental kingdoms. By tradition, each of the Elements ties in with certain nature spirits, of which the dryads are only one sort. They are:

Air

Raphael has as his servant Paralda, King of the Sylphs, who appears to clairvoyant vision as a tenuous form made of blue mist always moving and changing shape.

Fire

Michael is accompanied by Djinn, King of the Salamanders, who appears as a Fire giant composed of twisting living flame surrounded by fiery sparks which crackle and glow.

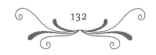

Water

Gabriel's servant is Nixa, King of the Undines, who is seen as an ever-changing shape, fluid with a greenish blue aura splashed with silver and grey.

Earth

Uriel is served by Ghob, King of the Gnomes, seen traditionally as a gnome or goblin who is squat, heavy and dense.

You do not necessarily have to call on these Elementals specifically in your rituals, but you should be aware of their energies in that they are the servants of the archangels and not yours.

PETITIONING THE ARCHANGELS

This spell uses the higher aspects of the guardians of the directions and petitions the four archangels according to their qualities – Michael for love, Gabriel for strength, Raphael for healing and Uriel for clarity. Uriel, the "light of God," is represented by the candles. When you perceive a lack of something in your life, petitioning the archangels helps to fulfil it.

You will need
• Four white candles
• Plate on which you have scattered sugar

Method

Stand the candles on the plate with the sugar all around the candles. Light the candles. Put the plate and candles in the highest place you can safely reach at home. This signifies the status we give the archangels. You may now ask for three wishes from your guardian angels St Raphael, St Gabriel, St Michael and St Uriel.

You might for instance ask one wish for business, one wish for love, one wish for healing, and one wish which seems unlikely to happen.

Bear in mind that you may only petition the archangels if it is really important.

If you like, address each of the archangels by name, or use the same invocation below. This is protective and protects you from inadvertently making silly mistakes. The words are:

Before me Raphael
Behind me Gabriel
On my right hand Michael
On my left hand Uriel
God be thanked.

Let the candles burn right out.

Share this spell with others on the third day (after you requested the wishes) and help to pass on the benefit of your gain. You should use this spell wisely and not make ridiculous requests with it. If what you wish does not happen, accept that it is not quite right for you to make that wish, and do not repeat the request.

SACRED SPACE

If you are going to be carrying out a fair number of rituals or spells, you will really need a sacred space or altar along with various other altar furnishings. Whether your altar is inside or outside does not matter. To set it up indoors, your altar and/or sacred space should preferably be in a quiet place in the home, where it will not be disturbed and where candles can be burned safely.

The space first needs to be dedicated to the purpose of magical working. You can do this by first brushing the area clean with an ordinary brush, concentrating your thoughts on cleansing the space as you work physically to bring this about. Mentally cleanse the space three times, imagining doing it once for the physical world, once for the emotional space, and once spiritually.

If you wish, you may sprinkle the whole area with water and with salt (which represents the earth). You might perhaps also burn incense such as benzoin, jasmine or frankincense to clear the atmosphere. Think of the space as somewhere you would entertain an honoured guest in your home – you would wish the room you use to be as welcoming as possible. You will later use your besom to keep the sacred space clear.

If you travel a lot or are pushed for space, you might dedicate a tray or special piece of wood or china for ceremonial working. This, along with your candles and incense, can then be kept together in a small box or suitcase. Otherwise, you could dedicate a table especially for the purpose. Ideally, you should not need to pack up each time.

You will also need a "fine cloth" – the best you can afford – to cover the surface. Place your cloth on your chosen surface and spend some quiet time just thinking about its purpose. You may, if you wish, have different cloths for different purposes or perhaps have one basic cloth, which is then "dressed" with the appropriate color for each ritual.

Setting up your altar

To turn your dressed table into a proper altar, you will need as basics the following objects:

1. Two candles with candle holders – you might like to think of one representing the female principle and one the male. In addition, you may also choose candles of a color suitable for the ritual or spell you are working.
2. An incense holder, and appropriate incense.
3. A representation of the deity or deities

you prefer to work with. An image of the Goddess, for instance, could be anything from a statue of the Chinese Goddess of Compassion, Kuan Yin, to seashells, chalices, bowls, or certain stones that symbolize the womb or motherhood.

4. A small vase for flowers or fresh herbs.

As already mentioned in the Tools section, there are other objects that you are likely to need for your ceremonial working. Briefly, these are:

1. An athame, which is a sacred knife for ceremonial use; it should never be used for anything else.

2. A white-handled knife (called a boline) for cutting branches, herbs, and so on.

3. A burin, which is a sharp-pointed instrument for inscribing magical objects such as candles.

4. A small earthenware or ceramic bowl, or a small cauldron, for mixing ingredients.

5. A bowl of water.

6. A bowl of salt or sand, representing Earth.

7. A consecrated cloth, or a pentacle, on which to place dedicated objects.

Some people also use bells to summon the powers of the Elements, while others have additional candles with the colors representing themselves or the work they wish to do. You can add other items to your altar, such as crystals, amulets and talismans.

You can do what you wish with your own altar. You should have thought through very carefully the logical or emotional reasons for including whatever you have there. You might, for instance, choose to have differing representations of the Earth Mother from diverse religions, or include a pretty gift to establish a psychic link with the person who gave it to you.

Dedicating your altar

Now you have turned your space into an altar, dedicate it in such a way that it will support any workings you may choose to do. One good way is to dedicate it to the principle of the Greater Good – that none may be harmed by anything that you may do. (Remember that traditionally any harm you instigate deliberately will return to you threefold, particularly when it comes from such a sacred space.) It will depend on your basic belief just how you choose to dedicate the altar further, perhaps to the Moon deity and all her manifestations, perhaps to the gods of power.

Try to put as much passion and energy into the dedication as you can, and remember to include a prayer for protection of your sacred space. Some people will need to cast a circle each time they do a working, while others will feel that just by setting the altar up in the way suggested, the space is consecrated henceforth. If you wish to follow the principles of feng shui rather than Wicca within your work, your placings will be slightly different, as they will also be if you

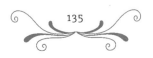

choose to follow the tenets of other religions. However, whatever you do, you should take care to dedicate all of your tools and altar furnishings to the purpose in hand. You are empowering them and making them usable only in ritual and magical work. If you try to use them for any other purpose, you will negate that magical power.

Consecrating altar objects

If you are not using completely new objects as the basic furnishings (such as candle holders) on your altar, you should cleanse them properly before you dedicate them to your purpose. Treat them in the same way as you would any crystals you use, by soaking them overnight in salt water to remove anyone else's vibrations and then standing them in sunshine (or moonshine) for at least twelve hours, to charge them with the appropriate energy.

When you are ready, hold each object and allow your own energy to flow into it, followed by the energy of your idea of Ultimate Power. (That way you make a very powerful link between yourself, the object and the Ultimate.) Ask this Power to bless the object and any working you may do with it, and perceive yourself as truly a medium or channel for the energy.

Hopefully, each time you use any of the objects, you will immediately be able to reinforce that link rather than having to reestablish it. It is like a refrain continually running in the background. Now place the objects on your altar in whatever way feels right for you.

Finally, if you wish, create and cast your circle (see below) so that it includes yourself and your altar. The magic circle defines the ritual area, holds in personal power and shuts out all distractions and negative energies. You now have a sacred space set up, which is your link to the powers that be. Again it is a matter of personal choice as to whether you choose to rededicate your altar and what it contains on a regular basis.

Casting a circle

Purify yourself first. You can do this by meditating, or taking a ritual bath. One way is to try to keep the water flowing, possibly by leaving the bath plug half in, or by having a shower. This reinforces the idea of washing away any impurities so you are not sitting in your own psychic rubbish. Ideally, your towel – if you choose to use one – should be clean and used only for the purpose of your ritual bath.

Wear something special if you can, something that you only wear during a ritual or working – perhaps your robes. You can always add a pretty scarf or a throw in the correct color for your working. This sets apart spell-working from everyday life.

Decide on the extent of your circle, which should be formed in front of your altar. Purify this space by sprinkling the area with water

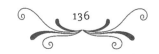

followed by salt – both of these should have been blessed or consecrated in some way with simple words.

Sit quietly for as long as you can inside the area that will become your circle. Imagine a circle of light surrounding you. This light could be white, blue or purple. If you are in a hurry and cannot purify and cleanse fully, reinforce the circle of light by visualizing it suffused with the appropriate color for your working.

Circle the light around, above and below you in a clockwise direction, like the representation of an atom. Feel it as a sphere or as a cone of power. Sense the power. Remember that you can create a "doorway" through which your magical energy may exit. You should always feel warm and peaceful within your circle. As time goes on, you will be able to differentiate between the various energies at play here.

Use your own personal chant or form of words, according to your own belief system, to consecrate your circle and banish all evil and negative energy, forbidding anything harmful to enter your space. Remember, you are always safe within your circle if you command it to be so.

If you wish, invite the gods and goddesses to attend your circle and magical working. Relax and be happy.

You can use objects on the ground to show the boundaries of the circle, such as candles, crystals, cord, stones, flowers or incense. The circle is formed from personal power. This may be felt and visualized as streaming from the body to form a bubble made of mist, or a circle of light. You can use the athame or your hands to direct this power.

The cardinal points of the compass may be denoted with lit candles, often white or purple. Alternatively, place a green candle at the north point of the circle, yellow candle at the east, red candle at the south and blue candle at the west. The altar stands in the centre of the circle, facing north in the direction of power.

An Alternative Method of Circle Casting

This method probably owes more to the practices of Wicca than any other way, though you do not have to be Wiccan to use it.

You will need

- Besom
- Ritual tools (athame, etc.)
- Candle to represent your working
- Altar candles to represent the Goddess and God
- Any of the ceremonial or consecrational incenses mentioned on pages 76–104
- Heatproof dish for the incense
- Compass (to work out directions)
- Candle snuffer

Method

Cleanse the sacred space symbolically with the besom.

Place the altar in the centre of the circle

facing north. Set up the altar as described on pages 134–5. Light the candles on the altar.

Start with the candle representing the Goddess on the left, then the God on the right. In the middle, follow with the candle which represents your magical working. Light the incense.

Move towards the northern edge of the area you are enclosing.

Hold your left hand out, palm down, at waist level. Point your fingers toward the edge of the circle you are creating. (You can, of course, use your athame if you have consecrated it.)

See and feel the energy flowing out from your fingertips (or the athame), and slowly walk the circle, clockwise. Think of the energy that your body is generating.

Continue to move clockwise, gradually increasing your pace as you do so.

Move faster until you feel the energy flowing within you. The energy will move with you as you release it.

Sense your personal power creating a sphere of energy around the altar. When this is firmly established, call on the Elements which rule the four directions.

Your circle is now consecrated and ready for you to use for whatever magical purpose you need. You will require the candle snuffer to safely close your circle after you have finished your magical working.

Ending your magical working

As well as all the preparations necessary for successful magical working, it is equally important to finish off correctly. When you have finished your ritual or working, remind yourself that you are as pure a channel for the energies that you have called upon as possible. These energies *must* be returned whence they came, so visualize them passing through you and being returned to where they belong. At the same time, remember that you are blessed by these energies and by the fact that you have used them with good intent.

Closing a Circle

Thank the Elements' rulers, if you have called upon them, for attending the ritual. If you used ritual tools, holding your athame, stand at the north. Pierce the circle's wall with the blade at waist level. If you wish, simply use your index finger to achieve the same end.

Move clockwise around the circle. Visualize its power being sucked back into the knife or your finger. Sense the sphere of energy withdrawing and dissipating.

Let the outside world slowly make itself felt in your consciousness. As you come back to the north again, the energy of the circle should have disappeared. If it has not, simply repeat the actions. If you have laid items to mark out the circle, remove them. If you have used salt and water, you may save the excess

salt for future uses, but pour the water onto the bare earth. Bury any incense ashes.

Put out the candles. Start with those that have marked the cardinal compass points, followed by any others used.

Next put out the one representing the God energy and finally the Goddess candle. Never blow them out (some say this dissipates the energy). Either snuff or pinch them out.

You may can leave the candles to burn out on their own if you wish.

Put away your tools respectfully if you are not able to leave your altar in place.

CORRESPONDENCES

Truly efficient spell-working requires a knowledge of the correspondences that were set up many eons ago when life was a good deal simpler. These correspondences meant that actions carried out at a certain time created very specific results. Through continual usage, it became clear that the position of the planets ruled various areas of life, creating the principle of the rulership of the planets and symbolism – an integral part of magical working today.

The table given overleaf lists some of those correspondences, including those of the angels and archangels. More detailed information on the archangels can be found on pages 131–3.

MOON PHASES

The Moon represents the feminine principle and is a symbol for the natural cycle of birth, life and regeneration. Her best personification is that of the Triple Goddess (Maiden, Mother, Crone) which is an image found in many early religions. The lunar phases (Waxing, Waning or Full Moon) can be made use of when planning your magical work. You will soon find that you become instinctively aware of these phases and can use them effectively.

It is always useful to have your rituals and spells coincide with the appropriate astrological influences. For example, spells and rituals calling on the Moon and involving the Element of Earth, should be performed during a time when the Moon is positioned in one of the three astrological Earth signs of Taurus, Virgo or Capricorn. Spells involving the Element of Fire should be done when the Moon is in Aries, Leo or Sagittarius; spells involving the Element of Air when the Moon is in Gemini, Libra or Aquarius; and spells involving the Element of Water should be performed when the Moon is in Cancer, Scorpio or Pisces.

You could also use the appropriate incenses for your rituals and there are other correspondences in the application of magic that might be utilized at these times:

Moon in Aries
Magic involving anything to do with authority, leadership, rebirth, moving on or spiritual conversion should achieve success.

Healing rituals for ailments of the face, head or brain are also best performed at this time.

Moon in Taurus

You can work magic for love, security, possessions and money. Healing rituals for illnesses of the throat, neck and ears are also undertaken during at this time.

Moon in Gemini

Magic for anything to do with communication, including writing, e-mails, public relations, moving house or office and travel is favoured. Ailments of the shoulders, arms, hands or lungs also respond well to healing rituals done now.

Moon in Cancer

This is the best time to work magic for home and domestic life, and also any nurturing activities. Healing rituals for ailments of the chest or stomach are best carried out now.

Moon in Leo

Courage, fertility and childbirth are all ruled by Leo, as is the power over others, so this is the best time to work such magic. Healing rituals for problems of the upper back, spine or heart all seem to have some success now.

Moon in Virgo

At this time magic worked for questions involving employment, intellectual matters, health and dietary concerns is much enhanced. Healing rituals for ailments of the intestines or nervous system are also best performed now.

Moon in Libra

Magic involving artistic work, justice, court cases, partnerships and unions, mental stimulation, and karmic, spiritual, or emotional balance receive a boost when worked at this time. Healing rituals for ailments of the lower back or kidneys have additional energy now.

Moon in Scorpio

This is the best time to work magic involving sexual matters, power, psychic growth, secrets and fundamental transformations. Healing rituals for difficulties with the reproductive organs are also said to be most effective during this period.

Moon in Sagittarius

This is the opportune time to work magic for publications, legal matters, travel and revealing truth. Healing rituals for ailments of the liver, thighs or hips are also done at this time.

Moon in Capricorn

This is an ideal time to work magic for ambition, career, organization, political matters and recognition. Healing rituals for the knees, bones, teeth and skin are best performed at this time.

SUN SIGN	PLANET	ELEMENT	DAY	MAGICAL USE
Aries (21 March – 19 April)	Mars	Fire	Tuesday	Passion and sexuality, energy, willpower, vigour, courage and strength. Determination
Taurus (20 April – 21 May)	Venus	Earth	Friday	Romantic love, friendships, beauty, courtship, artistic abilities, harmony
Gemini (22 May – 20 June)	Mercury	Air	Wednesday	Wisdom, healing, communication, intelligence, memory, education
Cancer (21 June – 22 July)	Moon	Water	Monday	Psychic pursuits, psychology, dreams/astral travel, imagination, intuition, reincarnation
Leo (23 July – 22 August)	Sun	Fire	Sunday	Power, magic, health, success, career, goals, ambition, drama, fun, authority figures, law
Virgo (23 August – 22 Sept)	Mercury	Earth	Wednesday	Wisdom, healing, communication, intelligence, memory, attention to detail, correspondence
Libra (23 Sept – 22 Oct)	Venus	Air	Friday	Love, partnership, marriage, friendship, beauty, courtship
Scorpio (23 Oct – 21 Nov)	Mars, Pluto	Water	Tuesday	Courage, energy, breaking negativity, physical strength, passion, sex, aggression, energy
Sagittarius (22 Nov – 21 Dec)	Jupiter	Fire	Thursday	Publishing, long-distance travel, foreign interests, religion, happiness, wealth, healing, male fertility, legal matters
Capricorn (22 Dec – 19 Jan)	Saturn	Earth	Saturday	Binding, protection, neutralization, karma, death, manifestation, structure, reality, the laws of society, limits, obstacles
Aquarius (20 Jan – 18 Feb)	Saturn, Uranus	Air	Saturday	Psychic ability, meditation, defence, communicating with spirits
Pisces (19 Feb – 20 Mar)	Jupiter, Neptune	Water	Thursday	Music, rhythm, dancing, spiritual matters, healing and religion, medication

COLORS	CRYSTAL	FLOWERS/HERBS	ANGEL
Reds, burgundy	Ruby, garnet, bloodstone, diamond	Gorse, thistle, wild rose	Samael
Blues, greens	Sapphire, emerald, jade	Violet, wild rose, red rose, coltsfoot	Anael
White, spring green, silver, yellow	Diamond, jade, topaz, aquamarine	Iris, parsley, dill, snapdragons	Raphael
Pale blue, silver, pearl, white	Emerald, cat's eye, pearl, moonstone	Poppy, water lily, white rose, moonswort	Gabriel
Gold, red, yellow, orange	Amber, topaz, ruby, diamond	Marigold, sunflower, hops	Michael
Pastel blue, gold, peach	Diamond, jade, jasper, aquamarine	Rosemary, cornflower, valerian	Raphael
Cerulean blue, royal blue, amethyst	Opal, lapis lazuli, emerald, jade	Violet, white rose, love-in-a-mist	Anael
Dark red, brown, black, grey	Ruby, garnet, bloodstone, topaz	Basil, heather, chrysan-themum	Samael, Azrael
Lilac, mauve, purple, amethyst	Sapphire, amethyst, diamond	Carnation, wallflower, clovepink, sage	Sachiel
Grey, violet, dark brown	Onyx, obsidian, jet, garnet	Deadly nightshade, snowdrop, rue	Cassiel
All colors	Zircon, amber, amethyst, garnet	Snowdrop, foxglove, valerian	Uriel, Cassiel
Purple, violet, sea green	Sapphire, amethyst, coral	Heliotrope, carnation, opium poppy	Sachiel, Asariel

Moon in Aquarius

This is the best time to work magic involving scientific matters, freedom of expression, problem-solving, extra-sensory abilities and the breaking of bad habits or unhealthy addictions. Ailments of the calves, ankles or blood receive benefit from healing rituals.

Moon in Pisces

Magic worked on the psychic arts involving dreamwork, clairvoyance, telepathy and music is enhanced at this time. Healing rituals for problems with the feet or lymph glands benefit from the flow of energy.

MAGICAL DAYS

The days of the week, because they are ruled by the various gods, create an energy which is best for certain types of magical working. Following is a list that, while not completely comprehensive, will give you some idea of when to perform your spells. Each day's planetary ruler and optimum colors are also given.

SUNDAY *(Sun – yellow, gold, orange):* ambition, authority figures, career, children, crops, drama, fun, goals, health, law, personal finances, promotion, selling, speculating, success, volunteers and civic services.

MONDAY *(Moon – white, silver, grey, pearl):* antiques, astrology, children, dreams/astral travel, emotions, fluids, household activities, imagination, initiation, magic, spiritual pursuits, psychology, reincarnation, religion, short trips, spirituality, the public, totem animals, trip planning.

TUESDAY *(Mars – red, pink, orange):* aggression, business, beginnings, combat, confrontation, courage, dynamism, gardening, guns, hunting, movement, muscular activity, passion, partnerships, physical energy, police, repair, sex, soldiers, surgery, tools, woodworking.

WEDNESDAY *(Mercury – purple, magenta, silver):* accounting, astrology, communication, computers, correspondence, editing, editors, education, healing, hiring, journalists, learning, languages, legal appointments, messages, music, phone calls, siblings, signing contracts, students, visiting friends, visual arts, wisdom, writing.

THURSDAY *(Jupiter – blue, metallic colors):* business, charity, college, doctors, education, expansion, forecasting, foreign interests, gambling, growth, horses, luck, material wealth, merchants, philosophy, psychologists, publishing, reading, religion, researching, self-improvement, sports, studying the law, travel.

FRIDAY *(Venus – green, pink, white):* affection, alliances, architects, artists, beauty, chiropractors, courtship, dancers, dating, designers, engineers, entertainers,

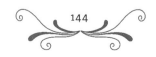

friendships, gardening, gifts, harmony, luxury, marriage, music, painting, partners, poetry, relationships, romantic love, shopping, social activity.

SATURDAY *(Saturn – black, grey, red, white):* binding, bones, criminals, death, debts, dentists, discovery, endurance, farm workers, financing, hard work, housing, justice, karma, limits, manifestation, maths, murderers, neutralization, obstacles, plumbing, protection, reality, sacrifice, separation, structure, teeth, tests, transformation, wills.

THE SIGNIFICANCE OF COLOR

Color is something that, over time, you will use as a natural adjunct in your magical workings. It can be used in your robes, to dress your altar, or in your candles as representative of the vibration you wish to introduce. By and large, the colors you choose for your workings will be those appropriate for your intention (the purpose of your spell). There are other uses of color in magic as well. Some simple color symbolism is listed for you below.

SILVER is almost always associated with the lunar goddesses and workings with the Moon, whereas **WHITE** symbolizes purity, chastity, spirituality, transformation and transmutation. It is said to contain within it all the other colors, so use white if you have nothing else available. Use it also when you want focus and a protective influence.

PURPLE, INDIGO and **VIOLET** are the royal colors and are therefore associated with wisdom and vision, dignity and fame. They are often used when honouring the Goddess in her aspect of Crone and the God as King, according to some traditions of magic. These colors command respect and promote psychic and mental healing. Purple connects with true creativity, with the mystic and with spirituality and is also to do with one's proper place within the overall scheme of things.

SKY BLUE signifies communication, not just between people, but also between the realms so is good for meditative practices and also for help with study and learning. It is also used to symbolize Water. Other shades of blue signify peace; strength; calm; recognition of the real self and the ability to express wisdom.

GREEN, which belongs to Venus, promotes love, fertility, beauty, wealth, prosperity and harmony – symbolizing balance and self-knowledge, that is, knowing our capabilities. Associated with the Earth in its guise of the Green Man and with the Great Mother in her nurturing form, it suggests emotional healing and growth.

GOLD and **YELLOW** represent vitality, strength and rejuvenation. They are used to promote physical healing, hope and happiness. Yellow inspires rational thought

and strong will. It is also an emotional color in the sense that it represents your relationship with the outer self and the world in which you live. Related to the Sun gods and the Element of Air, both gold and yellow may also be used for protection.

ORANGE has a healing vibration, particularly of relationships. It is also associated with material success and legal matters. A highly creative vibration, it often relates to childhood and emotional stability as well as imagination.

RED is recognized as being symbolic of passion and sexual potency and intensity. It is usually associated with Fire, with the quality of courage and with healing of the blood and heart.

PINK signifies friendship, love, fidelity and the healing of emotions. It also symbolizes creativity and innocence and is associated with the Goddess in her aspect of Maiden.

BROWN promotes the healing of the Earth, symbolizes the hearth and home, and is also connected with the animal kingdom. It can be used for the blending of several intentions.

BLACK is not a color but is the absence of both light and color. It can therefore be used to banish negativity. It is often seen as the color of the Goddess in her Wise Woman form.

CONSTRUCTING SPELLS

Traditionally, spells, formulas and rituals were recorded in the Grimoire which, of late, has become known as the Book of Shadows. There is often controversy over whether one's magical books should be called a Grimoire or a Book of Shadows. Really it depends on which tradition of magic you follow.

The word Grimoire simply means "a book of learning". It came to mean the records kept by true practitioners of magic, as they wrote down the secret keys they discovered as they progressed along the path of initiation. The best-known Grimoire was the translation of one made widely available at the beginning of the 20th century – that of King Solomon. This book was of great antiquity and traditionally is seen as the magical key to the Kabbalah. In truth, it was the key to the mysteries and has since formed the basis of other magical systems.

The first Book of Shadows is said to have been written by Gerald Gardner as he developed modern Wicca in the 1940s. The Book of Shadows does not serve as a diary, but reflects religious rituals, their modifications and any other workings that need to be recorded.

Both books were traditionally secret writings, often written in coded language. The Book of Shadows follows the same principle, although obviously with modern communication, much of what used to be hidden is more readily available. Most solitary practitioners will treasure the records of their workings, whether they choose to call it a Book of Shadows or a Grimoire. Either book becomes part of a rich tradition. Any self-respecting practitioner will both want and need to keep a record of all of these aspects of magic for future reference. You will need to find an easy way of remembering what you have done. Utilizing the worksheets and the respective headings below will help you to do this.

These can also be used, should you wish, with modern technology. Computer and software programs can be tremendously helpful in keeping records in a fashion that is suitable for passing on to other people.

SPELLS AND FORMULAS RECORD SHEET

TYPE OF SPELL OR FORMULA
This should state very clearly what the type of spell is, for example blessing, binding, and so on. When developing formulas for lotions and potions, for instance, you need to be clear as to the exact purpose.

DATE AND TIME MADE
This gives a cross reference should you wish to use the correct planetary hours or magical days within the working.

REFERENCE
You should develop your own system of reference; this might be, for instance, according to the time of year or alphabetically. Do also remember to keep safely somewhere a record of how you have developed your reference system, so that others may benefit from your experience.

ASTROLOGICAL PHASE
If you have an interest in astrology you will probably want to record where the planets are when you prepare the spell or formula. A decent ephemeris (list of planetary positions) can be of great help here, though there are also many free sources of information on the internet.

SPECIFIC PURPOSE
You should always state the specific purpose of the spell or formula very clearly. This is partly because it helps to focus your own mind, but also because it leaves no one in any doubt as to your intentions. Should you have more than one main purpose, you should also record these.

LIST OF INGREDIENTS AND/OR SUPPLIES NEEDED
Having all your ingredients to hand ensures that you are working with maximum efficiency and are not misusing or needing to adjust the energy by leaving the sacred space. Also, when you repeat a working you will need to replicate what you did the first time; even one small change in ingredients can make a tremendous difference to the final outcome.

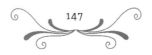

SPECIFIC LOCATION REQUIRED

You may well need to perform some spells within a certain area or setting. Also you may discover that your own energy responds to some locations better than others.

DATE, TIME AND ASTROLOGICAL PHASE WHEN USED

In all probability you will not want all your spells to take effect at the time you cast them. Let us suppose you have applied for a job and wish your spell to work at the time of interview. You would need to carefully calculate the date, time and astrological phase of the interview as well as the time you are actually casting your spell, and incorporate both sets of information into your working.

RESULTS

Record carefully all aspects of results you feel are associated with your working. This record should include how successful you consider the spell to be and how it might be improved. There will be some unexpected results, some that appear not to give a tangible result and others which come into play some time after they were expected.

DEITIES INVOKED DURING PREPARATION AND/OR USE

Often a particular god can be helpful in bringing about a needed result for a spell. You will chose the most appropriate for your purpose and can always petition a different one at another time.

STEP-BY-STEP INSTRUCTIONS FOR PREPARATIONS AND/OR USE

Often when spell-working, movements and words are intuitive and instinctive; the more you are able to remember what you did the more likely you are to achieve similar results. Also, should you require them for someone to work on your behalf or to undertake someone else's magical training, you will have an exact record.

ADDITIONAL NOTES

Here you should record for each occasion anything that seems strange, bizarre or noteworthy, so that you know what to expect next time.

In each of the spells throughout this book there is a list of ingredients and special articles which may be required to achieve a result for that particular spell. Because each

individual brings their own energy into the process, you may find that you intuitively want to change something, whether that is an ingredient, a container or the words used. This is absolutely fine, and means that your spell has a very personal feel to it.

Throughout the preceding sections there are various spells which have eased you into the world of magic. The information given touches on many subjects and aspects of spell working. You now have enough knowledge to permit you to develop your magical self. The second part of this book gives you some spells to try out that represent only a small selection of the wealth of opportunities available to you.

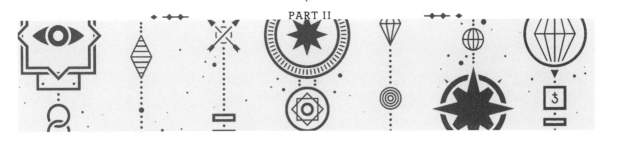

PART II
THE SPELLS

WHAT IS A SPELL?

In ancient Pagan communities the elders, or wise ones, had, by their very experience, an awareness of custom and a firm grasp of what had previously worked when trying to gain control over Mother Nature and other powers they did not fully understand. They had access to certain knowledge (and therefore power) that was not readily available to the ordinary individual.

The ancients recognized that words spoken in a certain way, according to custom, seemed to have more of an effect than those spoken on the spur of the moment. As a consequence, their words would have more power, yet the same words spoken by the uninitiated or those who did not understand, did not seem to have the same result.

There are three important aspects when reciting a spell. The first is that words spoken with intensity and passion do have a power all of their own. The next is that the speaker also has a power and an energy which, with practice, he or she may learn to use effectively. The third component, the forces and powers belonging to that which is "beyond the human being" also have a tremendous power and are

called upon, used or directed for a specific purpose. The use of all three of these aspects gives a very powerful spell indeed.

There are several kinds of spell, each of which requires a different approach.

LOVE SPELLS

Many people's first thought in this context is of love spells – ways of making another person find them sexually attractive and desirable. In theory, love spells should be unconditional and this type should be entirely unselfish and free from self-interest. However, most of the time they obviously cannot be so, unless they are performed by a third party, someone outside the longed-for relationship who is totally dispassionate.

To try to influence someone else directly may well go against the ethics of many practitioners and magicians, though such spells do tend to be the stock-in-trade of many practitioners for hire. Anyone who wishes to experiment with love spells needs to be aware that such spells come under the category of bidding spells and therefore must be used carefully. Love spells are

often accompanied by gifts or love philtres, which are also meant to have an effect on the recipient.

BIDDING SPELLS

These are spells where the spell-maker commands a particular thing to happen, but without the co-operation of those involved. Trying to make someone do something which they do not want to do, or which goes against their natural inclination, obviously requires a great deal of power and energy and can possibly misfire, causing the originator of the spell a good deal of difficulty.

For this reason, it is wise to preface such spells with words to signify that the outcome will only be in accord with the greater good – that is, that in the overall scheme of things no one will be harmed in any way whatsoever. This ensures that the intent behind the spell is of the purest and that there is not any maliciousness within the practitioner. It means that an able and responsible practitioner must choose their words carefully, even when they are not casting a spell.

One type of bidding spell that is allowable is when a curse or "hex" is being removed. A hex is a spell that ill-wishes someone and in many cases binds the recipient in some way. A curse is a spell with a much more

generalized effect. To remove such a negative spell, it is usual to turn it around and send the malign energy back to the person who summoned it in the first place. You command the energy to return from whence it came.

BLESSINGS

These might be counted either as prayers or spells and need a passionate concentration on bringing, for instance, peace of mind or healing to the recipient. They hold no danger for the practitioner but are sometimes more difficult to appreciate since they tend to be more general than other types of magical work. They may be thought of in terms of a positive energy from beyond the practitioner, being channelled towards a specific purpose.

Saying grace before a meal is a form of blessing preceded by an offer of praise and a prayer of thankfulness, an acknowledgement of a gift. The food is enhanced by the act and the blessing is given by drawing on the power vested in the expert. Thus one practitioner may call on the nature gods whereas another might call on the power of Jesus Christ.

HEALING SPELLS AND CHARMS

Within this type of spell it is wise to go beyond the presenting symptoms and to ask for healing on all levels of existence –

physical, mental and spiritual – because the practitioner may not have the knowledge or correct information to enable him to diagnose a condition correctly. The natural energies and specific vibrations are enhanced by invocations, incantations and blessings wherever appropriate.

Frequently, objects such as crystals are charged with energy and power to focus healing or other energies in a quite specific way, often to remind the patient's body of its own ability to heal itself.

INVOCATIONS

These call on what is believed to be the ultimate source of power, which differs from spell to spell. Quite literally, they call up that power and ask for permission to use this influence for a stated purpose. Meddling with this power and calling up negative forces is extremely unwise and very foolish.

Spells for selfish personal power or to gain power over others will often backfire and may cause damage to the individual who casts them. Invocations of positive forces can do no harm, except that the results can sometimes be highly disconcerting due to the sheer energy created, although the eventual outcome may be good.

INCANTATIONS

This type of spell prepares the magical worker and his helpers for further work by heightening their awareness. It does not set out to call up the powers, but appeals to gods, goddesses, powers of nature and so on for help.

Chanting, prayer and hymns are in many ways incantations, particularly when the intent is stated with some passion. An incantation is often very beautiful and rhythmic. Music has always been an efficient way of heightening awareness and altering states of consciousness.

THE ELEMENTS

In most systems of magical working you will find mentioned the four (or sometimes five) Elements, often in conjunction with their directions or, as they are known in magic, quarters of the universe or cardinal points. Together and separately they are extremely powerful sources of energy and can give a tremendous boost to your spell-making. Each Element also comes under the protection of one of the Archangels (see pages 131-3).

The four Elements are energies, and manifestations of energy, that make up the entire universe. They also influence our

personalities and therefore what we do. Magical working calls to each elemental kingdom and its ruler to protect each cardinal point and its properties. Each Element has an intrinsic power and is known for having certain qualities, natures, moods and magical purposes. Each also represents positive and negative traits.

Earth, Air, Fire and Water are the four Elements and you may well find that you work best using one of them in particular. People drawn to candle magic, for instance, are using mainly the Element of Fire, while those who work with incense are using Air with a fair smattering of Earth in the herbs and resins.

The fifth Element is that of spirit, which is the "binding principle" behind everything. Sometimes known as aether, it is, on the whole, intangible, yet is that which makes everything happen. You are both its representative and its channel, so in using the other Elements in magical working you have a responsibility to act wisely and well.

Earth

Traditionally the direction of this Element is north and the color associated with Earth is green. It is represented on the altar usually by salt or sand. Crystals, because they are totally natural substances, can also be used.

When invoking Earth and the powers of the north, you are looking for recovery and healing and perhaps trying to find answers to questions. These powers deal with gaining knowledge, blessing, creating and shielding. When working within a magical circle, this is the first corner or quarter on which you call for protection.

The principal nature spirits of the Earth are called gnomes. They are said to live underground and guard the earth's treasures. Other groups within the earth's nature spirits ruled by the god Pan are brownies, dryads, Earth spirits, elves and satyrs.

Air

The direction of this Element is east and the color usually associated with it is yellow. Incense is often used to represent Air, since the movement of the air can be seen in the incense smoke. When you are looking for inspiration, need new ideas or perhaps to break free from the past or undesired situations, you would use this Element. The quality associated with it is that of thinking or the use of the intellect. When working in a magical circle, Air is the second quarter on which you call for protection.

The sylphs are the Air spirits; their Element has the most subtle energy of the four. They are said to live on the tops of mountains and are volatile and changeable. They are usually perceived with wings and look like cherubs or fairies. One of their main tasks is said to be to help humans receive inspiration.

Fire

Fire is the Element of the south and is usually represented by a candle or a cauldron with a fire inside. Its color is red and its associations are to do with power, determination and passionate energy.

You would call upon this Element for protection from evil forces, cleansing and creativity. The quality associated with Fire is "doing" and it is a male principle. It is the third quarter or cardinal point on which you call for protection when working in a magical circle.

Without salamanders, the spirit of Fire, it is said that physical fire cannot exist. They have been seen as sparks or small balls of light, but most often they are perceived as being lizard-like in shape and about 30 cm or more in length. They are considered the strongest and most powerful of all the Elementals. As nature spirits they are greatly affected by the way that mankind thinks. If ever out of control, salamanders can be considered dangerous.

Water

Water is the Element of the west and is represented by a bowl of water or a goblet of wine or fruit juice. Its color is blue and, because it represents the giving of life, it is associated with the Elements of sea, rain, snow and rivers.

When you need cleansing, revitalizing, the removal of curses or hexes or change of any sort, you will call upon Water. It is to do with emotions, right through from the most basic passions to the most elevated forms of belief. It is predominantly feminine. It is the fourth and final quarter that you invoke in any magical circle.

The undines are the Elemental beings connected with Water and are beautiful and very graceful. The nymph is frequently found in a fountain and the mythical mermaid belongs to the ocean. Some undines inhabit waterfalls, others live in rivers and lakes. Smaller undines are often seen as winged beings, being able to emerge from the water on wings like those of the dragonfly. This has led people in the past to mistakenly identify them as fairies.

Spirit

When you feel you are sufficiently adept at using the other Elements, you may begin to use spirit – the fifth Element. This has no special space but is everywhere. It should never ever be used negatively because, particularly when you are weak and tired, it can rebound on you.

You may well find that you instinctively link strongly with the life force as spirit, in which case you are probably succeeding in bringing all the Elements together within yourself. There is no particular color associated with spirit – perception is all-important. If you choose to represent spirit on the altar, you may do so however you wish. You are free to use your intuition and you must have a very strong awareness of your reason for choosing that particular symbol.

DIFFERENT TYPES OF MAGIC

Elemental

In this particular type of magic the Elements of Fire, Earth, Air and Water are given their own directional focus to create added power and give extra energy to your spells. You will no doubt find that you tend to favour one particular direction but you should be able to use all of them.

Color

Perhaps the simplest form of magic is that which involves color. This method of working is also used in conjunction with various other forms of magic. Color can enhance, alter and completely change moods and emotions and therefore can be used to represent our chosen goal. At its simplest it can be used alone and in dressing an altar. (See pages 145–6 for some of the more usual color correspondences.)

Herbal

Herbal magic is often used alongside many other forms of magic. Used as talismans and amulets – for example in a pouch or bag – herbs become protective; the oil from herbs can also be used in candle magic. There are many different types of herbs available for use in this way. Each herb has its own specific use, but frequently is used along with many other herbs and oils to produce a desired result.

Candle

In candle magic, humans discovered the ability to control light and this is one of the oldest forms of magic as well as one of the most simple. Using candles to symbolize ourselves and our beliefs means that we have access to a power beyond

ourselves. Candle magic also forms an effective back-up for most other forms of magical working.

Crystal

Every stone or gem has its own attribute which can be used in magic. Crystals are used extensively in healing because of the vibrational impact they can have. Because of this, they lend themselves to the enhancement of any spell making or magical working. Even ordinary stones have their own power and can be used as repositories for all sorts of energies and powers.

Knot

Knot magic works partly with the principle of binding, which is a type of bidding spell, and also with that of weaving, which was traditionally a female intuitive occupation. It utilizes ribbon, rope, string, yarn, or anything that can be knotted or plaited. It is a type of representational magic, and is often used in conjunction with many of the other forms. The techniques of color, form and use of energies are all used in its practice.

Representational

Representational magic involves using an object that represents something or someone for whom you are working the spell. It helps in concentrating the energy and visualizing the desire and the end result. Representational objects should never be used for negative purposes and care should be taken to store or dispose of them correctly once the working is done.

Symbolic

In this system different symbols, rather than objects, are used to represent various ideas, people or goals. These symbols can be personal to you, or such things as Tarot cards, runes, Hebrew letters or numerology. You will often use symbolic magic in your magical workings and will soon develop your own preferred symbols.

Talismans, amulets and charms

These devices use all the other forms of magic in their formation, but principally representational and symbolic magic. They are "charged" (given power) magically and usually are worn or carried on the person for protection or good luck. Many are worn around the neck, perhaps as jewellery, or carried in a pouch. There are many types of each of these objects and you will gradually learn to differentiate between them.

FRIENDSHIP, LOVE AND RELATIONSHIPS

The majority of people probably first become aware of spell-making in an effort to influence someone else's feelings in their favour. While strictly this is apparently a misuse of energy, there is a place for such spells in that they help to make us feel better about ourselves and more confident in dealing with other people. They perhaps influence us as much as other people.

ATTRACTING A NEW FRIEND

Working magically can sometimes be a lonely business. However, we do have the means at our disposal to draw people towards us in friendship. This spell draws to you a friend rather than a lover – someone of like mind who enjoys the same things that you do. These can be very important relationships, especially if you are already partnered or happily single and just need new friendly energy in your life. It is best performed during a waxing Moon.

You will need
- Three brown candles
- Sheet of paper
- Pen

Method
Light the candles. On the sheet of paper, write down the attributes you would like your friend to have. Say each one out loud. Fold the paper in half twice. Light the edge of the folded paper from one of the candles and repeat the words below:

With heart and mind I do now speak
Bring to me the one I seek
Let this paper be the guide
And bring this friend to my side.
Pain and loneliness be no more
Draw a companion to my door.
With pleasures many and sorrows few
Let us build a friendship new.

Let not this simple spell coerce
Or make my situation worse.
As I will, it shall be.

Let the paper burn out then snuff out the candles. Use these candles only for the same type of spell.

Within the next few weeks, you should meet someone with some or all of the qualities you seek. Remember that you have called this person to you, so you can have the confidence and the time to explore the relationship properly. Never ever be judgemental about qualities in your new friend that are not ones that you have requested.

FREEZE OUT

There are many ways of "freezing people out," and this one which uses ice is good since it will only last as long as the ice remains frozen. The spell should only be used to prevent harm to yourself and others, not to bring harm to anyone else. It is only used if you know the name of the person involved. A good time to do it is the waning Moon.

You will need
- Magically charged paper and pen
- Water in a bowl

Method
Write the name of the person concerned in the middle of the paper. Fold the paper away from you at least four times all the while sensing the person's influence waning. Dunk the paper in the water until it is well soaked. Leave it overnight if necessary. Put the wet paper into your ice compartment or freezer. Leave it there until you feel the danger is over.

You then release the spell, by taking the paper out of the freezer and using words such as:

All danger passed
I set you free

Dispose of the paper in any way you wish.

Do note that you must never forget to set the other person free, lest you find yourself bound to them for longer than is healthy for either of you. By the laws of cause-and-effect you must do this to ensure that your actions do not rebound on you.

TO CLARIFY RELATIONSHIPS

The art of braiding is one which can be used in spell-making to represent many things. In

this particular spell it is used to signify the coming together of three people and in the unbraiding an amicable resolution. In the use of color the spell is focused either on the outcome or on the people concerned.

You will need

- 3 lengths of ribbon of suitable color
- You can use astrological colors to represent each person or you can use one color to represent the situation. For example:

    RED for a relationship soured by anger

    BLUE for a business relationship

    GREEN for a relationship in which finance is importance

    YELLOW where communication is difficult

Method

Decide before you begin what it is you are trying to achieve.

If it is important to bring people together, then as you are braiding you will concentrate on this. If it is seen as necessary for them to go their separate ways, while you are braiding you will concentrate on the intricacies of the situation and perhaps the ability to bring about open and frank discussion.

Once you have finished braiding, you have a completely new object which is a representation of the relationship between the various parties. You should now dedicate the braid to the best outcome for that relationship.

Put the braid somewhere safe for at least 72 hours, preferably in constant moonlight and sunlight. Only when the reason for the spell is fulfilled (e.g. reconciliation between people, full honest communication, a successful business partnership) can you think of dismantling the braid.

As you undo it ask that the people involved can go forward in life in whatever way is appropriate for them, gaining what they have needed from their association.

You may of course wish to keep the braid without undoing it. Remember you must not use the ribbons for other magical purposes.

A braiding spell comes under the heading of a knot spell and is a gentle way of affecting the outcome of a situation. It is, of course, not necessarily a quick way of resolving anything but is often surprising in its outcome.

TO WIN THE HEART OF THE ONE YOU LOVE

This is a very old folklore spell. Using a bulb is symbolic of love growing unseen and

unrecognized for a time, finally flowering at the right time. You cannot simply leave it alone, but must tend to it carefully if it is to grow successfully and give you the outcome that you desire.

You will need
- Onion bulb
- Your burin
- New flower pot
- Earth or compost

Method
Scratch the name of the one you love on the base of the bulb with your burine.

Plant it in earth in the pot.

Place the pot on a windowsill, if possible facing the direction in which your sweetheart lives.

Over the bulb, repeat the name of the one you desire morning and night until the bulb takes root, begins to shoot and finally blooms.

Say the following incantation whenever you think of the other person:

May its roots grow,
May its leaves grow,
May its flowers grow,
And as it does so,
[Name of person]'s love grow.

You do need patience for this spell and you may well find that you lose the impetus for the relationship before the spell is complete. This would suggest that this relationship may not be right for you.

CHOCOLATE AND STRAWBERRY DELIGHT

Chocolate is said to be an aphrodisiac, a mild euphoric, and helps to heal depression. It is therefore extremely effective in love potions and spells. In this spell two ingredients are brought together to help you to enchant your loved one. Strawberries are well known as lovers' fruits.

You will need
- Strawberry incense
- Pink candles
- A plate of strawberries
- Melted chocolate

Method
Be very clear in your own mind what you want to happen before you start.

Be aware that it is not right to influence the other person against their will or their natural inclinations. You should use this spell to prepare the ground for true relationship.

Light the candles and the incense. Dip each strawberry in the chocolate. As you do so, visualize you and the other person together enjoying one another's company, becoming closer and so on. Say the words below (or something similar) as you prepare the fruit:

Lover, lover, come to me
*   And even then you shall be free*
To come, to go just as you please
*   Until to stay your heart decrees.*

You may now enjoy the fruit together with your lover and build upon your feelings for each other with an open heart.

This spell can be quite powerful, particularly if you use the same pink candles when your lover arrives. Strawberries and chocolate both come under the rulership of Venus, the Goddess of Love, though there is a belief that Jupiter also has a connection with strawberries.

TO OBTAIN LOVE FROM A SPECIFIC PERSON

This spell uses fire as its vehicle, not as candle magic but in your cauldron. You use an incantation and can also use magical ink

and parchment if you so wish. The spell is best done at night-time and using the power of the number three is not just for lust but also for love.

You will need
- Your cauldron or a fireproof container
- A piece of paper
- Pen and red ink
- Fragrant wood or herbs to burn (you could use apple, birch or cedar)

Method
Light a small fire within your cauldron or a suitable container.

Cut out a piece of paper that is 10 cm x 10 cm (3 x 3 inches).

With the pen and red ink draw a heart on the paper and color it in.

Write the name of the person that you desire on the heart three times.

If you wish, do this from the edge to the middle in a spiral, to signify how deep your love goes.

While doing this be thinking of his or her heart burning with desire for you just like the flames of the fire.

Kiss the names on the heart three times.

Place the paper in the fire while saying these words three times:

Soon my love will come to me
This I know that it must be
Fire come from this wood
Bring love and caring that it would
Make our hearts glow and shine,
bringing love that shall be mine!

Sit quietly as the paper burns, visualizing your lover coming towards you.

After you are finished concentrating for a few minutes, extinguish the fire.

Say quietly three times:

So, let it be

Do not get impatient if nothing happens for a while. Simply have confidence that you will be given an opportunity to have a relationship with this particular person. How you handle the relationship thereafter is entirely up to you.

TO FOCUS YOUR LOVER'S INTEREST

If you find that your partner's attention seems to be wandering, try this spell. It is best performed on a Friday, since this is the day that is sacred to Venus, the Goddess of Love. You can perform at any Moon phase.

You will need
- A clean piece of paper
- A pen you like (you can use your magical implements if you like)

Method
Taking your pen, write your first name and your lover's surname on the paper. Draw either a square or circle around them. Use the square if you decide all you want with this person is a physical relationship, and the circle if you are utterly convinced this person is right for you.

With your eyes closed, say:

If it be right, come back to me.

Cut the square or circle out and place it inside your pillowcase for at least three nights. Your lover should show renewed interest.

This is one spell that occasionally does not work. It is said that Venus will not assist if there is any intrinsic reason for the relationship not to work out – for instance, if your partner no longer loves you, you may be unsuccessful in your aim. This you must accept, knowing you have done the best you can.

TO BRING ROMANTIC LOVE TO YOU
· · · · · · · ·

This spell is one that uses herbs, crystals, candle and color. The herb rosemary traditionally signifies long memory, the rose quartz crystal signifies love and the colors signify love and passion. It is designed to concentrate the mind and to attract love to you as opposed to a specific lover.

You will need
- Small box
- Red marker/pen
- Rose or vanilla incense
- A sprig of rosemary (for remembrance)
- A piece of rose quartz crystal
- Pink or red votive candle

Method
Sit in your own most powerful place. That might be inside, outside, near your favourite tree or by running water. Write in red on the box:

Love is mine.

Light the incense – this clears the atmosphere and puts you in the right mood. Put the rosemary and rose quartz in the box.

Put anything else that represents love to you in the box (drawings of hearts, poems, or whatever – be creative).

Remember, this spell is to attract love to you, not a specific lover so don't use a representation of a particular person.

Be in a very positive state of mind.

Imagine yourself very happy and in love.

Light the candle and say:

I am love
love I will find
true love preferably
will soon be mine
Love is me
Love I seek
my true love
I will soon meet.

Now sit for a little while and concentrate again on being happy.

Pinch or snuff out the candle and add it to the box. Let the incense burn out.

Seal the box shut and don't open it until you have found your true love.

When you have found your lover, take the rose quartz out of the box and keep it as a reminder.

Bury the entire box in the earth.

Because in this spell you reproduce a positive state of mind and you are imagining what it is like to be in love, you set up a current of energy which attracts like feeling. In sealing the box you are "capturing" the vibration of love and all things then become possible.

TO CLEAR THE AIR BETWEEN LOVERS

When communication between you and your partner seems difficult, you can forge a new link using this spell, which is representational. You will need to have confidence in your own power though.

You will need
• A crystal ball or magnifying glass
• Your partner's photograph

Method
Place the crystal or magnifying glass over the image of your partner's face.

Because the features are magnified, the eyes and mouth will appear to move and come to life.

Simply state your wishes or difficulties and what you feel your lover can do about them. They will get the message.

This way of working is very simple, but you do have to trust that you yourself are an able transmitter. Often we do not realize how difficult communication can be and here we are trying to make your partner understand how you feel, not to change them.

HERBAL HEARTSEASE

Broken relationships are extremely painful and the hurt often needs to be dealt with quickly. This spell, using three techniques, helps to keep things under control until you can look forward in a positive fashion.

Cleansing bath

You will need
• Handful of either heartsease, or/and jasmine, roses, hibiscus and honeysuckle flowers
• Essential oils in any of these perfumes
• Rose quartz

Method
Add the herbs to the bath along with the essential oils. Place the rose quartz in the bath. Soak in the bath for at least ten minutes allowing the hurt to be dissolved. Remove the rose quartz. Take the plug half out, so

the water begins to drain away. As it does so, replace with fresh water to signify new energy coming into your life. Carry the rose quartz with you or keep it under your pillow.

Healing sachet

You will need
- Two 10 cm squares of red or white material
- Needle with pink thread
- Herbs as above
- Small piece of rose or clear quartz
- Small quantity of dried beans for banishment

Method
Make a sachet by sewing together three sides of the material with the pink thread

Fill the sachet with the herbs, quartz and beans, then sew up the final side.

As you do so, know that the pain will pass.

Hang the sachet in a prominent position so that you can feel its healing vibration.

Healing face wash

You will need
- Herbs as above
- Boiling water

- Heatproof bowl (clear glass if possible)
- Glass bottle

Method
Infuse the herbs by pouring boiling water over them into the bowl and allowing the resultant liquid to cool.

If you wish, allow it to stand overnight in moonlight to absorb the power the Moon gives us.

Decant the liquid into a clean bottle and use as a face wash on cotton wool or tissue.

As you do so, remind yourself that you are lovable and will heal from this hurt.

At one and the same time, these techniques are gentle in their action and also offer support on an emotional level. Working in three ways, they allow body, mind and spirit to be relaxed and at peace.

CONFIDENCE IN SOCIAL SITUATIONS

Charm bags are a very efficient way of carrying reminders which can add extra zest to life. This one is used to help you overcome shyness, perhaps when you are meeting new people or doing something you have never done before. This spell is also

useful if you suffer from a lack of confidence in a general sense. It is best done during the waxing Moon.

You will need
• A small drawstring bag about 2.5-5 cm (1-2 inches) deep – you could use a color such as yellow to enhance communication
• Ground nutmeg
• Pine needles
• Dried lavender
• Piece of mandrake root

Method
Put a pinch or two of the nutmeg, pine needles, dried lavender and mandrake root in the bag and tie it closed.

Consecrate and charge the bag during the waxing phase of the Moon so that you can use positive energy. Wear the bag around your neck or keep it in your pocket. You should feel a surge of energy whenever you are in a social situation which you find difficult to handle. When you feel you no longer have need of the support your bag gives you, you can scatter the herbs to the four winds or burn them in your cauldron.

It is the consecrating of the bag which turns it into a tool for use in everyday situations, so choose your words carefully to express your particular need. Try to approach one new person every day or go into one new situation, until you lose your fear.

TO CREATE OPPORTUNITIES FOR LOVE

This is not a spell to draw a person to you, but more to "open the way" – to alert the other person to the possibility of a relationship with you. The spell should be performed on a Friday. The use of your mother's ring is symbolic of continuity.

You will need
• A wine glass
• A ring (traditionally your mother's wedding ring would be used)
• Red silk ribbon 80cm (30 inches) long

Method
Put a wine glass right way up on a table.

Make a pendulum by suspending the ring from the red silk ribbon.

Hold the pendulum steady by resting your elbow on the table, with the ribbon between your thumb and forefinger. Let the ring hang in the mouth of the wine glass.

Clearly say your name followed by that of the other person. Repeat their name twice

i.e. three times in all. Then, thinking of them, spell their name out loud. Allow the ring to swing and gently tap against the wine glass, once for each letter of their name.

Tie the ribbon around your neck, allowing the ring to hang down your neck, close to your heart.

Wear it for three weeks, and repeat the spell every Friday for three weeks.

By the end of the third week, the person you have in your sights will show an interest, unless it is not meant to be.

Let's assume there is someone in whom you are interested, but the interest does not seem to be reciprocated. This spell ensures there are no hindrances, but there has to be at least some feeling for it to stand a chance of working.

TO BECKON A PERSON

This is a very simple method of putting out a vibration which, if a relationship has a chance of succeeding, will make the other person aware of you. It does not force the other person to do anything, but simply paves the way.

Method
Say the following:

*Know I move to you
as you move to me.
As I think of you,
Think also of me.
As I call your name,
Call me to you.
Come to me in love.*

Say the person's name three times (if known).

You may need to recite the whole spell several times in order to feel the proper effect. You may also need to remember that a loving friend is just as important as a friendly lover.

TO DRAW A NEW LOVE TO YOU

Charm bags, talisman bags or mojos, whatever tradition they come from, are useful in bringing about a certain result. Friday is the day of Venus and her specific hours are the eighth hour of the day and the third and tenth hour of the night, so these are ideal times to perform this spell.

You will need
- A small drawstring bag
- 5 rose petals
- A couple of pinches of catnip
- Heather

- Vervain
- 1 inch (2.5cm) piece of jasper or rose quartz

Method

Your bag could be pink for love, or red for passion with your drawstring a different color to add other qualities.

During the waxing phase of the Moon at your chosen time, put all the ingredients in the bag, then consecrate and charge the bag. Wear it around your neck or keep it in your pocket.

FOR A LOVER TO COME TO YOU

This spell is reputed to work very quickly, so do not be too rash. Red candles represent passion, so you must take responsibility for whatever happens when you call your lover to you.

You will need
- Two silver pins
- A red candle

Method

Stick two silver pins through the middle of a red candle at midnight. Concentrate on your lover and repeat their name several times.

After the candle burns down to the pins, your lover will arrive. It is also said that if you give your lover one of the pins they will remain bound to you. If you wish companionship rather than passion, use a candle of a color appropriate to the other person's astrological sign.

This spell is one used to influence someone else, so be very careful how you use it. Pins were often used in magical work in times gone by, because they were readily available. One old custom was to ask a bride for the pins from her wedding dress, for which you must give her a penny.

TO ACHIEVE YOUR HEART'S DESIRE

This is quite an effective spell and does give you something to do while you are waiting for true love. It makes use of candles and of plant magic. Timing is important since it uses the rising of the sun, as also is color (red to represent passion).

You will need
- A fresh rose (preferably red and perfumed)
- Two red candles

Method

Find out the time of the next sunrise. Just before going to sleep, place a red candle on either side of the rose. The next morning at sunrise take the rose outside. Hold the rose in front of you and say:

This red rose is for true love.
True love come to me.

Now go back inside and put the rose between the candles again.

Light the candles and visualize love burning in the heart of the one you want.

Keep the candles burning day and night until the rose fades.

When the rose is dead, pinch out the candles and then bury the rose.

There are many spells for love and this one is extremely simple, except that it requires some effort to get up early in the morning. The concentration that you put into it as you burn your candles focuses your mind on the matter in hand.

TO FORGET ABOUT AN EX-LOVER

This spell is done best at the time of the waning Moon or New Moon. It is not done to get rid of a former partner, but to exorcize your bad feelings about them. It is sensible to finish the spell by sending loving thoughts to them. Woody nightshade is poisonous and you may not care to use it, in which case you can use a bulb of garlic.

You will need

• Photograph of your ex-partner
• Suitable container for burning the photograph (one in which the ashes can be saved)
• Root of bittersweet (woody nightshade, which is poisonous) or a bulb of garlic
• Red cloth or bag

Method

Place the picture of your ex-partner in the container. Set it alight.

Gather up all your hurt and pain as the picture burns down. Feel them flowing away from you as you say these words or similar:

Leave my heart and leave me free
Leave my life, no pain for me.
As this picture burns to dust,
Help me now, move on I must.

Repeat the words until the picture is burnt out and only ashes remain. Taking the herb

root or garlic, hold it first to your solar plexus (just above your belly button).

Allow the bad feelings to flow into the root or garlic. Touch the root or garlic to your forehead, indicating that you have converted the bad feelings to good.

Wrap everything, including the container of ashes, in your red bag or cloth.

As soon as convenient, bury it as far away from your home as possible.

If you have had a relationship which is argumentative and turned nasty it is often better to end it and move on. This must always be your choice but if you wish to try again you may like to try the To Stop an Argument spell on page 175.

TO HAVE A PERSON THINK ABOUT YOU

This spell works over time. A relationship that grows slowly generally has more chance of success than a whirlwind romance and that is what is represented here. Small seeds represent the many facets of a relationship. The spell is done on a waxing Moon.

You will need
• Packet of seeds of your choice
• Pot of soil (to grow them)

• A small copper object such as a penny (Copper is sacred to the Goddess Venus)

Method
On a night when the Moon is waxing, go outside and hold the penny in the moonlight. Bury the penny in the soil in the pot. Sprinkle the seeds on top to form the initial of the other person's name.

As the seeds germinate, love should also grow. Remember that just as plants need nurturing so does love, so you will need to look after the growing seeds.

It is said that the plants will grow and flourish if the love is meant to be, but will wither and die if there is no real energy in the relationship. For those who are not very good at plant care, you might choose to put a reminder to nurture somewhere prominent.

TO HAVE YOUR LOVE RETURNED

This spell is candle magic and also representational. It is a little more complicated than most because it requires an understanding of symbolism. It is best done on a Friday. The objects you use need not be the real things, but they can be miniaturizations such as cake decorations.

You will need

- Pink candle
- Blue candle
- Gold candle (to represent the relationship)
- Horseshoe (to represent luck in love)
- Key (to represent the key to your heart)
- Two roses
- An article of your love interest's clothing (failing that, use something of your own)

Method

Light the pink and blue candles (pink first if you identify as female, blue if you identify as male, or whichever your preference is if you're non-binary), followed by the gold.

Place the horseshoe and key on either side of the candles, with the roses between them.

When the candles have burnt down, wrap the flowers, the key and the horseshoe in the clothing.

Place the items in a bedroom drawer and leave them alone for fourteen days. If after this time the flowers are still fresh, this is a good sign. You should then bury them or put them (along with the horseshoe and key) in a pot pourri, if you prefer.

You might use this spell when you think a relationship with someone would be worthwhile.

If you cannot find an article of the other person's clothing, a handkerchief or some other small article will do as well. If that is not possible then use a square of pink material.

TO STRENGTHEN ATTRACTION

If you love someone but feel that they are not reciprocating, try this spell. Be aware though, that by using this spell you are trying to have a direct effect upon the other person. You are using representational magic because the hair stands for the person you are hoping to influence.

You will need

- A few strands of the person's hair
- A rose scented incense stick

Method

Light the incense.

Repeat the name of the one you long for several times, saying each time:

[Name] love me now.

Hold the hair on the burning incense until it frizzles away. As the hair burns, think of their indifference dissipating and being replaced by passion. Leave the incense to burn out.

Before you perform this you should have tried to work out why the other person feels indifferent and consider whether what you are proposing is appropriate. If, for instance, the person you want to attract has not learnt how to commit to a relationship, it would be unfair to try and influence them.

TO STOP AN ARGUMENT

This is a spell to stop an argument between you and another or to change their feelings of aggravation. You are using color and representational magic here. So that you do not let your own feelings intrude, you might take a ritual bath first. The plate is used for two reasons in this spell. Firstly, being glass it reflects back to the person, and secondly through its color it raises the whole question to its highest vibration.

You will need
• Glass plate (Deep purple if possible, but if not, clear will work just as well)
• Picture of the person with whom you have argued

Method
Place the picture face down on the plate for no more than 15 minutes. You do not want to over-influence the recipient, so spend a few moments remembering the good times you have had.

For this reason, if using an ordinary photograph you should also be aware of where the negative to the picture is so that you are only using positive energy.

The person should either drop in or communicate in some other way within 24 hours so you can resolve your difficulties.

If they do not, repeat the procedure for no more than 15 minutes.

If after a third time you still haven't heard from them, do try to give them a call or visit them because their feelings should have changed somewhat.

You will then know that you have done all you can to be on good terms with them.

It is often difficult to get back onto a normal footing with people after an argument, so do be prepared to apologize for any part that you have had in the difficulty. Remember that you are only dealing with that particular argument, not deeper issues within the friendship.

GARMENT SPELL FOR FIDELITY

This spell uses the combination of nutmeg and intimate garments in a form

of sympathetic magic, combined with herbal magic. It is said to keep a partner faithful. It obviously can be done at any time, particularly when you suspect that your partner may be open to temptation.

You will need
- 2 whole nutmegs
- A pin or your burin
- Wide red ribbon
- A pair of your and your partner's clean underwear
- Large white envelope

Method
Carefully scratch with your burin or the pin your partner's initial on one nutmeg and your own on the other.

Tie them together with the ribbon.

Wrap them in the underwear and then place in the envelope. Sleep with the envelope under your pillow if your partner is away or you are separated from them.

Nutmeg was at one time the most expensive spice available so one would have to be fairly serious about the relationship to be willing to lock away such an expensive commodity. This spell is not to be entered into lightly, nor is it designed to keep someone with you against their will.

TO RID YOURSELF OF AN UNWANTED ADMIRER

Occasionally people get into a situation where they are being pursued by someone whose attention is a nuisance. Rather than reacting in anger, it is often easier to open the way for the unwanted suitor to leave. This spell, done on a Waning Moon, often does the trick.

You will need
- Vervain leaves
- A fierce fire

Method
Light a fire. Pick up the vervain and as you do so call out the name of the offending person.

Fling the leaves on the fire and say:

Withdraw from me now I need you not.

There is a requirement to declaim passionately, and to use some force, in any spell that is designed to drive someone from you. Therefore, be very sure that you do not wish this person to be in your life in any way.

Ensure the fire is properly and safely extinguished. Repeat the action three nights in a row.

Preferably this spell should be performed outside, but it can be also be performed indoors if you have a suitable fireplace and provided you are careful. Strictly, one is supposed to gather the vervain leaves, though with urban living this is a bit of a tall order. Make sure you have at least a couple of handfuls of the dried herb.

TO FIND A NEW LOVER

This spell works best if performed at the time of the New Moon. You use everything new so that you change the vibration and can look forward with hope. It is representational and is carried out at the time of the New Moon for the same reason.

You will need
• Heart shaped rose petal or a red heart cut out of paper
• Clean sheet of white paper
• New pen
• New candle (preferably pink)
• New envelope

Method
On the day of a New Moon, cut a red heart out of paper or card.

Take the paper and with the pen write on it:

As this heart shines in candlelight,
I draw you to me tonight.

Bathe and change into nightclothes.

When you feel ready, light the candle and read the invocation out loud.

Hold the heart in front of the flame and let the candlelight shine on it.

Place the heart and spell in the envelope.

Seal it with wax from the candle.

Conceal the envelope and leave it untouched for one cycle of the Moon (28 days). By the time the Moon is New again, there should be new love in your life.

So many need companionship and partnership to boost their feeling of self-worth that to do a spell like this means, as always, that one must be willing to take on everything that a partnership brings. Compromise and compassion are key words whenever embarking upon a new relationship.

A LOVER'S TOKEN

This bottle is quite a nice one to give to your lover as a token of your love and to intensify the link between you. The herbs are all well known for their association with love, and because of the link between the bottles should help you to communicate.

You will need

For each token:
- A glass bottle with cork, any size will do
- A handful of dried rose petals (preferably from flowers given to you by your lover)
- Dried/fresh rosemary (for love and strength)
- Dried/fresh lavender
- Rose oil or water
- Wax (pink or red is good for love)
- Pink ribbon

Method

Crush the rose petals and place in the bottle. Put in the rosemary and/or lavender, then add the oil or rose water almost to the top, leaving some room for air to circulate.

Cork the bottle and drip wax over the cork to seal it. Make another token bottle in just the same way.

Lay the ribbon on a flat surface. Place the bottles at either end of the ribbon.

Gradually move them towards one another along the ribbon to signify you meeting with your lover.

When they meet, tie the ribbon round your partner's bottle and give it to them.

Place yours on a shelf, dresser or anywhere where it will not be disturbed.

These bottles are tangible evidence of the link between you and your lover. You may use them to remind you of the good times or soothe you in the bad. The ribbon signifies the link between you, so when you think of it you will have immediately connected.

HERBAL CHARM TO ATTRACT LOVE

This is a charm that uses both color, herbs and knots in its fashioning. Love is always of interest, but do remember that you need to be clear in your aspirations. Numbers are also used, seven being a particularly potent one.

You will need

- Acacia, rose, myrtle, jasmine or lavender petals, in any combination or singly
- A red heart cut from paper or felt
- Copper coin or ring
- A circle of rose or red colored cloth
- Blue thread or ribbon

Method

Place the petals, heart and coin or ring on the cloth and visualize the type of lover you are looking for.

Tie the cloth into a pouch with the blue thread or ribbon, using seven knots.

As you tie the knots you may chant an incantation, such as:

Seven knots I tie above,
Seven knots for me and love.

Hang the pouch close to your pillow and await results.

This charm is designed to draw someone towards you and does not guarantee that you will necessarily fall madly in love with the person who comes along – you have simply made yourself attractive to them. If this is so then be prepared to let the other person down gently.

FIDELITY CHARM

This spell uses the Elements combined with herbal magic. It is an old spell and comes from a time when every spell-maker would use what was easily available to them. The best time for performing this spell is around the time of the New Moon.

You will need
• 6 large ivy leaves (gathered at the time of the New Moon)
• Burin
• Granular rose or jasmine love incense
• Container suitable for burning the ivy leaves

Method
Using the burin inscribe one word of the following phrase on each leaf:

Keep my true love with me

Light the incense and in the container burn the inscribed leaves with the correct order of speech. Whilst you are doing this, say:

Goddess of love, God of desire,
Bring to me fidelity.

The above uses the Element of Fire. To use Water cast the leaves into a stream or other flowing water and say:

Message of love, I set you free
To capture a love and return to me.

Ivy traditionally highlights the quality of fidelity and is often used in handfastings. You should not use this spell if you are not prepared to offer fidelity in return.

TO BRING SOMEONE INTO YOUR LIFE

This spell can be used to attract love towards you or to draw a companion closer. It should be started on the night of a New Moon. It is representational in that the cruet set suggests a pairing, and also uses color.

You will need
• Salt shaker
• Pepper shaker (or two objects which obviously make a pair)
• A length of pink ribbon about one metre long

Method
Assign one article as the feminine principle and one as masculine.

Take the piece of pink ribbon, and tie the female object to one end and the male to the other, leaving a good length of ribbon between them. Every morning untie the ribbon, move the objects a little closer together, and retie the knots. Eventually the objects will touch. Leave them bound together for seven days before untying them. By this time, love should have entered your life.

There are several spells which make use of the idea that two people must travel along a set path.

This one is used to signify the path of love. It also suggests in the tying and untying of the ribbon the freedoms there are in the relationship.

TO REKINDLE YOUR LOVER'S INTEREST

This technique is worth trying when your lover is not paying you enough attention. You are using the laurel leaves to back up the energy that you are putting into making the relationship work. This spell uses herbal and elemental magic.

You will need
• A large quantity of laurel leaves
• A fire

Method
Sit in front of the embers of a fire and gaze into them, concentrating on your lover.

Keep your gaze fixed into the fire.

With your left hand, throw some laurel leaves onto the embers.

As they burn say:

Laurel leaves burn into the fire.
Bring to me my heart's desire.

Wait until the flames die down, then do the same again.

Repeat the actions once more.

It is said that within 24 hours your lover will come back to you.

Again this is a spell which must allow the person who you are targeting choices. To keep your partner by your side if they are unhappy would not be right. This spell does allow you to give careful consideration as to what fidelity and security you require within a relationship.

RESOLVING A LOVE TRIANGLE

Sometimes it is possible to get caught up in a situation where three people are in a love triangle. It would be wrong to influence anyone one way or another, so here is a way of resolving the situation that should not harm anyone. It is best done at the time of the Full Moon.

You will need
• Three lengths of string each about a metre long
• An open space where you will not be disturbed

Method
Form a triangle on the ground with the three pieces of string so that the ends are just touching.

Step into the middle of the triangle.

Appeal to the Triple Goddess in her guise of Maid, Mother and Crone. Use words such as:

Triple Goddess hear my plea
I ask you now to set us free
It's not a problem I can alter
So help me now lest I falter.

These words put you in touch with your own inner self which means that you make the decision which is right for you.

Wait for a few moments to allow the energy to build up then raise your arms in a "V" shape (the Goddess position) and say:

So let it be.

Allow yourself time to consider the problem from all perspectives before making a decision as to how you should act. Each time you consider the position, remember to repeat the first two lines of the verse above.

It usually takes a little time for a situation like this to reach some kind of resolution, but this spell allows you to feel supported and cared for. Gradually it will become apparent as to the action you must take and you can accept that it is the ultimately the best outcome for everyone.

TO EASE A BROKEN HEART

This spell contains many of the types of magic normally used in spells. There is candle, herbal and plant magic as well as representational. It is designed to make you feel better rather than have an effect on anyone else.

You will need
- I strawberry tea bag
- Small wand or stick from a willow tree
- Sea salt
- 2 pink candles
- Mirror
- Pink drawstring bag
- Quartz crystal
- Copper penny
- Bowl made of china or crystal that is special to you
- I teaspoon dried jasmine
- I teaspoon orris-root powder
- I teaspoon strawberry leaves
- I teaspoon yarrow
- 10 drops (at least) of apple-blossom oil or peach oil
- 10 drops (at least) of strawberry oil

Method
Charge all the ingredients before you begin.

On a Friday morning or evening (the day sacred to the Goddess Venus) take a bath in sea salt in the light of a pink candle.

As you dry off and dress, sip the strawberry tea. Use a dab of strawberry oil as perfume or cologne.

Apply makeup or groom yourself to look your best.

Cast a circle with the willow wand around a table on which the other ingredients have been placed.

Light the second pink candle. Mix all oils and herbs in the bowl. While you stir, look at yourself in the mirror and say:

Oh, Great Mother Earth,
Nurture and protect me now.
Let me use the strengths
I know I have.

Look into the mirror after you have finished mixing the ingredients and say:

Mother of all things,
All that is great is mine,
Help me now to be the person I can be
and let me overcome my difficulty.

Put half the mixture in the pink bag and add the penny and crystal.

Carry the bag with you until you feel you no longer need it. Leave the other half of the potion in the bowl in a room where you will smell the fragrance. Repeat this ritual every Friday, if you so wish.

Unfortunately, the break up of a relationship can truly knock our confidence. This spell is designed to restore yours as quickly as possible. It does not matter who is right or wrong, simply that you are able to go forward with dignity.

TO ASK FOR A COMMITMENT

There is no way to force someone to commit to you – and it wouldn't be ethical to do a spell to push for that outcome. However, you can ask the Universe to get your lover to commit to you if it is in everyone's best interests and reflects the true desire of their heart. This is best done on a waxing Moon.

You will need
• Magically charged paper and pen
• An ivy leaf

Method
Trace the outline of the ivy leaf on your charged piece of paper. Within the outline, write out, specifically, what it is that you feel

would be the commitment you want from your lover. It may be that you just want them to commit to see you twice a week or it may be a more traditional commitment such as a handfasting. Then put your initials and those of your lover at the end of the outline. Cut around the outline and take it to running water such as a stream, a river or an ocean. Cast the paper leaf into the water, saying:

Ivy true, Ivy faithful,
Pledge my love to me.

Then watch the paper leaf be carried away. Your lover should approach you regarding more commitment sooner rather than later.

The ivy is known as a plant connected to fidelity since it thrives when it clings. However, you should take care not to be too clingy within your relationship as even traditional handfastings usually only lasted a year and a day.

YEMAYA'S SEA LOVE SPELL

Yemaya is the Goddess of the Living Ocean and the source of all waters, thereby making her the mother of all, since we emerged from the seas in an evolutionary sense. She is a wonderful ally in bringing love to you. You

must remember though that appealing to her for help creates a link between you and the Goddess that must be honoured in some way, at least each year, if not more regularly. For this spell, it is very handy if you are based near the sea, but if not, a river or running stream will also work well. It is best performed during the waxing phase of the Moon.

You will need
- A white candle (it can be a tealight)
- Florida water or perfume that you like
- A blue ribbon
- Blue and white flowers
- Something sweet such as a biscuit or flat cake
- Natural twine

Method
With the twine, braid it into a circle. Around the edges of the twine circle, gently push in the stems of the flowers you have chosen. This should create a sort of bed in the middle of the twine circle. Lay your cake upon this and then tie the ribbon around your candle and put it in the middle of your offering. While gently flicking Florida water on the floral circle, say these words:

Yemaya, hear my cry
Beautiful Queen, hear my plea
Let the love I seek come to me
Move the oceans to let him see
Part the waves to hurry his passage
Let him cross your seas to me

Then take your offering to running water, ideally the sea, light the candle and float it on the water. Ensure there is nothing nearby that the candle can light and don't be disappointed if the candle goes out immediately. Yemaya will have heard your petition and, if your offering was made with pure intent, she will bring you the love you seek before the next new Moon.

The words for the spell above are addressed for those who wish to attract a man. You can adjust the words according to the gender of the person you wish to attract. Alternatively make up your own words for even more personal power.

EGG ROLL TO FORGET
Simple chicken eggs can be powerful ingredients in spells. This is because they represent potential, but also because they can "take on" the aspects of life you want to be rid of and can then be disposed of carefully

to rid you of the problem at hand. This spell is for ridding oneself of constant memories of an ex-lover so that you can forget and move on. It is best done on a waning Moon.

You will need
- Egg
- Fragrant bath salts

Method
This ritual is best done in the bathroom. Thinking about the person you want to forget, gently take an egg and roll it from the top of your head down your naked body. Roll or rub it under your armpits and especially around your genital area. Once you have rolled the unbroken egg all over yourself, crack it into the toilet, and say:

> *I bid you well*
> *But well away from me*
> *Leave me body and soul*
> *And blessed be*

Once you're done, take a bath with the fragrant bath salts and imagine a bright future for yourself.

This spell is quite powerful and should only be used when you are certain that you are done *with a relationship. A lover's tiff that is likely to be resolved is not the time to do this. It should also be done from a place of calm renewal rather than anger, fear or desperation.*

BUILDING FRIENDSHIPS AT WORK

It can be hard to make friends at work, especially if you work somewhere with lots of office politics. One of the clearest ways you can avoid falling into bad relationships at work is to avoid gossip and try and be kind and approachable to everyone. This spell is best done on a waxing Moon and it encourages friendships to form at work. You may find that you are invited to attend an outside work event soon after doing this spell.

You will need
- Salt
- A bowl of water
- A cloth

Method
Sit with some salt in a bowl on your altar. You may light a candle or some incense to build the atmosphere and make you feel like you are tapping into the Divine Consciousness. Then visualize a blue shimmering light

emanating from the salt. Imagine that it radiates outwards from the blue and infuses your whole altar with its blue light.

Then say out loud:

Light of friendship, Salt of the Earth,
Bring me your disciple to ease my path

Then dissolve the salt into a bowl of water. Imagine that the blue light has completely infused the water with its energy. You can now transfer that water to a water bottle and take it into work with you with the cloth. Discreetly wipe down your desk and your phone with that water, imagining the blue light energy covering your desk and your phone and any cabinets or shelves that are part of your workspace. When you have finished, clearly visualize the blue light coming from your workspace like a beacon to the rest of the office. You should soon find that friends emerge and ask you to meet with them.

It can be hard to bond with others at work, especially if you're new and everyone else already has their work buddies. Remember to be as helpful as possible and sometimes just a smile can prompt someone to want to come and talk to you.

REIGNITING THE FLAMES OF PASSION

Sometimes it can be easy to get stuck in a comfortable rut in a relationship and to forget how you felt about your partner when you first met and the love was young. You can feel that way again, but you need to ensure that both of you still feel the same way about each other. This is best done on a new Moon.

You will need
• A photo of you together from when you first met your partner
• A red ribbon
• A red candle

Method
Light the red candle and gaze upon it while enjoying the good memories of your relationship. Sit in meditation at your altar, looking at the photo of you two. Try and remember how you felt then, the excitement and passion you felt for each other. Then wrap the red ribbon around the photograph, saying, with each turn:

Our passion burns bright
The flames ignite

Once the photograph is fully wrapped in the red, kiss it three times, and put it away in a drawer where it won't be disturbed. Your connection to your partner should reignite with passion almost immediately.

Do not use this spell if you suspect that your lover is drawing away from you, only if you're both just suffering a loss of libido but not of love.

FINDING TRUE LOVE

True love can be elusive, but this candle magic spell will enable you to draw it toward you and it will ensure that you are open to the possibilities of love rather than blocking yourself off with judgement.

You will need
- Rose or gardenia essential oil
- A pink candle

Method
Take the candle and anoint it with the essential oil, working from base to the top. Using your burin or a pin, carve your name gently from base to top of the candle on its side. While doing this, you should hold in your mind an image of you happy in the sort of relationship you've always dreamed of having. Try to give the image (or day dream) as much detail and color as possible.

On the other side of the candle score it so that you divide it into seven roughly equal parts, leaving the base part as the largest. Then light the candle.

Sit in quiet contemplation of all the good things about being in love while the candle burns down. You should let it burn to the first score mark if you possibly can. If this takes some time, feel free to read a book or do something else, but don't leave it to burn unattended. Once it has burnt down to the first notch, snuff it out, saying "thank you" to whatever divine power you recognize.

For the next six days continue to burn the candle down one more notch each night, always concentrating on the positive elements of what love means to you. In this week watch romantic comedies, read famous love letters, clip out any images you see of loving couples. Once the candle has burnt down to its stub, bury the stub in your garden placing a little food like a sliced apple or something else appropriate on top of where you've buried it for garden wildlife to enjoy.

Finally, and most importantly, put yourself out and about a bit. The Universe helps those who help themselves so don't be shy, get out there and meet people.

HEALTH, HEALING AND WELL-BEING

The subtle energies which come together to give each person their unique makeup are very precious and can be conserved and enhanced. We as spell-workers have a responsibility to make ourselves as healthy and whole as possible and in so doing can also help others to overcome problems and difficulties. We learn to appeal to a universal energy and its various parts to help the world go round a little more easily.

TO FORM A HEALTHY HABIT

Sometimes we can want to behave in a way that we know is better for health and well-being, be that taking some form of exercise or eating well or even remembering to relax or meditate regularly. This spell uses nuts (or any other small edible if you are allergic to nuts) in order to allow you to visualize how far you've come in building your new healthy habit. Start this spell on a New Moon and bear in mind you must commit to it – and

your new habit – for 28 days, or, in other words, a full lunar month.

You will need
• 28 pine nuts (or small edible such as a chocolate button)
• A dinner candle
• burin

Method
Put the bowl of pine nuts on your altar. Then use your burin to mark 28 equal sections on your dinner candle. Light the candle and say these words:

With body and mind
I seek to find
A balance that is rightfully mine
A habit now I try to form
A break for good from my usual norm
Lady true, bring me health
Lady true, give me strength
So mote it be!

Now each day of the next 28 days, light the candle at the start of the day and meditate on what it is you want to achieve with your healthy new habit. It may be to be able to run for the bus without being breathless, if it is an excercise or healthy eating habit or it may be feeling relaxed at the end of a hard day without worrying about the dishes or giving yourself a hard time. Let the candle burn down to that day's segment. At the end of the day, when you have done your healthy habit, consume one pine nut. By the end of the lunar month, all the pine nuts will have been eaten and you will have a healthy new habit.

Habits can be hard to form, but if you do anything for a full lunar month, having evoked the help of the Goddess, you will definitely find it easier to stick to in future. The bowl of pine nuts will help you see how far you've come as you go through the month.

ACHES AND PAINS AWAY

You should always check with your usual healthcare professional if you have an ongoing health concern, but if you are just suffering from feeling run-down and have a few aches and pains, this bath will help restore your balance and will avoid over-reliance on pills for everyday aches and pains. This can be done at any time of the month as it is an immediate relief.

You will need
- Epsom salts
- Rosemary sprigs

Method
Run a hot bath and put in three generous handfuls of Epsom salts in the bath. These aren't true salts, but are very good for aches and pains. Take a handful of fresh rosemary sprigs and scatter them in the bath.

Then lie in the bath with your eyes closed. Imagine that a beam of healing golden light is entering the top of your head and is beaming down through your body eradicating any pain anywhere within your physical body. As the golden light reaches the parts that hurt, it soothes the pain until it is gone. Once you are ready, step out of the bath and imagine that as you are towelling yourself off, the light remains pulsating within your body but the beam coming into your head has now stopped. Express gratitude to the Universe for sharing its healing power and helping you in your daily life.

While the Epsom salts will be doing the heavy lifting in this bath in terms of the physical action of soothing your aches and pains, the spiritual

element of visualization is very important because physical manifestations of pain regularly begin in the subconscious mind. You should take a notebook in with you as well and make a note of any images or thoughts that pop into your head as you are taking this bath.

A HEALING WALK

We often live very sedentary lives that can impact adversely on our health and well-being. A mindful walk that uses magical techniques is an inspiring and wondrous way to improve your health while also making you more aware of the world around you.

You will need
• Nail scissors
• Comfortable shoes

Method
Take a look in an online or paper map to see where the most green area is around your home. Before leaving for your walk, repeat the words below:

Goddess, kind and true,
lead my feet
To an aspect of you.

Then embark on your walk with the thought of the Goddess in your mind. If you have a specific problem you need healing for, petition the Goddess directly to help you find relief from it. As you walk, stay alert to anything that draws your attention. It may be a feather on the ground or a particular plant or tree in a park. You may find the seeds of certain trees carpet your walk as you go, if it is in that season. Whatever calls to you, either take a tiny clipping of it with your nail scissors, giving thanks to the plant for helping you or pick up the gift from the ground if it has fallen already. When you return home, do some research on the treasure you found. Plants, trees and birds have many symbolic meanings and there may be a message for you and your own healing in the gift that you have been given.

It is useful to do this sort of a mindful walk on a regular basis, even if you don't particularly feel in need of healing. Witchcraft is nature-based and the quickest and easiest way to practice it is to become attuned to nature and the seasons.

TO GET RID OF WARTS

Warts have been said to be the mark of magic so you may wear yours with pride! If you find

them unsightly then try this simple, safe spell from folklore. Ideally done at the time of the waning Moon, this spell involves no pain and should not leave any trace of the wart.

You will need
- Higher vibration incense such as sandalwood
- Coin for each wart (ideally it should be a copper coin that you have had for a while)
- Spade or trowel

Method
Light the incense.

Prepare your coin by holding it in the incense smoke for no more than half a minute. Charge the coin with your personal energy. Rub the coin on the wart saying these words in your head for as long as you feel is needed:

Blemish begone, do not return
Leave no scar nor mark nor burn.

Visualize the wart transferring to the coin. When this is done bury the coin in the earth, this time saying the above words out loud. Forget about the coin and within a calendar month the wart should be gone.

This spell can be done on others. Modern day medicines can be harsh and wart remedies which burn them off usually burn the skin as well. Children especially may find the burning of warts uncomfortable and this is a safe alternative that can be fun to try.

A LIGHT SPELL

This spell enables us to practice in the safety of our sacred space, before venturing out into the everyday world. It is not so much a healing technique as an energising one. The closer we come to an understanding of the powers that we use, the less we need protection and the more we can become a source of spiritual energy for others.

You will need
- As many white candles as feels right
- (An odd number works well)
- Equivalent number of holders
- Anointing oil of frankincense

Method
Anoint the candles from middle to bottom then from middle to top. This is so you achieve a balance of physical and spiritual energy. Place the candles in the holders on the floor in a circle about six feet in diameter.

Standing in the circle, light the candles in a clockwise direction.

Stand in the centre of the circle and "draw" the energy of the light towards you. Feel the energy as it seeps throughout the whole of your body, from your feet to your head.

Allow the energy to spill over from the crown of your head to fill the space around you. It should feel like a cocoon around your body. Now, visualize this cocoon of light around you gently radiating outwards to the edge of your circle of candles.

When you feel ready, sit on the floor and allow the energy of the light to settle back within you. Ground yourself by sweeping your body with your hands in the shape of the above figure, but do not lose the sense of increased energy.

Snuff out the candles in a clockwise direction, and use them only to repeat this technique until they are used up.

Gradually, as you become used to the sense of increased energy, you should find that you are more able to cope with difficulties and to become more dynamic in the everyday world. It will become easier to carry the light within you not just within the circle of candles, and you may find that you perceive more ways in which you can "help the world go round".

A MEDICATION SPELL

As you begin to understand color correspondences, you can begin to use them in spells to keep you well. Many people have to take medication of one sort or another and this spell helps to enhance the action of your particular one. It does mean that you must take your medication at the times given by your health practitioner but you can add additional potency.

You will need
• Your given medication
• Healing incense (mixture of rosemary and juniper)
• Anointing oil
• Square of purple cloth
• White candle

Method
Anoint your candle with the oil. Light your candle. Light the incense and allow the smoke to surround you.

Sit quietly and imagine that you are well. Really feel what it is like to be functioning fully. Sense how the medication will help you. Pick up your medication and allow the healing energy to flow through you and into the medication.

When you feel it is charged sufficiently put it on the purple cloth and leave it there until the incense and the candle have burnt out. As you take your medication in future visualize the link between it and you as it helps to alleviate whatever your problems are. You can further help yourself if, before you take your prescription to the pharmacist, you place it under a white candle and ask for it to be blessed.

Do please remember that this technique is not a substitute for medication. You are asking for help in healing yourself and using everything that is available to you. The spell is designed to enhance the healing energy so that you can make maximum use of it. In working in this way, you will also be enabled to do all you can to make adjustments in lifestyle and diet.

CERIDWEN'S SPELL

This spell pays homage to Ceridwen, a Welsh Goddess and nurturer of Taliesin, a Druidic Bard. She is invoked here, and asked for the gift of inspiration, called Awen by the Druids. This brings poetic inspiration, prophecy, and the ability to shape-shift (become something else). In bringing about change, this becomes a spell for creativity in all its forms. One of Ceridwen's symbols is the cauldron.

You will need
- cauldron
- Seeds (preferably of wheat)
- White candle
- Incense made up of:
- 1 part rosebuds
- 1 part cedarwood chips
- 1 part sweet myrrh

Method
Blend your incense the night before you plan to use it.

Light your incense and the candle.

Place the cauldron in front of you and half fill with wheat seeds.

Stir the cauldron clockwise three times and let the seeds trickle through your fingers as you say:

Ceridwen, Ceridwen,
I seek your favour
Just as you searched for the boy Gwion
So I search for the power of Awen
Inspiration to be what I must,
to discover the known,
And to flow with change.
Grant, I pray, this power.

Since Awen is a threefold gift you should repeat the stirring of the cauldron twice more or alternatively once on each of the following two days.

When you have finished, tip the remains of the incense into the cauldron and bury the contents.

The candle may be snuffed out, but do not use it for anything else.

Ceridwen is said to have brewed herbs together to bring the gift of inspiration to her ugly son Agfaddu. Gwion was set to mind the potion but, in being splashed by the potion, absorbed its powers. In escaping the wrath of Ceridwen he became a seed of corn and was swallowed by her in the guise of a black hen. The Welsh bard Taliesin born nine months later was thus an initiated form of the boy. Artists, writers and poets can all seek this kind of inspiration.

CLEANSING THE AURA

This spell is a cleansing one which uses nothing but sound and can be done anywhere, although the open air is better. It will depend on your own sense of yourself what sound you use but the one given is known to be successful.

You will need
- An open space
- Your voice

Method
Find a spot in which you feel comfortable within your open space.

It will depend on what you are attempting to get rid of which spot is better. Be sure to take plenty of time over choosing this until it feels absolutely right. Settle yourself comfortably on the ground.

Take a big deep breath and then breathe out. Your breath out should be slightly longer than the in breath.

Do this three times to clear your lungs.

Now take a further deep breath and this time as you exhale say as loudly as you can:

Ahh... Ee... Oo...

Repeat the sounds at least twice more increasing in intensity each time until you are actually screaming.

If you can, continue for two more sets of three (nine times in all, though six is fine.)

Finally sit quietly, place your hands on the earth or the floor, re-orientate yourself in your surroundings and absorb fresh energy as you do so.

Become aware of the sounds around you. Leave the area in silence, feeling the resonance of your sounds in the air.

This is quite a powerful technique and you do need to be quiet for the rest of the day, so that you can allow the energy to settle. The technique is a good way to deal with the frustrations of your everyday world and often results in being able to look at things from a different perspective.

DRAWING OUT A LATENT TALENT

This charm is to bring out an existing talent and develop a potential, not give you one you don't already have. If you have a secret ambition you might try this spell. It uses herbs as its vehicle and could be done at the time of the Crescent Moon.

You will need
• A small drawstring bag about 10 cms (3 inches)
• deep
• Liquorice root powder
• Rose hips
• Fennel
• Catnip
• Elderflower

Method
Put a pinch or two of the liquorice root, rose hips, fennel, catnip and elderflower in the bag. Once assembled, hang the bag outdoors at dusk.

At midnight, remove the bag and place it around your neck. If you like you can make an affirmation before you sleep.

Say these words or similar:

As I sleep, I shall learn of my best potential.

You must then wear the charm bag for a full twenty-four hours to allow the spell to work.

After that time you can place the charm bag under your pillow the night before anything important is to happen when you feel you need some extra help in reaching your goals.

Sleeping and dreaming are often the best way we have of self-development. Most of us have secret ambitions but are prevented by doubts from succeeding. This spell helps to make those fears irrelevant.

FERTILITY SPELL

This spell uses symbolism in the use of the fig and egg, but also ancient methods

of acknowledgement in the offering to the Earth Mother for fertility. Crops were often offered to the goddess in the hope of a good harvest and in this spell that hope is for new life. The spell is best done at the time of the New Moon or in spring time when the Goddess of Fertility is commemorated.

You will need
- Frankincense and sandalwood incense
- White candle
- A fig (fresh if possible)
- A fresh egg
- A clear glass bowl
- A marker pen
- Your boline
- A trowel

Method
Light your incense and the candle. Put the egg on the left and the fig on the right, the bowl in the middle.

Draw a symbol of your child on the egg. Very carefully break the egg into the bowl and place the empty shell on the left side again. Make a small cut in the fig with your boline and carefully scrape the seeds into the bowl.

Place the remains of the fig into the egg shell to represent the physical baby within the womb and again replace it on the left side.

With your finger, stir the contents of the bowl clockwise three times and say:

As these two become one
May the Goddess and the God
Bless our union with child

Leave the bowl in the middle and allow the candle to burn out. Take the bowl and the eggshell with its contents to a place where you can safely bury them. (Your own garden is good if you have one otherwise a quiet secluded spot.) Place the eggshell in the ground and pour over it the contents of the bowl. As you cover it with earth say:

I offer to Mother Earth
A symbol of fertility
In love and gratitude for her bounty

Now await developments without anxiety.

This spell is full of symbolism. The fig represents not only fertility, but also is thought to feed the psyche – that part of us that some call the soul. The egg is an ancient symbol of fertility and indeed of the beginning of life. Bringing the two together acknowledges your sense of responsibility for the continuation of life

HEALING THE BODY

This spell works on a simple principle, that of identifying within the body whether the pain it is suffering is physical, emotional or, as is often the case, has a more deep-rooted spiritual component. It uses visualization and color as its vehicles and calls on Raphael the Archangel of Healing for help.

You will need
- Large piece of paper
- Red, yellow and purple felt tip pens
- Black marker pen

Method

Draw three concentric circles. The inner one should be purple, the middle yellow and the outer red. Add a circle for the head and lines for the legs, so you have drawn a representation of yourself.

Now, thinking of any health difficulties you have, with the black marker put a small mark on the drawn "body" to represent that pain. Keep your pen in contact with the paper and ask Raphael for help.

You might say:

Raphael, Raphael, Angel of ease
Help me to understand this pain please

You should find that your mark is closer to one circle than the other.

Remembering that this Method is not a self-diagnostic tool at all - it is simply designed to help you to come to terms with the pain or difficulty - note which color this is:

Red represents pain that is purely physical
Yellow usually signifies an emotional root
Purple tends to have a more spiritual basis
Sit quietly and draw that color into yourself as though you were marking within your body where the pain is.

Next mentally flood that part of your body with white light.

For the next two days sit quietly and make the invocation to Raphael again.

Repeat the drawing in of color and the flooding with white light.

At the end of that time you should begin to have an understanding of the causes of your pain and how your body is reacting to trauma.

It must be stressed that this method is not designed as a substitute for medical diagnosis. It is a method of pain management which links with subtle energies to bring about healing on different levels.

GOOD HEALTH WISHING SPELL

This spell is worked at the time of the New Moon and is incredibly simple to do. Bay leaves possess a great deal of magical power and are used for granting wishes. This spell can be used to fulfil a range of desires, and here is used to bring about health and happiness.

You will need
- 3 bay leaves
- Piece of paper
- Pencil or pen

Method
During a New Moon, write your wish on a piece of paper and visualize it coming true. Fold the paper into thirds, placing the three bay leaves inside. Fold the paper towards you.

Again visualize your wish coming true. Fold the paper into thirds a second time, thus forming an envelope.

Keep it hidden in a dark place. Reinforce your wish by repeatedly visualizing it coming true. When the wish comes true, burn the paper as a mark of thanks.

This little envelope of power can also be included in a mojo or talisman bag to add more power to

it. In that case try to be as specific as you can in your wish. You can, using it this way, impose a time limit on the spell coming to fruition, though it is often better not to do so.

SELF IMAGE SPELL

In many ways this spell is one which is about loving yourself, hence the use of pink candles and love oil. By using incantation, you are making a link with the principle of beauty and with the Goddess of Beauty in one of her many forms.

You will need
- At least one pink candle, more if you prefer
- A handheld mirror
- Love oil

Method
Dress the candle(s) with the love oil, working towards you since you want to feel differently about yourself.

Have in mind your ideal qualities of beauty as you do so. Light the candles and stare deeply into the mirror. See first the person you are now. Visualize the change you want. Then "see" the person you would like to be.

Recite this incantation out loud:

Sacred flame as you dance
Call upon my sacred glance.
Call upon my better self,
Give me [your request]
Blessed flame shining brightly,
Bring about the changes nightly
Give me now my second chance
My beauty and glamour please enhance
Power of three, let them see, let them see,
  let them see.

You can now snuff out the candle and relight it the next night, burning it for at least an hour. Repeat the incantation at least three times over three consecutive nights.

The power of visualization is a very strong tool. Each of us has an inner beauty which if we work with it is a tremendous help in daily life. Once we are prepared to recognize it, it becomes evident to others. This spell accomplishes that recognition.

DISPERSE NEGATIVE EMOTION

Here is a simple technique for dealing with negative energies such as anger and resentment. It uses the Elements and their qualities in a very positive way. The circle of light links with spirit, the dark stone represents Earth and the water acts in its cleansing capacity.

You will need
- A dark stone

Method
Visualize a circle of light around yourself.
  Hold the dark stone in your hands.
  Place it over your solar plexus.
  Allow the negative emotion, perhaps anger and resentment, to flow into the stone.
  Try to decide what color the emotion is, and how it arose in the first place. It sometimes helps to counteract such an emotion by changing its color.
  Raise the stone first to your forehead to signify clarity. Next, place it over your heart (this helps to raise the healing vibration to the correct level).
  If it seems right, use words such as:

With this stone
Negative be gone,
Let water cleanse it
Back where it belongs.

This reinforces the idea of the stone holding your anger.

Concentrate and project all your negative emotion (anger, resentment etc) into the stone. Visualize the emotion being sealed inside the stone.

Take the stone to a source of running water in the open air and with all your energy throw it as far as you can. It also helps if you can get up to a high place to throw your stone away, since this way you are using Air as well.

Here you are deliberately using the Elements to clear away negative emotion. This leaves space for positivity and good new things to come into your life. Under no circumstances should you allow the anger and resentment to build up again as this will negate the positivity created.

OVERCOMING YOUR SHADOWS

This spell, which signifies letting go the hurts of the past in a way that allows you to move forward with fresh energy into the future, can be performed at the time of the New Moon. By carrying it out every New Moon you are gradually able to cleanse yourself of the detritus of the past.

You will need
• Cedar or sage smudging stick or cleansing incense
• Bell
• Athame or ritual knife
• White candle
• Cakes and wine or juice

Method
Cast your circle using the smudge stick or incense to "sweep" the space as you move around the circle clockwise.

Think of your space as being dome-shaped over your head and cleanse that space too. Ring the bell. With your arms raised and your palms facing upwards, acknowledge the Goddess and say:

Great Goddess,
Queen of the Underworld,
Protector of all believers in you,
It is my will on this night of the new moon
To overcome my shadows and bring about change.
I invite you to this my circle to assist and protect me in my rite.

Hold your athame or knife in your hands in acknowledgement of the God and say:

Great God,
Lord of the Upper realms,

Friend of all who work with you,
It is my will on this night of the new
*   moon*
To overcome my shadows to bring about
*   change.*
I invite you to my circle to assist me and
*   protect me in my rite.*

Light the candle and say:

Behind me the darkness, in front of me
*   the light*
As the wheel turns,
I know that every end is a beginning.
I see birth, death and regeneration.

Spend a little time in quiet thought. If you can remember a time either in the last month or previously when times have not been good for you, concentrate on that.

While the candle begins to burn properly remember what that time felt like.

Now concentrate on the candle flame and allow yourself to feel the positivity of the light. Pick up the candle and hold it high above your head.

Feel the energy of the light shower down around you, the negativity drain away.

Now draw the power of the light into you and feel the energy flowing through you.

Pass the candle around you and visualize the energy building up. If you wish, say:

Let the light cast out darkness.

Now ground yourself by partaking of the food and drink. Thank the God and Goddess for their presence. Withdraw the circle.

This is a very personal way for you to acknowledge the God and Goddess in your everyday life. While on first acquaintance it appears to be a protection technique, it is actually one to enhance your energies and to allow you to be healthy and happy in all levels of existence.

HEALING A DEPRESSION

Depression is not an easy illness to handle and you should not regard spells such as this as a substitute for medical care. However, a mojo or talisman bag can be of tremendous support in the process of getting better and has the effect of continually "topping up" the energy needed to overcome difficulty.

You will need
- Your burin or a pin
- Piece of angelica root for a woman
- Pine cone for a man

• Clary sage oil to dress the objects and to use as incense
• Sprig of rosemary
• Small dog tag, lucky coin or token
• White candle
• Red flannel pouch or talisman bag

Method

If the person you are helping is a woman, then inscribe her initial on the angelica root and dress it with some of the clary sage oil.

If a man then do the same with the pine cone. If a person is non-binary, use whichever they prefer the smell of.

When using a lucky token, charm or sprig of rosemary take care to dedicate it specifically to the person concerned. Say something like:

May this token of good luck bring healing to [name of person].

With the dog tag inscribe it either with the person's initials or their astrological sign. Repeat the words above as you do this. Place the objects in the pouch. Light your candle and the incense.

Dress the bag by dropping a little oil on it. Pass the bag and its contents over the candle three times whilst visualizing the person well and happy and also asking your favourite deity to help you in your task. Give the bag to the person concerned asking them to keep it with them at all times for at least a week.

Your subject should sense an improvement in mood within the week. You can reinforce the bag's efficiency every now and then by burning a candle for a short while and directing the energy at the bag. If you are not able to give the bag to the person concerned then hang it somewhere prominent so you are reminded of them occasionally and can send loving energy their way.

HEALING IMAGE SPELL

This spell uses the very old technique of representing a person as a poppet or small doll. Remember that healing takes place in the way that the recipient needs, not necessarily in the way we think it should happen.

You will need
• Poppet
• Blue candle
• Salt water

Method

Create your poppet to represent the person you wish to help already completely healed and whole. Take the doll into your sacred

space. Light the blue candle (to represent healing). Sprinkle your poppet with the salt water and say:

> *This figure I hold made by my art*
> *Here represents [name person],*
> *By my art made, by my art changed,*
> *Now may he/she be healed,*
> *By art divine.*

Pass the poppet quickly through the flame of the candle and visualize the person being cleansed of their problem.

Hold the poppet in both hands, breathe gently on it and visualize first the poppet and then the person being filled with Divine healing energy.

Pay particular attention to the areas in the physical body of your friend with which you know they are having difficulty.

Imbue the poppet with the idea of being healed from a mental perspective.

Think of spiritual energy infusing the doll, and therefore your friend, with the spiritual help that they need.

Visualize the person concerned being completely filled with white light, well, happy and filled with energy.

Keep the poppet in your sacred space until it is no longer needed.

At this time, enter your sacred space, take the poppet, sprinkle it with water and say:

> *By Divine art changed,*
> *By my art made,*
> *Free this poppet from the connection*
> *with [name].*
> *Let it now be unmade.*

If the poppet contains direct links with the person - such as hair - burn it in an open fire. If it does not, dispose of it in any way you wish.

If you have used a crystal at any point in this spell, this should be cleansed by holding it under running water and perhaps then given to the person as a keepsake or for protection.

We are not just asking for alleviation of the symptoms, we are asking for help from a holistic perspective. You do have a responsibility if you are working on someone else's behalf to do nothing which will make matters worse for them, therefore think very seriously about using this method.

HEALING OTHERS

This is a spell using crystals, candles and incense. It is also representational in that you use the paper to represent the person

you are healing. If you use an altar then work with that, but the spell can also be completed by recognizing that the space between the candles is sacred.

You will need
- 3 candles:
- Blue for healing
- White for power
- Pink for love
- Healing incense (1 part allspice, 1 part rosemary)
- Paper with name of the person you wish to be healed
- Clear quartz crystal

Method
Place the candles on the altar or in your sacred space in a semi-circle, with the white candle in the middle.

Place the incense on the left if the recipient is a woman, on the right if male. Light the incense.

Place the paper with the person's name in the centre.

Put the quartz crystal on top of the paper.

Be aware of your own energy linking with whatever you consider to be the Divine.

Breathe in the incense and feel your energy increasing. When you feel ready, release the energy. Imagine it passing through the crystal - which enhances it - to the recipient. As you are doing this, say:

> *[Name] be healed by the gift of this Power*

Remember that healing energy is used by the recipient in whatever way is appropriate to them. A physical condition may not necessarily be healed, but you may have started an overall healing process. Often the person is given the emotional strength to withstand their trials and tribulations so that an inner healing occurs.

PHYSICAL BODY CHANGE

In this spell you use the power of the crystal to make changes. By bringing the problem into the open you are creating a way to a change on an inner level which brings healing with it. This can be done at the time of the New Moon.

You will need
- Small piece of paper
- Pen
- Quartz crystal
- String

Method
Take the piece of paper and write your name

on it. Draw on it what part of the body you want changed and what you want to look like.

If you want to change more than one area, draw the whole body and mark what you would like to change.

Hold the paper in your hands and imagine the body-part changing from what it looks like now to what you want it to look like.

Fold the paper up any way you like and tie it to the crystal.

Once more visualize the body part changing again.

When you feel that changes are taking place, untie the string, tear the paper up and scatter it to the wind.

If you wish, you can bury the crystal to signify the fact that you have internalized the changes you have made.

This spell is very good for changing aspects you don't like. It may take a few days or even longer to see results, so please be patient. The spell should not be used to try to heal serious conditions of a medical nature.

PURIFYING EMOTIONS

This spell is one that helps you to release negativity and distress that may build up when you do not feel that you are in control of your life. It uses the four Elements to do

this and may be performed on any evening during a waning Moon. It has been kept deliberately simple so that you can spend more time in learning how to make your emotions work for you rather than letting them overwhelm you.

You will need
- White candle
- Bowl of water
- Bowl of salt
- Dried herbs (such as sage for wisdom)
- Vessel in which the herbs can be burned

Method
Stand in your sacred space, light the candle and say:

> *I call upon the Elements*
> *in this simple ceremony*
> *that I may be cleansed from the*
>   *contamination of negativity.*

Wave your hand quickly over or through the flame and say:

> *I willingly release negative action in my fire.*

Rub the salt on your hands and say:

> *I release stumbling blocks*

and obstacles in my earth.

Put the herbs in the container and light them. Wave the smoke in front of you, inhale the perfume as it burns and say:

I clear my air of unwise thoughts.

Dip your hands in the water and say:

I purify this water.
Let this relinquishing be gentle.
Purified, cleansed and released in all ways,
I now acknowledge my trust and faith
in my own clarity.

Spend a little time thinking about the next few weeks to come.

Recognize that there may be times when you need the clarity you have just requested. Now dispose of the ingredients immediately in the following way.

Put the salt in with the ashes then pour the water on the ground so that it mingles with the ashes and salt.

It is often helpful to find some sort of ceremonial way of releasing energy which enables you to let go of an old situation which is still troubling you. A good time to do this is just before a New Moon, so that you can begin a fresh cycle with renewed vigour.

TO CURE SICKNESS

Knot magic is good for getting rid of illnesses; this spell is one that will help to do this. It works on the principle of binding the illness into the cord, so is a form of sympathetic magic combined with positive thought.

You will need
- 20 cm (8 inch) length of cord
- Pen and paper
- Container of salt

Method
Mark the cord six times so that you have seven equal lengths.

Take a few deep breaths and feel your energy connecting with the earth.

Repeat the following words six times and tie a knot in the cord each time:

Sickness, no one bids you stay.
It's time for you to fade away.
Through these knots I bid you leave,
By these words which I do weave.

Put the cord in the container of salt (this represents burying in the earth). Create a seal for the container with the above incantation written on the paper. Dispose of the container, perhaps in running water.

The number six has particular relevance here: it is widely accepted as the number of the Sun, which is restorative and regenerative.
Again, this can never be a substitute for seeking medical assistance.

THE SPELL OF THE SHELL

This is a lunar spell which calls on the power of the Moon and the waves. It is also representational because the shell is a long accepted symbol for the Goddess and signifies her ability to take all things to her and effect changes. You can use this spell for healing if you choose a symbol that means this for you; otherwise, it can also be used for other purposes. It is performed at the seaside.

You will need
• Shell
• A symbol of your desire
• Fine nibbed marker pen

Method
To perform this spell, you must find a suitable shell in shallow water.

Take the shell and dry it thoroughly. Draw your chosen symbol upon the surface of the shell. Place the shell upon the shore so that the tide will bring the waves across the shell.

When the shell is in place, draw a triangle in the sand, enclosing the shell completely.

The symbol upon the shell must be facing upwards (towards the Moon). Meaningful words, or phrases, may be placed upon the shell also, or simply written in the sand (inside the triangle).

Finally, face the Moon and say the following words of enchantment:

Goddess of Moon, Earth and Sea,
Each wish in thy name must come to be.
Powers and forces which tides do make,
Now summon thy waves, my spell to take.

Leave the area now and the spell is set. Once the waves come, then your wish will be taken out to the spirits of the sea.

It will usually take about seven days for a lunar spell to begin to manifest, but it can take as long as 28 days.

This type of magic is what we called "little works" and belongs to the folk-magic level of spell-making. Take care to note the phase of the Moon (waxing for the gain of something, waning for the dissolving of something). You are using natural objects which to the uninitiated mean nothing. Ths means these spells can be performed quite discreetly.

RADIANT HEALTH

This spell uses invocation to enable a person to attain and maintain radiant and perpetual health. You can enhance the energy by finding an open space, free of pollution. and using sunlight, moonlight, wind or rain as part of the process. Sunday is an ideal day to perform this spell as this is the day that health matters are highlighted.

You will need
• An open space or your sacred space
• Coriander seeds tied in a small muslin bag

Method
In your sacred space or the open space, first sense your own aura - your subtle energies which make you unique.

Hold your hands over your heart area and then move them down to just below your solar plexus. You should sense a change in energy in your hands. This is the point in your body sometimes called the "point of power," the place where your life energy resides.

Now, facing the east with your arms spread wide and the palms of your hands upwards, say the following:

*Great God of the Heavens, and Lord of
All Power,*

*Grant me the right to feel and perceive
the true life force that is mine,
So that I may have everlasting well
being.
Grant me, O Great God, this favour.*

Now run your hands around your body from top to toe in a sweeping motion, not quite touching your body.

Raise your arms again and visualize the Universal healing energy sweeping towards you as you repeat the incantation above.

Take a deep breath, visualizing and feeling the energy being drawn in and down to the solar plexus.

As you slowly exhale, see the energy travelling to your extremities and filling you with power and healing.

Do this at least three times or for up to fifteen minutes at a time.

Place your hands on your point of power and repeat the incantation a third time, this time sensing the energy settling into your point of power. If you are in an open space become aware of the power of sunlight, moonlight, wind or rain.

Finally take a ritual bath into which you have put the coriander seeds.

*The purpose of this spell is not to cure you of
any ailment but, by enhancing your energy,*

to help your health overall. Please always seek the services of a qualified doctor or health practitioner if you know, or suspect, your health is compromised in any way.

BALANCING YOUR ENERGIES

This spell principally uses the energy of the earth and of candles. The spell can be performed either during the day if you particularly appreciate the light, or at night when you honour the Moon. Often it is good to perform it outside as an appreciation of energy returning to the earth.

You will need
- Fresh flowers for your sacred space
- Single white flower
- Bowl of water large enough to hold the flower
- Green and yellow candles
- Jasmine or rose incense

Method
Prepare your sacred space as usual, making sure you use plenty of fresh flowers to decorate. Float the single white flower in the bowl of water, thinking all the time of its beauty.

Light the candles, thinking all the while of the freshness of Mother Nature's energies.

Light the incense and become aware of the differing perfumes created. Quietly consider the cycle and power of Nature.

Stand with your feet about 18 inches apart.

Become aware of your connection with the earth, mentally reaching towards the centre through the soles of your feet.

Feel the energy rising through you towards the light. Reach towards the light and feel its energy moving downwards through you.

Let those energies mingle with those of the earth. Allow the new energies to swirl around and through you, cleansing, healing and balancing. Say:

Lady of flowers and strong new life
Be born anew in me tonight.

When you feel refreshed ground yourself by running your hands over your body from head to toe. Sit quietly for a short while and contemplate how you will use your new energy. Finally, allow your energy to settle in your solar plexus.

This spell is designed to replace old stale energy with new vital force. You should come away feeling refreshed and invigorated. While this spell has similarities to rituals to Ostara, the single white flower also represents the Moon and therefore feminine energy.

ISIS GIRDLE

This spell is one based on knot magic and is used to ensure that your energy is at the right level for your magical work. Buckles, belts or girdles were often associated with Isis or Venus and therefore aspects of femininity. They represent physical well-being and moral strength. It can be performed on a Wednesday and at any Moon phase.

You will need
• 3 lengths of cord, each about 3 metres (9 feet) long

Method
Decide before you begin the purpose of your girdle. To specifically use one for health issues you might choose the color blue, or to work from a spiritual perspective choose purple or white.

Begin braiding the cord and as you do so bear in mind that you are fashioning three aspects of self, body mind and spirit to become one source of power in all that you do. In this way the braid becomes an extension of you and also a protector of your being. Call on the power of Isis as you do so to give you strength and determination

Tie a knot in both ends to tie in the power. Now consecrate the girdle by holding it in your left hand and circling it three times anticlockwise with your most powerful hand, while saying words such as:

Isis, Mistress of the words of power
Cleanse this girdle for my use

See it surrounded by bright light and glowing brightly. Let the image fade.

Next circle the girdle clockwise three times with your power hand and say:

Isis, Goddess of the Throne
Protect me from all ill

Again perceive the girdle surrounded by light. Next put the girdle round your waist and say:

Isis, Goddess of Perceived Truth
Thy wisdom is reality

This time feel the energy pulsating in the girdle and say:

I stand ready to do thy work

In future, each time you put on the girdle you should be able to sense the energy, giving you the power to carry out your chosen task.

This is quite a powerful spell to do. Not only does it protect you from illness, it also prepares you to be able to help others as they require it. Since Isis rules intuition, you find that you are in a better position to understand others pain and distress.

KNOT SPELL

To rid yourself of problems or a troublesome situation, you can use a representation of the problem in a tangled and knotted length of yarn. There are then differing ways of getting rid of the problem. This spell is best done at the time of the Full Moon and is in two parts.

You will need
- Biodegradable string or cotton yarn
- Ingredients for a ritual bath (including candles and a purification oil)
- Three candles – one in your astrological color, one in a color you dislike (to represent negativity), and one in a color you like (to signify a life without problems)

Method – PART ONE
Your string needs to be biodegradable because it reinforces the idea that your problems will dissolve.

The string or yarn can be in the appropriate color for the problem to be solved (green for money, red for love, etc).

Sit quietly and think of all your fears and problems. Let them pass into the yarn.

Tie this in knots to symbolize how mixed up your problems makes you feel.

One way of dealing with your difficulties is to take the knotted yarn to a high place and let the wind blow it away, along with your negativity.

A second way is to bury the yarn in soft ground, though this method will mean that the resolution of your problems may come slowly.

A third way is to begin to untie the knots and as you do so ask for help in seeing and understanding solutions.

This last method does not have to be done all at once but can be done over time.

Method – PART TWO
Whichever method you use make sure you take a ritual bath or shower cleansing after working with the string. Anoint the candles with a purification or blessing oil. Anoint the candle that represents negativity from the end to the wick to remove bad luck. The others are done from the wick to the end to bring you what you desire. Have your ritual bath as usual.

This spell has two parts, first getting rid of the

problems then cleansing yourself of the effects. Only then can you decide how you are going to make changes in your life so that you do not attract yet more problems.

MARS WATER

Water charged with iron was at one time considered to be a healing potion, creating a way of treating anaemia. Today it is considered to be more of a protective device and, when under attack, to enable you to send a curse or hex back where it belongs.

You will need
- Iron nails or filings
- Large jar with lid
- Enough water to cover the nails

Method
Put the nails or filings in the jar and cover them with water.

Close the jar and leave undisturbed until rust begins to form. The jar can be opened occasionally to check on its condition, which helps the formation of rust. This should take about seven to ten days.

After this time the jar may be shaken and the water then strained and used as appropriate. Keep adding water as necessary to the jar thereafter to maintain its potency.

You should not need to renew the nails unless the concoction begins to develop mould, in which case throw everything out and start again. When using the water you may like to give acknowledgement to Mars by using a form of words such as:

Mars, God of War protect me now as I [state task]

You can use some of the water in your ritual bath or to cleanse and empower your hands before an important event. A business situation which required you to be more than usually aggressive might need a crystal charged in Mars water to make it especially powerful.

SELF ESTEEM

This spell uses visualisation, candles, cord and color, and requires very little effort, though it takes a week to finish. It is a spell that men can do very easily and feel tangible results. It works on the self esteem and on virility.

You will need
- Seven short lengths of cord, about six inches long
- Seven tea lights
- Seven small squares of red paper or cloth

Method

On returning from work, place a tea light on one red square. Surround the tea light by the cord, laying it on the red square. As you do so say:

> *This represents me and all I feel myself to be*
> *I wish to be [strong, virile, at ease with myself —*
> *your choice of words]*

Let the tealight burn out. Next morning knot both ends of the cord saying as you do:

> *This cord carries my intent to be [your choice of words]*

Carry the cord with you and when you need to, remind yourself during the day of your intent. Repeat the procedure for seven nights using the same words and either the same intent or another which feels more appropriate. Repeat the same procedure as the first morning also. At the end of the seven days either tie the cords together in one loop (end to end) or tie them so they form a tassel. Either way hang them by your mirror where you cannot fail to see them. Each morning for about six weeks choose which affirmation you wish to use that day and make sure you have acted accordingly.

This spell has a long-term effect on your personality. Each time you make the morning affirmation you are calling on the power of the whole to assist you in being the sort of person you want to be. Any behaviour which does not fit that image, soon drops away.

SLEEP WELL

Smoky quartz is sometimes known as the "Dream Stone". It is an able tool for meditation, and helps you to explore your inner self by penetrating the darker areas with light and love. Because of this, it is effective in releasing negativities like grief, anger and despair by removing depression. It is mildly sedative and relaxing and a good balancer of sexual energy. The cairngorm stone beloved of the Scots is a form of smoky quartz.

You will need
- Piece of smoky quartz
- Piece of paper
- Pen
- Your bed

Method

When you have prepared your sleep environment, sit quietly holding the smoky quartz and bring to mind any old hurts, anger, depression and difficulties you may have. Do not be afraid that doing this will bring on depression, because with this technique you are aiming to rid yourself of the depression these things bring.

Put aside the quartz for the moment and write down on the paper all that you have considered and thought about. Now pass the quartz three times over the bed to absorb any negativity. Wrap the paper round the quartz and place it under your pillow with the intent that it will help you to overcome your pain and hurt.

Go to sleep, and in the morning, remove the paper and dispose of it by tearing it up and flushing it away or burning it.

If you wish you can repeat the process for the next two nights, by which time you should find you feel much relieved.

Finally cleanse the stone under running water and keep until you need it again or dispose of it as you do in Disperse Negative Emotion on page 199.

Another use for smoky quartz is to reflect an intrusive energy back to the person concerned. If you are receiving unwanted attention from *someone, place a piece of smoky quartz or cairngorm in your window and know that you can sleep protected.*

TO FIND THE TRUTH

Without the truth one cannot make sensible decisions. As one's intuition grows it becomes easier to tell when people are not telling you the truth. Until that time a simple spell like this ensures that the truth is revealed in the right way. It uses herbs and candles.

You will need
- Handful of thyme
- Red candle
- Flat dish or pentacle on which to put the herbs

Method

Place the thyme into the dish and say:

Clarification I now require
So that truth is spoken
Let what is hidden now
*   Be brought into the open.*

Light the candle and say:

Speak truth with passion
And goodbye to caution

As the truth is said
May I not be misled.

Allow the candle to burn down until the wax drips into the herbs.

Bury the cooled wax and herbs, preferably at a crossroads, having first blown any loose herbs to the wind.

The herb thyme is said to bring courage, which is often needed to bypass our inhibitions. The color red often represents sexual passion, but here is much more the passion for truth. Do remember therefore that sometimes the truth can hurt, and you may have been being protected.

TO REMOVE OBSTACLES

In this spell Ganesha, the Hindu elephant-headed god, is invoked to ensure the success of any difficult task and to grant wishes. Because he represents a combination of strength and shrewdness, he is able to get rid of the most intimidating of barriers. The spell can be adjusted to encompass all sorts of life decisions.

You will need
- Yellow candle
- Red candle
- Your favourite flowers
- Sandalwood incense
- Figure of Ganesha or of an elephant
- Cooked rice
- Pen and paper

Method
Light the incense and place the flowers and the rice in front of the figure.

With your hands together and fingertips pointing to your forehead, bow to the statue and say:

Greetings, Ganesha.
Welcome to my sacred space
With your help, all success shall be mine.
I come to you, knowing you will grant
*   my wishes*
All impediments are removed.
I honour your presence,
Good fortune be with you and with me
*   and mine.*
I praise you Ganesha!

Light the candles and tell Ganesha what you most desire. Now commit your wishes to paper and place the paper under the statue. Say:

God of wisdom, God of strength
Loving bringer of success
Take now these wishes of mine.

*Mould them, shape them, work them
Till together we can bring them to
    fruition.*

   Bow as before and put the candles out. Repeat for the two following days, finally letting the candles burn themselves out. Afterwards, do not disturb the statue for three days and never keep asking for the same thing twice.

Before long, a new way will be shown to enable you to achieve your objective. Give thanks by sharing your good fortune with others and making a further offering to Ganesha who appreciates effort made.

TO SLOW DOWN A SITUATION

When things are happening too fast and we feel that life is running away with us it is possible to slow things down. For this we use the power of Saturn and his control of time coupled with the idea that if something is frozen it allows us time to think and consider our actions.

You will need
- Paper
- Black pen and ink
- Your freezer

Method
On the front of the paper either write a few words about, or draw a representation of, the situation you feel is moving too fast.

   On the back of the paper draw the symbol for Saturn.

$$\hbar$$

Pop the paper into your freezer or ice-making compartment and leave it until you feel you can handle your problem again.

   Tear the paper into small pieces and flush away or burn it safely.

This spell is similar to "Freeze Out" except that we use the power of Saturn, the Roman god of Time and agriculture. By using the freezer we are bringing this spell up to date and utilizing the idea of solidifying something rather than allowing it to flow.

A HEALING TECHNIQUE FOR SOMEONE ELSE

There is a whole art in knot tying which actually arose among the Celtic people and later became an illustrative art. If you are able to do it the reef knot - beloved of scouts and woodcrafters - is the ideal knot for this spell, since it will not come undone.

You will need
- A length of grass, string or ribbon

Method
This requires you to tie a double knot in your chosen material. In using material which will return to the earth and rot away you must also think of the pain or difficulty as dissolving. Tie one knot going first from left to right and saying words such as:

Pain begone
Tis now withdrawn

Now tie a knot in the opposite direction and use words such as:

This pain is held
Its effects dispelled

Now bury the knot, preferably well away from the person concerned.

As you bury it, give a blessing such as:

Bless this place and make it pure
Ill gone for good we now ensure

Now you can leave nature to do its work.

In this spell you tie your knot with the idea of binding the pain and then getting rid of it.

*This may be a slow process if the condition is a long-standing one and sometimes we have to remember that there are spiritual lessons to be learned through sickness. **Obviously, the person concerned should also have medical help**, so part of your responsibility is to ensure that this happens. Do not feel that the spell has failed if changes are not seen; they may be taking place at a much deeper level.*

RE-ENCHANTING THE WORLD RITUAL

It is easy when you have demands on your time and energy to forget about ritual and spell-work. Suddenly you have no idea what phase the moon is in and it has been weeks since you did anything magical. You might even start feeling depressed and wondering what it's all for anyway.

This is the time to stop and rebalance yourself. The dense energy of the world is clinging to you and weighing you down.

Begin with a proper declutter of your physical space. Then avoid news and politics for a while by turning off the TV or radio, not picking up a paper and not engaging with online distractions such as social media or news websites. This will help you reconnect to your own intuition rather than be buffeted by the opinions of others.

After your physical declutter, visualize a golden sparkling energy coming in through your front door (even if it is closed) and whooshing around your home, clearing away anything that isn't meant to be there. Then do this prayer on a waxing Moon.

You will need
- White or gold candle

Method

Sit where you won't be disturbed for a while. Light the candle. Close your eyes and place your hands, palms facing upwards, beside you or in your lap.

Call on the god or goddess you most affiliate with to guide you. Ask what you should do to make your experience of life more magical.

Sit in this space for a while, thinking about the answers that you are being given. Then turn your palms downwards and rub them against your legs and open your eyes. Write down the answers you've been given.

Review your answers two weeks later and see how they relate to what has happened over the last fortnight.

Now that you have opened the doors of communication with your divine guide, you will also find that you receive powerful, transforming dreams and experience strange, delightful coincidences.

This ritual or prayer asks for help from the divine to access a place of inspiration in your life and to beat everyday blues. However, another vital cure for feelings of disconnection is to get out in nature. Dragonflies become fairies in disguise. Trees speak to you in rustling voices. That rabbit that darts out across your path has a message for you, as does the fox following swiftly behind it. Brother Crow wants you to be happy. And spending time with all these elements might just get you there.

THUNDER, PERFECT MIND SPELL

In the Nag Hammadi scriptures, there is a beautiful poem, or rather invocation, that is the Great Goddess revealing herself in all her contradictory glory. Here is an excerpt from it:

For I am the first and the last.
I am the honoured one and the scorned one.
I am the whore and the holy one.
I am the wife and the virgin.
I am the mother and the daughter.
I am the members of my mother.

I am the barren one and many are her
*   sons.*
I am she whose wedding is great.
And I have not taken a husband.
I am the midwife and she who does not
*   bear.*
I am the solace of my labour pains.
I am the bride and the bridegroom,
And it is my husband who begot me.
I am mother of my father and the sister
*   of my husband,*
And he is my offspring...
Give heed to me.
I am the one who is disgraced and the
*   great one.*

To connect with the Great Goddess, you can meditate on the deeper meaning of this invocation while in front of your altar. You can connect with the Goddess at any point in the lunar month so there is no particular phase that is necessary.

You will need
- A white candle
- A bead

Method
Light the candle and take a few deep, cleansing breaths to centre yourself. Take the bead between the thumb and forefinger of your non-dominant hand and roll it around. Gazing into the flame, petition the Goddess to help you in whichever area of life you require her help in. Once you have finished, snuff out the candle and keep the bead with you as a reminder that the Goddess is always with you.

This spell not only enables you to connect with the Goddess, but also to keep a memento with you that links in to that connection. It will be a comfort to you at times when you are stressed or worried.

THE EVIL EYE

The evil eye is an ancient, widespread and deeply held belief in more than one third of the world's cultures, but is particularly strongly feared even today in countries of Mediterranean origin, and also in Celtic countries. Different cultures have different ways of dealing with this nuisance.

In Greece, it is thought that it doesn't take much to get the matiasma, or the evil eye. If anyone so much as admires your shoes, even from a distance, this envy can put a spell on you. Anyone with blue eyes is particularly suspected of being able to cast the evil eye. It is believed that mothers have a particular ability to remove it if their son is afflicted. Though the knowledge is passed from mother to daughter, a woman will not always learn the prayers necessary to do this until she becomes a mother herself. At that time she is prayed for herself thus, since she is considered vulnerable:

... and with bright, shining Angels enfold
and cherish her,
guarding her round about
against every attack of invisible spirits;
yea, Lord, from sickness and infirmity,

from jealousy and envy,
and from the evil eye.

A mother can diagnose and then remove an attack of the evil eye in the following way.

DIAGNOSIS OF THE EVIL EYE

You will need...
- Olive oil
- Bowl of water

Method

Drip three drops of olive oil on the surface of the water. Watch what happens.

If the drops remain distinct there is no evil eye. If they run together there is.

Dispose of the oil and water safely.

There are many ways of removing the evil eye. The following is just one method used for the removal of the evil eye.

REMOVAL OF THE EVIL EYE

You will need...
- Lemon
- Iron nails

Method

Drive the nails with some force into the lemon. Visualize the evil eye being pierced.

Keep the lemon for three days, by which time it should begin to rot.

If it does not, repeat the procedure. Here you have externalized the difficulty, checked that the spell worked and repeated the procedure if not. You could then repeat the diagnostic procedure to ensure that you are clear.

The Greek Orthodox Church does forbid people to go to "readers" or other individuals for use of magical rituals to overcome the evil eye. It is stated quite categorically that such people take advantage of the weakness of superstitious people and destroy them spiritually and financially by playing upon their imagination. However, Vaskania – which is another word for the evil eye – is recognized simply as a phenomenon that was accepted by primitive people as fact. It is the jealousy and envy of some people for things they do not possess, such as beauty, youth or courage. Though the Church rejected Vaskania as contradicting divine providence, the prayers of the Church to avert the evil eye are an implicit acceptance of its existence.

In Scotland it seems that the evil eye was more often associated with women and therefore inevitably with the crone, or wise woman, than with men. Anyone with a squint or eyes of different color could be accused of possessing the evil eye and of using it to cause harm or illness. A charmed burrach or cow fetter could be used to protect animals. Other preventative measures could also be taken, some using plants and trees – such as rowan and juniper – and others using horseshoes and iron stakes. This next technique explains one of the most-loved pieces of Scottish jewellery.

ANTLER CHARM

You will need...

- Piece of deer's antler
- Hair from a black mare's tail
- Silver tip for the antler
- Cairngorm stone (a type of smoky quartz)

Method

Wind the horsehair around one end of the antler at least nine times.

Fix the silver tip to the antler. This ensures that there is a balance of male and female energy, which repels the evil eye.

If you wish to make your own jewellery, the gemstone adds additional protection,

particularly from fairies. If you wish, you can then consecrate your creation.

It is said that if the antler breaks you have been attacked and you should bury the broken pieces in the earth.

This charm demonstrates how much arcane knowledge can be lost, without people appreciating the real reasons for certain actions. In other cultures the shark's tooth is equally protective.

While the owner of the evil eye did not necessarily need to be a witch, the curse did require the services of a magical person to remove it. In Scotland such arcane knowledge was, and in some cases still is, passed from father to daughter and mother to son. The word *orth* was used for an ordinary spell but a ceremonial magical spell among the Gaelic Celts was signified by the word *bricht*. It is interesting that this word also means "bright" in dialect – perhaps such a ceremony required an exceptionally bright moonlit night.

CLOVE REMEDY FOR THE EVIL EYE

Cloves have traditionally been used throughout the Middle East and the Indian subcontinent in the removal of the evil eye.

Here they believe children and babies to be particularly vulnerable to attack and an unresponsive or lethargic child with half-closed eyes is suspected of having fallen foul of the evil eye. The diagnosis and cure are both the same procedure.

You will need
• 3, 7 or 9 cloves
• A fire

Method
Taking the cloves in your closed right hand, pass them around the head of the child (or whoever is suspected of suffering from the evil eye) anti-clockwise three times. Then burn the cloves on the open fire. If there is no scent, it is said to be an indication that the evil eye is at play. The burning of the cloves should revive the sufferer immediately. Keep an eye on them for a while to ensure that the evil eye does not return.

This remedy is so widely practised that it is not even considered to be a spell, more a basic First Aid kit for spiritual ailments. Cloves should always be part of your magical larder as this spice is thought to be a spiritual cure-all and has been used in many different traditions for all manner of spell-making.

HAMSA AMULET FOR THE HOME

The Hamsa symbol is used throughout the Middle East and North Africa and has a place in many different traditions. Both Jewish and Muslim cultures have embraced the charm, calling it the Hand of Miriam and the Hand of Fatima respectively.

While popular culture has adopted this symbol for everything from t-shirts to jewellery, the original purpose of this amulet was to protect against the evil eye. It was originated in a protective gesture made to deflect and return the evil eye to anyone you suspected of wishing you harm. This is also why the hamsa occasionally features an eye in the palm of the hand.

The name comes from the Arabic meaning "five" and this "hand" is used in many forms throughout North Africa. You can create your own version of the amulet to hang in your home to protect all who dwell there.

You will need
- A piece of cardboard or a canvas
- Brushes
- Paints featuring blue, white and black

Method
Place your right hand on the cardboard or canvas and draw around it. This makes the amulet personal to you.

In the centre of the palm draw two circles within one another to represent the eye. cardboard and draw around it, thus making the amulet personal to you. Paint and decorate this image as it pleases you, but remember to draw one of the circles in black outline and to incorporate a turquoise or lapis lazuli hued blue into the circles of the eye in the middle of the hand. If you are feeling artistic, you can decorate the hand as much as you like.

Once you have finished, frame the cardboard or canvas and hang it opposite your front door so that anyone entering your space sees the amulet immediately.

It is said that amulets such as this protect a house not just from the evil eye, but also from burglars, flood and fire. These are the misfortunes that can befall a house so it is always good to increase your protection in this area.

BLACK CORD PROTECTION FOR ANIMALS AND HUMANS

Often animals and younger humans are unwilling to stand still long enough for you to use the clove remedy opposite. In

such a case, it is possible to have the same effect through consecrating a piece of black cord and tying it around the animal's neck or the human's wrist. This is a form of knot magic that is enchanced with some divine invocations for protection. It is best done on a waning Moon.

You will need
• A piece of black cord long enough for how it will be worn
• A black or white candle
• 3 cloves

Method
Light the candle on your altar. Black is traditionally the color for binding protection spells, but if you feel uncomfortable with it due to popular culture's mistakenly connecting it with Satanism, you can use a white candle instead.

Using a fireproof bowl and possibly a pair of tongs, light each clove in turn inhaling its scent as it burns. Holding the cord in your left hand, say these words:

Goddess of Shining Light and
the Comforting Dark,
Protect the wearer of this cord
from all harm, for now and forever

Sit for a while as the candle burns down thinking about the recipient of the cord and imagining them protected with a cloak of shining light. Oddly enough, you may see that cloak as a black shimmering light cloak rather than one of white – this is perfectly fine and normal.

Then tie the cord around the recipient and say a blessing for them, whether in your mind or out loud. They should not remove the cord until it breaks. Then it may be buried or cast into moving water.

We must get away from the idea that black is a bad or evil color. Our prejudices against this color have held back much protection from us in the past. In the East, black is used in the kohl that rims eyes to protect from the evil eye and in the black marks that are often tattooed as marks of protection on skin or in dye on animals. This is a magical use of the color and it is a color that is much beloved of the Goddess.

SALT METHOD FOR REMOVAL OF EVIL EYE

You can also remove the evil eye through the use of sea salt. This is placed on your altar and consecrated as "goddess salt" – the culmination of your prayers to the

goddess and your meditations at your altar. Remember to keep your salt on your altar for a whole lunar month before using it.

You will need
- A bowl of sea salt

Method
Having consecrated your sea salt and placed it on your altar, you should end every working with a short request to the goddess that she embue the salt with her protective qualities.

After one lunar month, your salt will now be ready to be used in the removal of the evil eye.

Simply say a prayer of gratitude to the goddess whenever you have need of the remedy and take a few grains of the salt and put it in the mouth of whoever has need of it.

Note that this salt can be used in a variety of different remedies including for healing and for protection. It is not just for the evil eye.

Finally, it is also important to note that you should avoid accidentally giving anyone else the evil eye by not envying anyone and always saying "bless him/her/them" whenever you praise them or something they have. This simply puts out to the Universe that you intend them no harm and that you have their best interests at heart.

In some cultures and religions, it is considered poor form to compliment others without adding a blessing as it is seen to attract the evil eye and a subsequent loss of the quality that you are praising.

MONEY, LUCK AND CAREER

It might be easier to think of this section under the title of Resources. Most of us need – or at least imagine that we need – more money or the wherewithal to do more with our lives and the spells in this section are designed to help you do just that. Mainly they will help you to move away from the so-called "poverty mentality" and perhaps help you to realize that you deserve to be rewarded for living according to your principles.

BASIL FOR BUSINESS

Many Hindu families keep a tulsi or Holy Basil plant in a specially-built structure, which has images of deities installed on all four sides, with an alcove for a small earthenware oil lamp. Here basil is used very simply to enhance business matters. Just how widely it is used throughout the world is shown by the use of the second technique, which is said to ensure that you will always be prosperous. This latter technique owes a great deal to vodou and the technique of floor washing.

You will need
• Basil seeds and plant
• Pots containing compost
• Small oil lamp

Method
Place the pot and plants where they can be safely left.

Carefully nurture the seeds to maturity. Whenever practical, light the oil lamp and keep it burning. This action honours the goddess Tulsi who fell in love with Krishna and calls upon her beneficence.

To attract clients and prevent theft

You will need
• Glass jar or metal container
• Handful of mature basil leaves
• One pint of boiling water

Method
Shred the basil leaves into the container. Pour the boiling water over the leaves. Allow to steep for four days.

Strain out the leaves and reserve the remaining liquid. Sprinkle the liquid over the thresholds and windowsills of the business premises and anywhere else the public is likely to go.

The nurturing of the seeds obviously has significant symbolism in the growing of the business, so it is good to have plants in various stages of development. As you can see, this spell uses information gained from several cultures, showing how universal herbal magic can truly be.

ATTRACTING EXTRA MONEY

This is a representational spell since the money in your pocket is representative of a greater fortune. Use this only at the time of a New Moon and make sure you are in the open air. It is said that the spell is negated if the Moon is seen through glass.

You will need
• Loose change

Method
Gaze at the Moon. Turn your money over in your pocket. As you do so, repeat the following three times:

Goddess of Light and Love, I pray
Bring fortune unto me this day.

You will know that it has worked when you find extra money in your pocket or your purse or come across money unexpectedly.

In previous times the Moon was recognized as much as the Sun as being the bringer of good luck. This spell acknowledges that and allows you to make use of her power. It is said to ensure that you have at least enough for bed and board until the next New Moon.

FOOTWASH FOR MONEY

This is a folklore recipe and would strictly only become a spell if an incantation or invocation were added. Black Cohosh is better known as a herb to be used at the time of the menopause, but here is used as a footwash which will lead you to money.

You will need
• Black Cohosh root
• Cup of boiling water
• Small bottle

Method
Soak the root in the cup of boiling water for

fifteen minutes. Strain the water and throw away the root. Put the liquid in the bottle for seven days and leave it alone.

On the eighth day, rub the liquid all over the bottom of your shoes.

Be alert to your own intuition until money comes your way.

It is said that you will either find money, win it, or gain it in some legal manner. This, by its method, cannot really be used to gain a specific amount, but you can bear in mind what your needs are.

MONEY DOUBLING SPELL

This spell is representational and helps double any denomination of paper money that you have. You are asking that the money be increased so you may also use a herb which has this effect. You are also appealing to the highest authority in asking the Angels to help you.

You will need
• Paper money (preferably new and as much as you can spare)
• White envelope
• Cinnamon powder
• Wax to seal the envelope

Method
Place the money in the envelope, along with the cinnamon powder, and seal it with the wax. Fold the envelope, leave it in your sacred space and say once, every day, for seven days:

Hear me, angels in your glory,
Hear me now Zacharael.
I see the need for the common good
And ask for this to be increased.

Hold the envelope up, and perceive that it feels heavier than it was.

Keep the envelope in your bedroom for safety. After you receive more money, open the envelope, and share what was in the envelope with others.

Zacharael means "remembrance of God" and is the angel who reminds us not to be bound by material concerns. For this reason, when we have truly shown that we understand both the value and the illusions associated with money we should never go short.

HOW TO SPEED UP A HAPPENING

Sometimes we find ourselves in a situation that is not happening quickly enough for us, such as a business deal or house purchase.

We can then use our knowledge of color and herbs and spices to speed things up. We may not always know what other circumstances surround the problem, so it is wise to bear in mind the words "if it be right" or "An it harm no-one".

You will need
- Red candle
- Fast luck incense
- Cinnamon powder
- Papers associated with, or representative of, the problem

Method
Sprinkle each of the papers with cinnamon powder. Arrange in a pile. Place the candle on top of the papers.

As you do this repeat the following words three times:

Time passed, time fast
Let this [event] happen

Light the incense and the candle and allow them to burn out.

When doing this spell, be sure to keep a close eye on the candle so that the papers are never in danger of being set alight.

A CASE FOR COURT

This spell should help you to obtain the verdict you wish for in a court case. It is simple to do and can also give you the confidence to face your ordeal with courage.

You will need
- Several pieces of paper
- Pen (all magically charged if possible)
- Orange candle (for legal matters)
- Fireproof dish
- Scissors

Method
Sit in a quiet space and light the candle.

Breathe deeply several times to help clear your mind. Look at the issue from the perspectives of the other people involved (your opponents, the judge, jury and so on).

Try to think of all possible scenarios which might occur, being realistic in your assessments.

Write down each one on a single piece of paper. See yourself handling each scenario calmly and factually.

Concentrating on the candle flame, call on your own favourite pantheon of gods and ask for right action. You might for example petition the Egyptian goddess

Ma'at, Themis the Greek goddess, or Forseti the Norse god. Ask that there will be clarity, honesty and justice in the situation.

Take a brief look at each of the scenarios again and write down any new ones which then come to mind. Now choose the outcome you most desire and put that piece of paper under the candle while it burns out. Take the rest of the papers and cut them up into small pieces. Set light to them in the fireproof dish by first lighting one piece from the candle. When these have burnt out, flush them away under the tap or blow them to the four winds.

When you go to court, take the paper with your desired result, put it in your pocket, and when you find yourself in difficulties hold the paper unobtrusively in your hand to give you courage.

This spell does not automatically ensure that you will win your case, particularly if there is dishonesty involved. Remember that you are asking for justice, which may involve some kind of penance or penalty on your part.

A MAGICAL POMANDER

As our knowledge of herbs and magic increases, we are able to use old-fashioned ideas and charming customs and perhaps return them to their original use. Pomanders, aromatic spheres that are prepared by studding oranges with cloves, have been used since medieval times in a practical way to keep bad smells at bay. Magically they can be used to attract money and for protection and – when they have lost their fragrance – as an offering through fire to the gods.

You will need
- An orange with an oily skin
- A nail or knitting needle
- A good quantity of whole cloves
- Cinnamon powder
- Plastic bag
- Ribbon
- Pins

Method
Stud the orange with whole cloves complete with stems, bud side out. It is easier to insert the cloves if you poke a small hole first with the nail or knitting needle. Space the cloves evenly in a pattern that pleases you, leaving room to tie the ribbon. The cloves will move closer together as the orange dries out. Keep your intent for the pomander in mind.

Place the powdered cinnamon in the plastic bag, and shake the pomander inside

the bag until it is well coated with the powder.

Leave in a warm place to dry out, which may take up to six weeks.

Check frequently that the orange is not going mouldy, but try not to open the bag.

Lastly, tie the ribbon around the pomander, fixing it securely with the pins.

Hang the pomander where you can both see it and enjoy the fragrance.

When you come to dispose of the pomander, throw it into a fire. Say:

As I return this to its Element
Sun, Jupiter, Venus
I thank you for your help.

Made in this way the pomander can last up to a year before its fragrance completely fades.

This pomander is multi purpose. All the components are ruled by the element of Fire and the relevant deities and planetary influences are Sun for the orange, Jupiter for the cloves and Venus for the cinnamon.

ACHIEVING A DREAM JOB

Candles always work well when dealing with aims and aspirations. This spell introduces some of the techniques beloved of those who believe in using the Element of Fire, which represents drive. This particular spell is best begun on the night of a New Moon.

You will need
• 2 brown candles (to represent the job)
• Green candle (for prosperity)
• A candle to represent yourself (perhaps your astrological color)
• Prosperity incense such as cinnamon
• Prosperity oil such as bergamot, or blended patchouli and basil

Method
Light your prosperity incense. Anoint the candles with the prosperity oil from wick to end, since you want the good things to come towards you.

Place one of the brown candles in the centre of your chosen space.

Place the green one on the right, with your personal candle on the left. (These candles should be in a safe place; they have to burn out entirely.) As you light your personal candle, say:

Open the way, clear my sight.
Bring me chance, that is my right.

Light the green candle and say:

Good luck is mine and true victory,
Help me Great Ones, come to me.
Light the brown candle and say:
Openings, work, rewards I see,
And as I will, So Must it Be.

Leave the candles to burn out completely.

Each night for a week – or until the candle is used up – light the second brown candle for 9 minutes while contemplating the job and the good to come out of it.

You need to identify exactly what you mean by "a dream job". It is of little use aiming for something which is beyond your capabilities, though you might go for one initially which will begin to take you to where you want to be.

ACTIVATING A WISH

It is easy to categorize the granting of wishes as a separate area of spell-making, but, depending on the offering you make, it could be classified as crystal, candle, herbal or symbolic. Timings and other correspondences can be according to your wish or need.

You will need

• Your chosen gift to the Elements, spirits or deities (this might be an appropriate crystal, plant, rune or piece of metal)

• A suitable place to make that offering (perhaps a quiet woodland, a running stream, a high place, or in urban areas a park, waterway or high building)

Method

Before you begin you will need to have given some thought to your wish.

Be very specific in stating what you want otherwise you may get more than you bargained for.

State your wish clearly and as briefly as possibly, addressing your deity or spirit by name or title if you can, for instance:

Pan and spirits of the woodland
Hear now my request
I wish for health, love and happiness
For [name]

When you make your offering, be appropriate. For example:

If your wish is for material goods or finance you could use a crystal or coin and bury it to signify the tangibility of your desire.

If your wish has an emotional content then you might throw your offering into running water.

If your wish is for knowledge or information then signify this by getting up to a high place and using the currents of air.

You might for instance choose to scatter some plant seeds to help restore the ecological balance.

If choosing to use the Element of Fire outside then be responsible, use only dead wood and never place your fire close to plants or buildings.

Repeat your wish three times. This is so that any negative attached to your desire should have dropped away by the third request and by then you will also be more aware of your own feelings and whether you really want what you are asking for.

Making wishes is a quick way of making things happen within your everyday world, often without having to carry out a full-blown ceremony. As you get to know your own capabilities you will be able to take advantage of the moments which are presented to you.

FOR STUDY AND CONCENTRATION

It is sometimes important to go right back to basics to gain the help we need. This is a herbal and color formula spell which also calls on the powers of Bridget, the goddess of poetry, or on Sarasvati, the goddess of knowledge. Your sachet will be purple for the former and white for the latter.

You will need
- 2 parts rosemary
- 2 parts basil
- 1 part caraway seeds
- 1 part dried rind of citrus fruit
- (a part equals one quantity)
- Small bowl to mix the herbs
- Small cloth bag about 15cms in size
- Silver thread or cord

Method
Combine the herbs thoroughly while chanting either:

Bridget, Brighde fashioner of words,
Help me now as I seek your aid
Let me now bring you honour
In what I have to say today.

Or, for Sarasvati:

Sarasvati, divine consort of Brahma
Mistress of knowledge
Teach me to use words wisely and well
My doubts and fears I pray you dispel.

Now put the herbs in the bag, tying it securely with the silver cord. Place the sachet somewhere within your work area where you can see it.

You should find that simply by focusing on the sachet you are able to free your mind from distractions and find inspiration as you study for exams or write your articles and masterpieces. If you become really stuck then pick up the sachet and allow some of the fragrance to escape, remembering to tie it back up when you are finished.

LEGAL SUCCESS

This spell is based on ancient herb and folk magic. To influence the outcome of legal procedures, the associated papers are "dressed" to give added power to any decisions that have to be made. The technique is very simple and, of course, can also be used in business proceedings, but in this case should probably be carried out away from the office.

You will need
- *Your documents*
- *Dressing powder, consisting of:*
- *unscented talcum or powdered chalk*
- *Deer's Tongue leaves*
- *calendula flowers*
- *ginger or cinnamon powder*

Method
Combine the leaves, flowers and ginger or cinnamon powder in equal measures with the talcum or chalk. Place your documents on a flat surface and sprinkle them thoroughly with the mixture.

Draw your fingernails through the powder in wavy lines from top to bottom. Concentrate as you do so on the desired outcome.

Leave the papers overnight then in the morning shake off the powder.

This spell does not seem to work if there is any dishonesty or deliberate nefarious dealings on your part. However if you are completely above board it is possible to turn things in your favour. "Dressing" papers can also be carried out if you have important exams or studying to do.

ELIMINATING PERSONAL POVERTY

A modern-day adaptation of an ancient formula, this spell ensures that you always have the necessities of life, such as somewhere to stay and enough to eat. Because it becomes

part of your everyday environment, you simply need to refresh the ingredients when you feel the time right.

You will need
- Small glass container containing equal quantities of:
- Salt, sugar and rice
- Safety pin

Method
Fill the container with a mixture of the salt, sugar and rice. Place the open safety pin in the centre of the mixture.

Put the container in the open air where you can easily see it. Occasionally give the bowl a shake to reinvigorate the energies.

Though this spell has no particular timeframe, the more confident you become in your own abilities the quicker it will work. Rather than using salt, sugar and rice you can use a pot-pourri of your choice. Shaking the container also keeps the energies fresh and you must use your intuition as to when they need changing.

FAST LUCK OIL

This oil contains herbal essences, all of which have the effect of quickening up a spell. However, there is need for a word of warning, since many people nowadays have sensitivities to so many substances. Wintergreen if ingested internally is highly toxic so you should be extremely careful when dealing with it and cinnamon oil can irritate the skin. When it is used to dress a candle, the combined oils are an efficent and speedy way of making things happen.

You will need
- A small bottle
- 10 drops wintergreen oil
- 10 drops vanilla oil
- 10 drops cinnamon oil
- Carrier such as almond oil
- (If you wish you can suspend a small piece of alkanet root [Bloodroot] in the bottle for a deep red color and extra power)
- You can also, for money spells, add gold or silver glitter

Method
Carefully combine the essential and carrier oils in the bottle.Shake well and repeat as you do so at least three times:

Fast Luck, Fast Luck
Bring to me my desire.

Now add the other ingredients if you are using them and leave the bottle in a cool dark place for at least twenty four hours for the oils to blend. After this time you can use the oil to dress your candles.

Remember that, as you are drawing luck towards you, you should dress the candle from the top down. If you are using Fast Luck Oil for a money spell concentrate on money coming towards you, use a green candle and repeat the words above.

Use a brown candle if you have a business deal you need to accelerate, but this time it is wise to add a few flakes of silver or gold glitter.

To bring love into your life use a pink candle, visualize your ideal person coming into your life and repeat the words above, adding:

If it be right for all concerned.

Let the candles burn out safely.

You should have some indication that this routine is working within about thirty-six hours. If there is none, then you must consider what obstacles there are to progress. These may have come to light since you began the spell and you can attempt to remove them before carrying out the procedure again.

GAMBLING SPELL

This spell activates a good luck charm which can be used whenever you gamble. The acorn is a symbol of fertility and good luck and takes on the quality of its parent tree, the oak, which is considered to signify strength and power.

You will need
- Acorn
- Gold paint
- Narrow paintbrush

Method
Sit quietly for a few moments, holding the acorn in the hand you consider to be your most powerful and visualize yourself receiving your winnings.

Now carefully paint the acorn with the gold paint.

Make sure that you completely cover it.

Repeat the following at least three times while doing this:

When chance's dice I choose to throw
Little seed of acorn grow
As I gild thee here and now
Bring me gold and silver

When the paint has dried keep the acorn in your pocket or wallet.

Remember that you have used a living plant and should therefore return an offering to the earth in some way – perhaps plant another acorn in a wild place.

Do not expect to win large amounts of money using this spell. It is much more likely to be a steady trickle, through whatever way you choose to gamble. Occasionally for best results you should share some of your winnings with others, so that your good luck is passed on.

MONEY BOTTLE

Spell bottles were originally created to destroy the power of an evil magician or witch thought to have cast a spell against the bottle's creator. The bottles consist of a container, usually glass, filled with various objects of magical potency. All are concentrations of energy, created and empowered for specific magical purposes.

You will need
- Tall, thin glass bottle
- 5 cloves
- 5 cinnamon sticks
- 5 kernels of dried corn
- 5 kernels of dried wheat (or 5 teaspoons of wheat flour)
- 5 pennies
- 5 10p pieces
- 5 20p pieces
- 5 sesame seeds
- 5 pecans
- 5 whole allspice

Method
Put the ingredients into the bottle, making sure the top is secured tightly.

Shake the bottle for five minutes while chanting words such as:

Money gain, silver and herbs
Copper and grain hear my words.

Place the money bottle on a table somewhere in your house. Leave your purse or wallet near the bottle when at home so that the power is transferred.

You should find that money will come to you, perhaps in unexpected ways.

The number five is used to effect change. In financial matters it suggests movement into another phase of material gain.

You can if you wish bury this bottle close to your home rather than actually keeping it

indoors. If you do this however it is a good idea to acknowledge it in some way every time you pass it. You can do this by leaving a small gift such as a pretty pebble or some wildflower seeds.

MONEY CHARM

This is more properly a charm rather than a spell because you have formed a different object (the bag) and given it power through incantation. As always, a money charm like this relies on the energy set up between you and the money. If you recognize that money is a resource, you can adjust the spell to ask for resources rather than money itself.

You will need
- A square of green cloth
- Allspice, borage, lavender and saffron
- Crystals (such as garnet, ruby and emerald or rock salt)
- Three silver coins
- Gold and silver-colored thread

Method
Hold the three silver coins in your hands. Breathe on them four times and say:

*To the spirits of Air I say
bring some money my way.*

Put the herbs, crystals and coins on the cloth. Tie the cloth into a bag using eight knots in the thread. (It is probably easiest to fold the thread into two and tie knots round the neck of the bag.)

Hide the bag in a safe, cool, dark place, away from prying eyes for eight days. After eight days money should be coming in.

Be as realistic as possible, imagining what you will do with the money and how best it will be used. Once you have made the bag, meditate daily on what you want. By using the three silver coins and four breaths you create the vibration of the number seven which is considered to be both a lucky, and spiritual, number.

MONEY SPELL

This is a spell to help you come to terms with money and your attitude to it and should be performed around the time of the Full Moon. Most of us at some time or another have financial problems. We may not have enough, we may not manage it very well, there may be demands on us that we can't or don't feel we can meet.

There are two versions of this spell and you should choose the one you are most comfortable with. If you are really hard up

you will find it simpler to use play money, however if you are very brave you may choose real money. Choose the largest denomination of money – either pretend or otherwise – that you are comfortable with.

You will need

- Green taper candle
- Mint or honeysuckle oil
- Play money of various denominations or a single note of the largest denomination of real money you can afford

Method

Two days before the Full Moon, take the green candle to your sacred space.

Carve several pound signs on the candle, thinking of a more prosperous life as you do so. Anoint the candle with the essential oil. Place it in the holder and set it in the middle of your sacred space. Light the candle.

If using play money:

Spread out your "money" in front of the burning candle.

Handle it, sort it, play with it. Spend at least 5 to 10 minutes thinking about your attitude to money, how you would use it if it were real. Extinguish the candle. The next night, light the candle again.

Play with the money again, thinking about how you might make it grow. After 10 to 15 minutes, extinguish the candle.

The third night, the night of the Full Moon, do the same again; think about how you would help others. Before the candle burns out completely burn a large denomination note of your play money after you have finished sorting it.

This is your offering to the Gods but it also represents your acknowledgement that money is simply an energy to be used.

If using real money:

The ritual is the same except that during your meditation on the first day you should think about how you wish to spend the money you are going to accrue.

During the second ritual visualize it growing and becoming more. See yourself going to the bank to put money into your account or some such action.

On the third night you have a choice: You can either burn the money, place it somewhere safe, perhaps on your altar as a reminder of your good fortune, or give it to charity. Do not use it for your own purposes.

This spell does require a certain amount of courage, but having the confidence to take a risk

and burn money – play or real – really can open up your mind to the opportunities for prosperity.

REMOVING MISFORTUNE

This spell uses plant magic combined with folk magic and the meaning of numbers. Burying an object binds the energy of what it represents and reciting prayers raises the vibration to the point where any negativity is nullified. The instruction "Within sight of a church" suggests that the bad luck then is overseen by the Angels.

You will need
• Three small jars (small jars such as honey or baby food jars work well)
• Nine cloves of garlic
• Nine thorns from a white rose or nine pins

Method
Pierce the garlic cloves with the pins or thorns saying forcefully while doing so:

Misfortune begone from me.

Put three of the cloves and pins in each jar. Bury each jar within sight of a church.

Say the Lord's prayer each time you do this.

Walk away and don't look back at what you have done.

This spell can give impressively fast results. As soon as you become aware of the misfortune you are suffering, look for a common theme – i.e. are the problems financial, love etc – and actually name them in the words you use. Because you have addressed it three times it cannot remain.

SILVER SPELL

This spell relies on the use of candles and takes about a week to perform. Before you begin, believe you have prosperity and that you have no money worries. Consider your attitude to money. You will probably find that the spell is best begun on a Friday.

You will need
• A small bowl
• Seven silver coins
• A green candle and holder

Method
Place the bowl, the candle and its holder on a flat surface in your home, where it will be passed every day. For the next seven days put

a coin in the bowl. After seven days, take the candle in your hands and imagine prosperity coming to you. Sense the opportunities that you will have with money.

Be aware of the energy that has been given to money. Place the candle in the holder.

Pour the seven coins into your left hand.

Draw a circle with your hand around the coins. Put the first coin right in front of the candle. As you place it, say these or similar words:

Money grow, make it mine
Money flow, Money's mine.

Place the other coins around the candle one by one and repeat the incantation.

Finally light the candle and allow it to burn out. Leave the money in position for at least three days.

It is better you do not spend this money if at all possible.

This spell is another one which is designed for long term security. Just as you built the energy very slowly, so the gains will build slowly too. A variation of this spell is to take a scallop shell which represents the Great Mother and place the coins in that, leaving them as an offering.

TO BANISH YOUR DEBTS

This particular spell uses candle and incense magic and, if you wish, the art of magical writing. You could choose incense or oil for purification or protection, whichever seems right for you. It is suggested that you perform this at the time of the waning Moon as this can be used to help take away the difficulty.

You will need
- Incense of your choice
- Purple candle
- Oil of your choice
- Rolled parchment or paper, 6cms wide and as long as you like
- Black pen or pen with magical black ink
- A pin or your burin
- Unbreakable candle holder

Method
Light the incense and dress the candle with the oil. List all your debts on the parchment.

Draw a banishing pentagram on the back of the parchment. This is drawn lower left point to top to lower right to top left to top right and back to lower left.

Carve another banishing pentagram with the pin or burin on the candle. Place the

rolled parchment in the candle holder then tighten the candle on top. Do this carefully since your candle will eventually set the paper alight.

Concentrate on banishing your debts. Visualize your happiness and relief when the debts are banished.

Light the candle.

Take the candle to the east and ask that the Spirit of Air acknowledges your intention to be debt free.

Replace the candle in the holder, making sure it is safe to burn out where it stands.

In your own words, ask for the debts to be banished and replaced with prosperity.

Allow the candle to burn out completely, but as it comes to the end make sure that you are present.

The paper will catch fire and flare up, so it must be properly attended to.

As you do this, be aware of the lifting of the burden of debt.

You should not expect your debts to simply disappear, but the wherewithal to clear them should come your way quite quickly. This might be, for instance, in the form of an unexpected gift or the opportunity for some extra work. Once your debts are cleared you are honour-bound not to create the same problems again.

WANT SPELL

Since Mother Nature supplies our most basic needs, this spell uses the cycle of her existence to help fulfil your wants. The leaf is representative of her power and you are using natural objects to signify that all things must come to pass.

You will need
- A marker pen
- A fully grown leaf

Method
Write or draw on the leaf a word, picture or letter that represents the thing that you want.

Lay the leaf on the ground.

As the leaf withers, it takes your desire to the Earth. In thanks, Mother Nature will grant your wish.

You may also throw the leaf into running water or place it under a stone if you wish.

This is a spell which owes a great deal to folk magic and an appreciation of the cycle of growth and decay. In such spells, it is usual to use a leaf that has fallen rather than pick one from a tree. If you do the latter you should thank the tree for its bounty.

STRING SPELL

This spell is another representational one and is very simple to do. It pays homage to the art of knotting and makes use of your sacred space if you are able to leave your altar in place. Otherwise simply use a windowsill in broad sunlight or moonlight.

You will need
• A length of string long enough to outline your material desire

Method
Sit quietly with the piece of string and pour your wish into it. Try to have a clear picture in your mind of what you want.

Tie a knot in one end of the string and say:

With this knot the gods I implore
Bring this [your desire] my way, for sure.

Tie a knot in the other end and say:

With this knot I lock it in
*   With thanks for the gift that it will*
*   bring.*

Lay the string on a flat surface and fashion it into as close a picture of your material desire as you can. Leave it in place for at least three days.

When your wish has manifested, thank the gods either by giving something to charity or offering your skills to your local community.

This spell seems to work best if you actually need the object you are representing. The gods do not grant their favours without some effort on your part so use your gift wisely and well. Your relationship with the gods is always a two-way street.

OPEN SESAME

Sesame seeds are said to have the power to open locks, reveal hidden passages and to find hidden treasures. They also are used in magic to induce lust. However here they are used in a much more mundane way, to attract money.

You will need
• A pretty glass or ceramic bowl
• Handful of sesame seeds

Method
Place the sesame seeds in the bowl. Put the bowl somewhere near the door of your home

in a safe space. Each time you pass the bowl on the way out, give it a stir with your Apollo finger (the ring finger) of your right hand.

Change the seeds every month, and dispose of the seeds by burying them or throwing them into running water.

When going for a job interview try to ensure that you have some sesame oil. Decide what salary you want, then touch a little of the oil on the pulse spots on your wrists. Be confident in asking for the required sum.

SUCCESS IN FINDING A JOB

When you submit a job application, manuscript for publication, or anything that requires paper there are several things that you can do, using herbs and crystals as well as some techniques based on ancient beliefs. One or all of the parts of the techniques can be used, but first you must make your combined incense and dressing powder base. This spell is similar to Legal Success on page 234, but uses different herbs for a slightly different result.

You will need
- 1 tsp ground cinnamon
- 1 tsp ground ginger
- 1 tsp ground lemon balm
- Few drops of bergamot oil
- Bowl

Method
Mix all the ingredients together in the bowl.

For a dressing powder add a carrier such as powdered chalk or talcum powder which should be unscented.

To use as incense leave it as it is, and burn it on a charcoal disc in a heatproof burner.

For the spell proper

You will need
- Your papers (application form etc)
- Any supporting documents (e.g. your CV, covering letter)

Method
Light your incense. Before you begin writing or filling in your forms "smoke" the paper on which you will write. This consists of wafting the required amount of paper or the application form in the incense smoke and asking a blessing for the process you are about to start.

You may wish to place a crystal on your desk to help in the writing or you could place it on or near your printer.

You might use tiger's eye for clearer thinking or tourmaline to attract goodwill. Be guided by your own intuition.

Once you have completed the forms or the writing you can "dress" each page individually. On the back of each page sprinkle the dressing powder.

Draw your four fingers through the powder in wavy lines from top to bottom so they leave very clear tracks.

Leave for a few moments, then shake off the powder, all the while visualizing the success of your project.

Finally, you can leave the papers in front of the image of your chosen deity if you have one, or offer them for a blessing overnight.

When you have done this, you know that you have done as much as you can to ensure success as is humanly possible. It is literally now in the hands of the gods. Obviously, you will already have done or will be doing any necessary research into your project on a physical level.

TO CREATE OPPORTUNITY

This spell appeals to the Roman goddess Ops who used to be petitioned by sitting down and touching the Earth with one hand, since she was a deity of prosperity, crops and fertility. During the Full Moon, using sympathetic magic, a wish doll (poppet) representing health and happiness is made to draw opportunities towards you.

You will need
- A bowl of sand (to represent the earth)
- Green cloth
- Needle and thread
- Pen
- Cinnamon or cedar incense
- Dried camomile, vervain or squill
- Mint and honeysuckle oil

Method

Make a poppet out of the cloth. While concentrating on the opportunities available to you, write your name on the poppet and stuff it with the dried herbs that have had a few drops of the oils added. Sew the figure shut. Light the incense.

Hold the poppet in the incense smoke. Say:

Goddess of opportunity,
Bring good fortune now to me
Guide me by your gentle hand
For I am as worthy as
*   these grains of sand.*

Let the sand trickle through your fingers to signify touching the earth.

Repeat this an odd number of times (seven works very well).

Keep your poppet safe, you do not have to have it with you at all times, just with your possessions or papers.

For the spell to continue to work, renew it every Full Moon.

This is a good spell to use for business opportunities, since the poppet can be kept unobtrusively in a drawer or cupboard and hopefully will become imbued with the excitement of your day-to-day work. It can also be used when you wish to enhance your career prospects.

TO HELP MAKE A DECISION

This spell uses color and candles to allow you to make a decision over two opposing outcomes. You are in a sense taking the dilemma to the highest authority in order for the best outcome to become apparent. Do the spell at the time of the New Moon if there is a new beginning involved.

You will need
- Two yellow candles
- White candle or your astrological candle
- Length of purple ribbon just over half a metre long
- Two pieces of paper
- Pen

Method
This spell takes three days to do in total.

Place the white candle on the exact middle of the ribbon. This ribbon signifies the highest possible spiritually-correct energy. Place the two yellow candles either end of the ribbon.

Write the two possible outcomes on the pieces of paper and fold them separately. Place these two papers under the yellow candles on top of the ribbon.

Light the middle (white) candle first and then the two outer (yellow) ones.

Acknowledge the fact that you will be extinguishing them as part of the spell.

Burn the candles for at least an hour, so that a link is properly made. Consider both decisions carefully.

Snuff the candles out and next day move the papers and the outer candles closer to the middle candle. Roll the ribbon in towards the centre against the candle bases.

Relight the candles and again burn for at least an hour, considering your two options carefully.

Each day repeat until all the candles are grouped together. (This should take at least three days, and, if time allows, longer.)

Ensure that you have at least an hour's burning time left for the final day.

Allow the candles to burn out and within three days you should find it easy to make a decision.

This process allows due consideration of all the pros and cons of the various options. It provides the energy for the correct decision and allows you to be rational and objective while still taking account of the emotional aspect. It keeps your mind focused on the matter in hand. You do not then "stand in your own light" – get in the way of your own success.

TO IMPROVE WORK RELATIONSHIPS

This is a combination of a candle and mirror spell and is designed to improve the work environment. It works equally well for all levels of work relationship. Often spells to do with work are best done at home and a reminder taken in to reinforce it. The spell is carried out for seven days and then reinforced once a week. Tuesday or Thursday are good days.

You will need

• Small mirror that will fit unobtrusively in your drawer
• White candle
• Oil such as jasmine for spiritual love or ylang ylang for balance

Method

Anoint the candle. Light the candle and burn it for at least an hour.

Concentrate for a few minutes on the image of your boss or colleague as they are when they annoy you.

Look in the mirror and visualize them being pleasant and calm. See yourself working with them as an efficient team.

Carry on doing this each evening for a week then do it once a week thereafter for at least six weeks.

In between times keep the mirror in your work desk drawer and reinforce the positive visualization of your colleague or boss being calm every day.

You should see an improvement after a week – others may also notice a change as time goes on. As you become less stressed you may find you become more creative and can deal with other petty annoyances.

WEAVING SUCCESS

The use of ribbons is an extension of knot magic and is often used in binding or protection spells. However, this one is an unobtrusive way of enhancing the energy of your business as well as ensuring its security. Braiding three strands links us with the triple-aspected Great Mother – Maid, Mother, Crone.

You will need
• Three equal lengths of ribbon: dark blue for success in long-term plans, and clarity yellow for mental power, wealth, communication and travel brown for grounding, stability, and endurance
• A large safety pin

Method
Pin the three ribbons together at the top to make braiding easier.

Braid the ribbons neatly together.

As you do so, repeat the following words as often as you feel is right remembering the significances of the colors:

Great Mother Great Mother
Come to me now
As these strands weave and become one
May this business grow

Now loop the braid around the front door handle so that anyone who comes into the business must pass it.

You should find that the qualities you have woven into the business begin to bring results very quickly. Combinations of different colors will have different results; red will bring vitality and willpower, orange success and prosperity through creativity and yellow communication, mental power and wealth.

REFLECTIONS

Chinese coins often have a square hole in them which is symbolic of manifestation of prosperity. They can nowadays be obtained through the internet. The eight-sided mirror is a device used in feng shui to represent different aspects of life and, like the coin, to intensify or redirect energy. Here you can use both to bring you tangible gain. This is best done in the open air at the Full Moon.

You will need
• Chinese gold-colored coin
• An eight-sided feng shui mirror

Method
Ideally, the light of the Moon should pass

through the central hole of the coin and reflect on to the mirror. You will need to use your own intuition to judge when you have the best reflection.

Concentrate on the reflection and say:

Lady Moon, behold thy power
I capture this and ask this hour
Thy bounteousness on me you shower
Bring me silver, bring me gold
Long before the Moon grows old
I ask a blessing

Ch'ang O (Lady Moon) is the Chinese immortal who lives on the Moon. In one story, she is banished to the earth when her husband, Houyi the Archer, shot down the extra nine suns which were scorching the earth. She then ate the pill of immortality, and now lives on the Moon, betwixt and between two worlds. It is she who is petitioned here.

BAY LEAVES OF PROSPERITY

Bay leaves are traditionally plants of wealth and luck. If you are lucky enough to have a bay leaf tree in your garden, you are almost always assured of some form of good luck around money. However, even bay leaves bought from a supermarket have the potential to be powerful allies in your quest for financial fortune.

You will need
- 3 bay leaves
- gold pen
- A gold candle

Method
Light the candle and sit in meditation for a while in front of it, while thinking on why you want more money. Money is simply a medium of exchange so what you do want to exchange that money for? It may just be a feeling that you'd like to experience such as financial freedom and an end to worry.

Whatever it is, think deeply on this for some time as the gold candle burns. Then, taking the gold pen, write your name and the sum of money you wish to attract on each leaf. Carefully place all three leaves in your wallet and await the money. When it comes to you, give thanks to the Universe for its bounty, and bury the leaves in your garden or a windowsill box. Try and ensure that the leaves stay in your possession as they break down.

If you find this spell works particularly well for you, it will be enhanced if you buy yourself a bay

leaf tree and put it at your front door or toward the front of your home on a balcony, if you live in an apartment for example.

THE MANIFESTING WATERFALL

Imagine if you could simply visualize your way to wealth? This ritual uses nothing except your own imagination to bring forth whatever material good you require. It may be that there is a piece of furniture you need or an expensive dental treatment. This enables you to manifest the outcome rather than the means to achieve it so you concentrate on the outcome rather than how much money you will need to make it happen. You will find that miraculous opportunities to get just what you need begin to appear.

You will need
• Just yourself!

Method
This ritual can be done anywhere, but it is obviously more potent when done in front of your altar. However, if you find that you're away from home and have some time for meditation and a manifestation would be useful to you, you can perform the ritual anywhere and at any time. Sit on a straight-backed chair and steady your breath by taking three gently deep breaths. Place your hands with the palms facing upwards on your lap.

Then close your eyes and imagine a beautiful waterfall above your head over your head that is allowing for a gentle spray on your face. Imagine that the spray is the water blessing you and promising you that you will always have what you need.

If you feel that it is appropriate, think about the thing you want to manifest. It is often better not to think about anything specific and to allow the waterfall to manifest what you need according to its own laws. Sometimes we think we need one thing when really it is quite something else.

When you have finished spending the time you want to under the waterfall, thank the spirit of it, and placing your hands palm downwards on your lap and rubbing them on your thighs until you are ready to open your eyes and go about your day.

A regular meditation practice will make this sort of ritual even more potent since your mind will automatically go to the state it needs to be in.

GRAINS OF WEALTH

Grain has been used in harvest festivals to denote prosperity and good living for

millennia. It is also good to use in fertility spells. Here we use it to encourage a good living to be acquired.

You will need
- A bag of grains, wheat or spelt
- A large scarf or cloth
- A green candle
- A length of green ribbon or string

Method
Light the candle on your altar. It is important that you use a green candle as this indicates to the Universe that this is a wealth spell. Put the cloth on your lap (you can either be seated on a chair or, if possible, sit on the floor with your legs crossed so that the cloth forms a receptacle on your legs). Taking a handful of the grains in your right hand, slowly pour them onto the cloth, while saying:

Richest of grains, hear my plea
Give me the means to set myself free

Do this another two times so that you have three handfuls of grain in the cloth on your lap. Draw the corners of the cloth together so that it forms a pouch. Tie the top with the ribbon or string. Put this pouch of grains in a safe place and tap it on any CV or business loan application you make. You are sure to see success as soon as it is right for you to have it.

You can substitute the grain for lentils, rice or pulses if that is your preference. It should ideally be a grain that you regularly eat.

CINNAMON CAKE SPELL

Cinnamon has long been associated with abundance and wealth. It is ruled by the Fire Element, which makes it good for fast working spells. It is a delicious treat as well!

You will need
- Your favourite sponge cake recipe
- Cinnamon powder
- A cinnamon stick

Method
When you have the cake batter ready from your favourite sponge cake recipe, sprinkle a teaspoon of cinnamon into the bowl, saying:

Fire spice, Fire spice,
wealth and love are in your gift
Let all who eat feel your bounty
So mote it be

Stir in the cinnamon with the cinnamon stick clockwise three times. Then bake the

cake. Once it is out of the oven and coolled, cut a slice for your ancestors and place it on your altar. This portion should not be consumed but put out for the birds after 24 hours.

Then slice the cake and share it with members of your household. Think about where you want more abundance in your life as you eat the cake.

This is an enjoyable spell as it is as much a nourishing blessing as it is a ritual for bringing more prosperity into your life.

SPELL FOR A PROMOTION

If you are feeling stuck at the level where you are in your workplace, this spell will help you get ahead. Beware though that it should only be used if you have a legitimate reason to think that you should be promoted (needing more money isn't enough!) – you must have worked hard enough or made enough money for your company to make a promotion a fair outcome for your efforts.

You will need
- A green ribbon
- A green candle
- A sprig of rosemary
- Basil oil

Method
Anoint the candle with the basil oil working from the bottom to the top. Light this and sit in front of it in meditation for a while, considering carefully the reasons why you want that promotion. Is it for reasons external to you, such as worrying about your status among your peers? Or is it a genuine desire to hold more responsbility and progress in your career? Examine your thoughts and make sure that a promotion is really what you seek and that it would make you happy.

Take the sprig of rosemary and tie the ribbon around it, while saying:

Bring me now to greater height
Raise me up if it be right

You can now tie your rosemary sprig to either the base of your computer monitor at work or leave it in your drawer at work. Whenever you doubt that a promotion is coming, take it out and rub it between your hands, inhale the fragrance and know that sucess is on its way.

While rosemary is often connected with healing, it can also be used in prosperity spells, especially ones where there is an element of justice involved. It is the herb of luck that is earned as much as it is a boon of fate.

PEARL MONEY MAGNET SPELL

Pearls have long been associated with wealth due to the difficulty of procuring a true (rather than cultured) pearl. This spell uses those associations to draw money to you like a magnet. The "pearl" essentially becomes a charm.

You will need
- A pearl or bead that looks like a pearl
- A white candle
- A green candle
- A dish of sea salt

Method
Place the dish of sea salt on your altar and put the pearl or bead on top of it. Light and set the white candle to the right of your altar as you are facing it. Place the green candle to the left and light it.

Raise your arms above you to form a "Y" with your body with your palms facing upwards and imagine pure white light coming down from the heavens and entering into your palms. Let that light pool at your hands until it is a sphere of pulsating light. Then place the light upon the pearl in your dish. Say:

Goddess of light, She who is perfect
Bless this sphere with your generosity

When you have properly visualized the light merging with the pearl, bring your hands together and close the working by thanking the Goddess and letting the energy recede back inside you. Try "earthing" yourself for a bit by walking barefoot around the room.

Then take the pearl and keep it in a bag or pocket you always have when you're out and about. It will continue to work in the background, attracting money and new opportunities for wealth to you.

Pure energy work such as this requires a lot of work on yourself to ensure that you do not "leak" energy or leave yourself energetically vulnerable. Therefore you must remember to do your ritual baths and always close down your energy work properly by grounding yourself in some way. Even eating a carb dense snack such as a piece of toast can help.

SANTERIA BATH FOR SUCCESS

The Santeria religion uses beautiful ritual baths for many different outcomes. Like many West African religions, you work with both deities and ancestors. Here you can adapt the tradition according to which spiritual power most resonates with you. As long as it is done with respect and acknowledgment

of the powerful tradition you are borrowing from, you can gain insight into your own spiritual journey as well as honouring your ancestors and patron deities. This is a very typical bath that can be used both for healing and for attracting success to you. This is best done on a waxing Moon.

You will need
- A cup of goat's milk
- A bunch of yellow or white flowers (not roses)
- Florida water
- Honey
- 2 coconuts

Method
Carefully crack open one coconut and empty its water into a large bowl. Add the goat's milk, Florida water and the petals from the bunch of flowers. Leave covered with a white clean cloth overnight, ideally in a spot that moonlight falls upon.

The next morning, add the contents of the bowl to a warm bath. Standing in the bath, take the water from the second coconut (best to crack it open before you get in) and pour that water over your head, imagining that it is blessings that are showering down upon you. Then, still standing, rub the honey all over your body and then sit in the bath to allow it to wash away. You can shower as normal afterwards, although it is good to keep the scent of the Forida water in your bathroom to remind you of the ritual bath.

This bath is even more potent when someone who loves you does it for you. So perhaps a partner or a sibling you trust pours the coconut water over your head and rubs your body with the honey before you bathe in the enchanted water.

You are embodying a spiritual Queen when you bathe in this way and success will come to you as your birthright.

ANIMAL ALLY FOR BUSINESS SUCCESS

Shamans have known for millennia that there are spirits that can help us in our everyday lives. The greatest part of their work for a community was to commune with those spirits to bring back healing for the people that needed it. In the same way, you can "journey" to find animal allies that embody qualities that can help in your career. A Full Moon is a good time for this work.

You will need
- A shamanic drumming CD or a sound file of shamanic drumming

- A blanket
- A representational totem (see below)

Method

On the night of a Full Moon, lie down on your bed and state your intention for your journey, in this case, it could be something like "I am journeying to meet my power animal who can be an ally to me in my business life." Then play the shamanic drumming. Put the blanket over you to ensure you feel warm enough as the journey continues. The drumming will lead you to the World Tree, in your imagination.

From there, you should journey downwards through the roots to get to the Lower World where you can meet your power animal.

It may be that the animal you encounter is not the one you thought you would have. You may have been thinking of a glamorous, fierce lion when instead you meet a small squirrel. It doesn't matter what the animal is, you should check that it shows you itself from three sides, ask it its name, and thank it for its help.

As the drumming changes to a higher tempo, you can then return up through the sky of the Lower World, through the roots of the tree, to our world. Finally, you should feel yourself back in your bed. Wiggle your toes and fingers to bring yourself back to the here and now. Sit up and drink a glass of water if you need it.

Having secured the help of a power animal, you should now discover the message it has for you. That aforementioned squirrel might be a message for you to prepare for the winter by storing your "nuts" aka your money and resources. It may be its wise counsel to prepare for leaner times. Researching the qualities and concerns of the animal that came to you can give meaning to the journey and to how you can gain help in your business life.

You should also try and find a small figurine of the animal in question to carry with you as a totem. If you cannot find one, use a small stone to represent it and keep it with you as you go about your day.

Animals can help us in our daily lives. They are more intuitive than humans and can often show great kindness. Do keep an eye out for any animal helpers in your daily life and check their behaviours to see what you can learn from them.

HONEY JAR TO SWEETEN COLLEAGUES TO YOU

Honey is almost universally used to "sweeten" outcomes in spells. If you want to get really

into the use of honey in magic, it is useful to know which plants/areas the bees that made the honey collected their nectar. For example, if you want to continue to work in a particular company or area, choose honey from hives local to it. Alternatively, if you require a potent money, Arabian honey is the one to use. Experiment until you find a honey variety that suits you best.

You will need
- A jar of honey
- A piece of paper
- Tape or glue

Method
Write "I am loved and admired" on the piece of paper and tape it to the bottom of the jar of honey. Take the jar into work and eat a little of it daily (either a spoonful if you like the taste) or spread on toast if that is too strong for you. If a colleague asks to have a bit of your honey, it is fine to give it to them. You must keep the honey at work and imagine that everyone at work adores you whenever you ingest the honey.

This is an ongoing useful item to have and the ease with which you can "charge" the honey with your intent means that it is relatively easy to do.

FIGS AND HONEY SPELL

You can add figs to increase the potency of a spell using honey. The idea is to impress upon the world that you have the means to luxuriate in food items that would have been costly in times gone by and indicated a wealthy person.

You will need
- A plump, ripe fig
- A jar of honey
- A small plate

Method
You begin this spell by cutting the fig into slices and putting it upon the small plate and drizzling it with honey. Put this plate on your altar. Then say:

Honeyed be this fig
And honeyed be my words
Sweetest success stick to me
And so mote it be

You can now eat the honeyed figs, giving thanks for all the bounty in your life and all the many things for which you are grateful. Doing this spell once a month is a good way of expressing gratitude for all that have and thereby inviting more to come.

BLESSED NUTMEG

Nutmeg was once an eye-wateringly expensive commodity that gentlemen would keep with them to grate into their drinks when out and about in town. This spell uses the magical properties of this spice as a signifier of wealth and prosperity. It is done on a waxing Moon and is particularly good to do in winter.

You will need
- A nutmeg
- A nutmeg grater
- A green candle
- Nutmeg essential oil

Method
Anoint the candle with the nutmeg oil, moving from bottom to top. Light the candle on your altar with the nutmeg and grater placed there too. Licking your right index finger (the finger of Jupiter), touch the nutmeg and say:

Blessings be upon this spice
Blessings be, wealth to entice

Then place the nutmeg and grater in your bag or coat pocket. The next time you buy a coffee or a hot chocolate, grate a tiny bit of nutmeg onto it and think about how luck you are. It has been shown that the more people think of themselves as lucky, the luckier they get.

The use of spit in the licking of the finger and placing it on the nutmeg connects that particular nutmeg to you. Saliva is often used in a number of traditions as all bodily fluids tie magic in to you personally and become a source of your personal power. If you dislike working with such substances, you can achieve a similar result by holding your Jupiter (index) finger to your belly button and imagining a small ball of light emerging from there and sticking to your finger. You can then transfer that ball of light to the nutmeg.

MONEY PLANT MANTRA

As a money, luck and career cure-all, nothing beats a money plant. If you can obtain one, tend to it carefully and connect with it by chanting this mantra to your plant on a daily or weekly basis:

Kindest of allies
Show me your skill
Partner with me
And bring us our fill

HOME AND PERSONAL PROTECTION

Almost inevitably protection spells form an integral part of any spell-worker's armoury. When you are working with powers which are not well understood you can open yourself up to all sorts of negativity, and sometimes sheer goodwill is not enough to protect your own personal space – you need a little extra help. Equally as you develop your own abilities it becomes possible to protect those around you from harm.

ANIMAL PROTECTION SPELL

When we work with Nature we are often called upon to protect her creatures. These would range from our own pets to animals in the wild and also those animals which have become our totem animals. This spell uses photographs to represent these animals or you could use small figurines. The candles are used to focus your energy and the oil to create a safe environment.

You will need
- Two green candles
- One white candle
- Picture or figurine of the animal
- Protection oil
- Consecrated salt and water
- If protecting your pet, include its favourite treat

Method
Light the two green candles being conscious of the conservation issues in regard to your animal. Light the white candle to represent the animal concerned.

Put the photograph under the white candle or the figurine next to it and say:

Spirit of fire burning bright,
Give your protection here this night.
The moon above for this animal dear
Gives shelter and so freedom from fear,
Draw close all spirits of the same

Come hither! Come hither!
Power of the wild and strength so great!
Defend and safeguard this one's fate.

To complete the spell, either give your pet its treat or scatter the crumbs outside for other animals to enjoy.

The animals you are drawn to are believed to be the ones who in return for your care will also protect and teach you. By being aware of their needs you become part of the cycle of Nature and of life.

ANIMAL STONES

The ancients were very good at perceiving shapes in stones and wood and believed that such shapes could be made to hold the spirit of the animal "trapped" in such a way. Many artists today are still able to do this, and we too as magic makers can make use of this art. When on your wanderings you find an interesting stone or piece of driftwood, look at it with fresh eyes and turn it into a fetish – the correct meaning of which is an object that is believed to have magical or spiritual powers. Your fetish will help you as an ally and, over time, will become more powerful and connected to you.

You will need
• A pleasantly shaped stone or piece of wood
• Paints and brushes
• Decorations such as beads and ribbons
• Glue or fixative
• Incense such as benzoin or frankincense
• A small box

Method
Light the incense. Sit quietly with your object and let it "speak" to you.

Allow the ideas to flow as to what it might become – your totem animal, a bear, a horse or perhaps a dog or cat.

Decorate the object appropriately, taking care to enhance the natural shaping rather than to change it.

You can now consecrate it in one of two ways. Pass the object quickly through the smoke of the incense three times to empower it with the spirit of the animal.

Or
Place it in the box with an appropriate image or herbs and bury it for three days or place it on your altar for the same period. This allows the metamorphosis to take place and the spirit of the animal to enter your now magical object.

It is now ready for use, perhaps to help you access the wisdom of the animals, as a healing device or for protection.

Ancients believed that the fetish must be fed appropriately so that it retained its magical powers. Today, corn is an appropriate "food," as is pollen, although you can use your imagination, since it is your creation. Should you not feed (energize) it for a period you may need to consecrate it again for it to work properly.

BANISHING POWDER

Most herbs can be pulverized either in a pestle and mortar, a coffee grinder or in a blender to make various powders for specific purposes. In an emergency you can also use commercially dried spices and blend them yourself. The following powder is designed to get rid of pests, both human and otherwise.

You will need
- Equal quantities of peppercorns
- (black, white, cubeb, paprika etc)
- Similar quantity of ginger
- Wasabi (Japanese horseradish) powder

Method
Grind all the ingredients together. As you do so visualize the pest walking away from you into the sunset. Sprinkle the resulting powder sparingly around the edge of the area that you wish to protect.

You can also sprinkle the powder where you know it is where the pest will walk.

There is no need to make it obvious that you have sprinkled this powder. Indeed, the more unobtrusive it is the better. You should be aware however that since the spell uses the idea of heat, all the ingredients are "hot" the powder should not be used when you are angry, and you must be very sure you do not wish to have any contact with your "pest".

ANIMAL PROTECTION COLLAR

A simple way to protect an animal is to plait your own collar for it to which you can attach various objects. Try to use natural materials wherever possible. Using the same principle as Mesopotamian cylinder seals you may like to make your own protective device, or you could use an inscribed pet tag, or a small charm bag. Choose the colors of the cords carefully according to the animal's temperament, e.g red for a terrier, silver for a nocturnal cat or a mix of colors.

You will need

- Three pieces of cord slightly longer than the circumference of your pet's neck, to allow for braiding and tying.
- A small cylinder name tag or a disc inscribed with the animal's name and address.
- A small charm bag about 10cm (3 inches) square with cord or ribbon tie
- Small quantity of child's clay
- Small piece of flint
- Small piece of coral
- Small crystal of rose quartz
- Your burin
- Pen

Method

Carefully braid the cord, while calling on your chosen deity for protection for your animal, and weaving in the intention for good behaviour.

Form a rough cylinder from the child's clay and before it dries out completely, inscribe it with a protective symbol or the name of your preferred deity.

Attach it to the collar you have woven, or place it in the charm bag.

If you are using the cylinder type of dog tag, write a protective symbol (see pages 281 – 298 on amulets) on the back of the paper in the cylinder; if using a circular disc inscribe it on the back.

Place the flint, the coral and the rose quartz in the charm bag and attach it to the collar. Put the collar round the animal's neck again calling for protection.

Sometimes an animal needs protection as much from its own behaviour as anything else. This spell gives you a starting point and a foundation from which to work, including further training if appropriate.

BLESSING FOR THE HEART OF THE HOME

This is a candle, crystal and representational spell which calls upon Hestia, goddess of the hearth and home, to bring her qualities of constancy, calmness and gentleness to bear on your home. Hestia is supportive of the family and home and was praised by the poet Homer in ancient Greece.

You will need

- Lavender candle
- Small silver or brass bowl in which to stand the candle
- Lavender flowers
- Small piece of amethyst

Method

Before placing the candle in the bowl raise the latter above your head and say:

*Hestia, you who tends the holy house
of the lord Apollo,
Draw near, and bestow grace upon my
home.*

Place the candle in the bowl, making certain the candle will stand firmly. Light the candle and when it is properly alight pass the amethyst three times through the flame and say:

*Hestia, glorious is your portion and your
right.
Place the amethyst in your hearth or
close to your fireplace.*

(If you have no fireplace then as close to the centre of your home as possible.) Sprinkle some of the lavender flowers across your doorway to keep your home safe. Say:

Hail Hestia, I will remember you.

Allow the candle to burn down and then place some of the lavender flowers in the bowl, leaving it in a safe space.

At times when the atmosphere in the home becomes somewhat fraught, this spell can bring a period of peace and tranquillity. The bowl, lavender flowers and amethyst are all sacred to Hestia and remind you of her presence.

CLEANSING THE BODY OF NEGATIVE ENERGIES

This spell uses candle magic and an appeal to the Elements. One aspect needs to be noted. Black candles were once associated with malevolence but today are used in many different ways, some positive and some negative. This is an old spell and so the association with negativity remains, but you may use a dark blue candle if you prefer.

You will need
• White or yellow candle (for positive energy)
• Black or dark blue candle (for negative energy)
• Green candle (for healing)

Method
In your sacred space, place the candles in a triangle with the green candle closest to you. Clear your mind of everything except what you are doing.

Light the white candle, being aware of its symbolism and say the following:

Earth, Fire, Wind, Water and Spirit;
I ask thee to cleanse my body of all
negative energies.

Light the black or blue candle, being aware also of its symbolism.

Repeat the words above and pause to let the energies come to a natural balance.

Light the green candle and again repeat the above words.

Sit back, keep your mind clear and be peaceful for at least 10 minutes.

When the time feels right either snuff out the candles or allow the green one to burn right down so that you are filled with healing energy.

You should feel rested and relaxed and more ready to tackle problems as they arise. Make this part of your weekly routine till you feel it no longer to be necessary.

TO REVERSE NEGATIVITY OR HEXES

Try this candle spell using the element of Fire to reverse any negativity or hexes you become aware of being sent in your direction. Anger from others can often be dealt with in this way, but deliberate maliciousness may require more force. You need to be as dispassionate as you can when dealing with a hex, which is defined as "an evil spell".

You will need
- Purple candle
- Rosemary oil
- White paper
- Black ink
- Fire-proof dish such as your cauldron or an ashtray

Method
Visualize all blocks in your life-path being removed. Anoint your candle with the oil.

On the piece of paper write in black ink:
All blocks are now removed.

Fold the paper three times away from you.

Light the candle and burn the paper in your dish.

Invoke the power of Fire and its Elemental spirits by repeating three times:

Firedrakes and salamanders,
Aid me in my quest,
Protect me from all evil thoughts
Turn away and send back this hex.

After the third repetition close the spell in whatever way is appropriate for you.

A simple statement is enough:

Let it be so.

No-one has the right to curse or malign another person and all you are doing with this spell is turning the negativity back where it belongs. When you use the power of Fire you are harnessing one of the most potent forces of the universe, so be sure you use it wisely and well.

HOUSEHOLD GODS

Household gods are found in most folk religions. In Rome, the penates were household gods, primarily guardians of the storeroom. They were worshipped in connection with the lares, beneficent spirits of ancestors, and, as guardians of the hearth, with Vesta or Hestia. This spell is representational and pays due deference to them for protection from harm.

You will need
• A representation of your household gods (a statue, a picture or something significant for you)
• Representations of your ancestors

(perhaps a gift from a grandparent, an heirloom, a photograph)
• Fresh flowers or taper candles
• Incense sticks of your choice
• A bowl of uncooked rice
• A bowl of water

Method
This technique offers food to the gods and the ancestors.

Place your representational objects either close to your kitchen door or near the cooker, today often considered the heart of the home.

Light your incense and place the bowls in position in front.

Light the candles or place the flowers so that you have created a shrine.

Spend a little time communing with the penates and the lares.

Welcome them into your home and give thanks for their help and protection. (In Thailand a sometimes quite intricate "spirit house" is provided away from the shadow of the house for the ancestors.)

Their presence is acknowledged each day in order that they do not become restless.

Replace the water and rice weekly.

Remembering to honour the household gods and the ancestors means that their spirits will look

favourably upon us. Often if there is a problem, taking it to the household gods for consideration is enough to have the resolution become apparent.

INVOKING THE HOUSEHOLD GODS

This ritual is best performed during the Waxing Moon. It could be considered a kind of birthday party, so feel free to include food and drink as part of it, if you so wish.

You will need
• Pine cones, ivy, holly, or something similar
• Symbol appropriate to your guardian (e.g. a crescent moon for the Moon Goddess)
• Small statues of deer or other forest animals
• An incense that reminds you of herbs, forests and green growing things
• Green candle in a holder
• Your wand

Method
Decorate the area around your guardian symbol with the greenery and small statues.
   Clean the guardian symbol so that there is no dust or dirt on it. If the symbol is small enough put it on the altar, otherwise leave it

nearby. Light the incense and candle. Stand before your altar and say:

> *Guardian spirits,*
> *I invite you to join me at this altar.*
> *You are my friends and I wish to thank*
>   *you.*

Take the incense and circle the guardian symbol three times, moving clockwise and say:

Thank you for the help you give to keep this home clean and pleasant.

Move the candle clockwise around the symbol three times and say:

> *Thank you for the light you send to*
>   *purify this*
>   *space and dispel the darkness.*

With the wand in the hand you consider most powerful, encircle the symbol again three times clockwise and say:

> *I now ask for your help and protection*
>   *for me,*
> *myfamily and all who live herein.*
> *I ask that you remove trouble makers of*

all sorts,
incarnate and discarnate.
I thank you for your love and
understanding.
Stand with your arms upraised. Call upon your own deity and say:

[Name of deity] I now invoke the
guardian of this
household whom I have invited into my
home.
I honour it in this symbol of its being.
I ask a blessing and I add my thanks for
its
protection and friendship.

You can change the "its" to "his" or "her" if you know the gender of the guardian. If you have more than one guardian, change the "its" to "their". Spend a few moments caressing the symbol, sending out the thought that the guardian is important to you.

Be aware of the subtle changes in atmosphere which occur as the protective spirits become part of your environment.

TO PROTECT A CHILD

By the time a child is about seven he or she is beginning to venture out into the world away from home often without either of the parents being present. Teaching your child a simple protection technique is helpful for both you and them.

You will need
• Your child's imagination

Method
Discuss with your child the best image they can have of protection. This might be a shield, a cloak, a wall or more effectively being surrounded by a cocoon of light.

Working with their own visualization image, have them experience what it is like to feel safe and protected. Agree that whenever they are frightened or under pressure they can use this visualization.

Now whenever you have to be separated from them, repeat these words or similar to yourself three times:

Forces of light, image of power
Protect [name of child] till we meet
again.

Now perceive them surrounded by light and know that they are as safe as you can make them. Reassure your child that he or she is protected, always.

You may need to reinforce for the child the idea of them feeling protected by their own image, but coincidentally you are teaching them to have courage and to experience their own aura and circle of power. You may well find that your parental antennae tend to be alerted quite quickly when your child is having a problem.

TO PREVENT INTRUSION INTO A BUILDING

In this spell you use visualization and power to create a barrier to protect your home or a place of business. This means that only those who you want to enter do so and anyone else will be driven away. The spell can be reinforced at any time.

You will need
• The power of your own mind

Method
Sit in your sacred space and gather your energy until you feel extremely powerful.

In the main doorway to the building, face outwards and visualize a huge wheel in front of you.

Put your hands out in front of you as though grasping the wheel at the positions of twelve o'clock and six o'clock with your left hand on top. Visualize the energy building up in your hands and forming a "light rod" or laser beam between them.

Bring your hands through 180 degrees so they change position (right hand now on top).

Pause with your hands at nine o'clock and three o'clock and again build up a light rod between them.

As you do so say something like:

Let none with evil intent enter here.

Again feel the energy build up between your hands and say:

May those who would harm us,
stay away.

Bring your hands together level with your left hip and "throw" the energy from your hands to create a barrier in front of the door.

This powerful spell should be sufficient to prevent all intrusion, but you could reinforce it by treating all other entrances in the same way and could also visualize small wheels at the windows. You might vary the technique by tracing a banishing pentagram on the door itself.

FIRE PROTECTION SPELL

This spell uses the Element of Fire to protect you and create a visual image which you carry with you throughout your daily life. It requires a clear space outside of about twenty feet in diameter initially and you must be careful not to set any vegetation alight through the heat of your fires. You can also perform this spell on a beach if fires are permitted on your local beach.

You will need
- Enough fallen wood to feed four fires
- Dry brushwood or paper to start the fires
- Matches
- Water to douse the fire

Method
You should make sure that you only gather fallen wood or driftwood.

Make sure you have enough to keep each of the fires burning for about half an hour.

Taking up one of the sticks of wood, draw a rough circle about eleven feet in diameter.

Determine the four directions North, East, South, and West (use a compass, the sun, moon, or stars).

Lay a small pile at each point just inside the circle but do not light them.

Reserve any spare wood safely beside each pile to keep the fires burning for at least half an hour.

Walking to the South first, light the fire proclaiming as you do:

Nothing from the South can harm me
Welcome Spirits of the South.

Wait until one of the pieces of wood is burning, pick it up and move to the West. Light the fire and say:

Nothing from the West can harm me
Welcome Spirits of the West.

Again take up a burning branch and move to the North.
Light the fire while saying:

Nothing from the North can harm me
Welcome spirits of the North.

Again take up a burning piece of wood and take it to the East.
Light that fire and say:

Nothing from the East can harm me
Welcome spirits from the East.

Take up a burning branch and carry it to the South.

Thrust it into the southern fire and choose a new branch.

Trace an arc with it above your head from South to North, saying:

Nothing from above can harm me
Welcome spirits from above.

Finally, throw the wood down in the centre of the circle and say:

Nothing from below can harm me
Let spirits come who wish me well.

This last stick represents Aether or spirit and this technique has created a sphere of energy which you can call on whenever you need it.

You can replace that piece of wood into the southern fire if you wish, or contemplate it as it burns out.

Replenish the fires from the reserved wood pile as necessary.

Sit in the centre of the circle and recognize that the fires are purifying and cleansing your personal environment on every level of existence.

Watch each fire carefully to see if you can perceive the spirits of the Elements:

Salamanders for Fire Gnomes, Dryads or Brownies for Earth Sylphs for Air Undines for Water

Revel in the warmth of the fires, appreciate their light and sense their protection.

Remember these feelings for they are what protects you as you leave this space.

When the fires begin to die down, douse them with the water and bury the embers to prevent them flaring again.

Erase the markings of the circle and leave the space.

This spell or ritual (depending how ornate you wish to make it) as it is done in the open air creates a barrier of protection for you, but may also make you more conscious of how fire works. In this case it consumes that which is dead and finished with, leaving only its power in its wake.

PROTECTION BOTTLE

The idea behind this protection bottle is that it is made very uncomfortable for negativity and evil to stay around. As you progress and become more aware you become very conscious of negativity, while at the same time needing protection from it. This will help you achieve a good balance.

You will need
- Rosemary
- Needles
- Pins
- Red wine
- Glass jar with metal lid (a jam jar is ideal)
- Red or black candle

Method
Gather together rosemary, needles, pins and red wine. Fill the jar with the first three, saying while you work:

Pins, needles, rosemary, wine;
In this witches bottle of mine.
Guard against harm and enmity;
This is my will, so mote it be!

You can visualize the protection growing around you by sensing a spiral beginning from you as its central point.

When the jar is as full as you can get it, pour in the red wine.

Then cap or cork the jar and drip wax from the candle to seal.

Bury it at the farthest corner of your property or put it in an inconspicuous place in your house. Walk away from the bottle.

The bottle destroys negativity and evil; the pins and needles impale evil, the wine drowns it, and the rosemary sends it away from your property. It works unobtrusively like a little powerhouse and no one need know that it is there.

PROTECTING YOUR VEHICLE

If you are a passenger, the first method given below is a simple unobtrusive way to protect you and your driver. If you yourself are driving, the second enhanced method may give you more peace of mind.

You will need
- The power of visualization

Method
Visualize a sphere or bubble of light around the vehicle and mentally seal it with the sign of the equal armed cross above the bonnet.

Enhanced technique

You will need
- Few drops of frankincense oil
- Stick of frankincense or other protection incense
- If desired a small charm such as a dolphin or eagle

Method

Before any long journey, put a few drops of frankincense in water and wipe over the wheel arches with a sponge dipped in this water. Burn the stick incense inside the vehicle and pass the charm through the smoke to bless it.

Hang the charm in a prominent place or put it in the glove compartment. Finally protect the vehicle as in the simple technique.

You can expect to feel happier and to feel safer through having carried out the protection spell, but this does not mean that you can afford to take risks with your driving and you should observe all other safety precautions as well.

For some people travelling can be a real ordeal. These three techniques can protect the traveller and give considerable peace of mind during what is, after all, a period of transition. When you arrive safely at your destination it is always worthwhile making a small offering to the powers that be that have helped you in thanks.

TO PROTECT YOUR LUGGAGE

In these days of greater security at airports, you should never leave your luggage unattended, however, this technique will protect it even as it travels separately from you in the hold. You can expect it to avoid taking detours to other destinations.

You will need
- A sprig of rosemary
- A purple ribbon

Method

Place the rosemary inside your case. Trace the sign of the pentagram over each lock.

Weave the ribbon securely round the handle. Say three times:

> *Protected is this case of mine*
> *Return now safely in good time.*

Practically, you should recognize your luggage anywhere, and if you do have to lose sight of it, for instance when flying, it has been made safe. Thieves are unlikely to think that it is worth stealing and it is not likely to get lost.

PROTECTING YOURSELF PRIOR TO THE JOURNEY

You yourself are also in need of protection when embarking on a journey and this simple technique will help you to feel that you have an aura of protection around you at all times.

You will need

- Four tealights
- Few drops of protective oil such as sandalwood or vetivert
- 1 pinch of sea salt
- 1 clear quartz crystal
- A coin or bean for luck
- A square of indigo cloth
- One white cord

Method

Take a leisurely bath placing the tealights securely at each of the four corners of the bath. Add the essential oil to the bathwater.

Visualize all your cares being washed away and at some point begin concentrating on the journey to come.

Do this without anxiety just savouring the enjoyment of the journey.

To this end you might light a yellow candle for communication and ask that you be open to opportunities to enjoy new experiences, get to know new people and understand the world in which you live.

You can blow the tealights out when you have finished your bath and relight them when you return home as a thank-you for a safe journey.

Now prepare a charm bag with:

- 1 part basil
- 1 part fennel
- 1 part rosemary
- 1 part mustard seed

If liked, add a representation of a wheel and/or a piece of paper with the name of your destination

Spread the cloth so that you can mix the herbs quickly.

Hold your hands over the herbs and ask for a blessing from Njord the Norse god of travel or Epona the Horse goddess who accompanied the soul on its last journey.

Gather up the herbs and the representative objects in the cloth and tie it into a bag, making sure it is bound securely with the white cord.

Keep this bag secure about your person throughout your journey.

You should find that your journey is accomplished without too much trouble and that people are eager to assist you when you need help. You may well find that you are observing more than is usual or are being asked to participate in experiences which might otherwise pass you by.

TO MAKE BAD LUCK GO AWAY

This spell can be adapted to use any of the Elements you choose to help the energy to work. Remember that Fire consumes, Air dissipates, Water washes away and Earth eliminates. You might do this spell at the New Moon to signify new beginnings or on a Saturday to change blockages into valuable experiences from which you can learn.

You will need

• Square piece of paper at least 10 cm x 10 cm (3 x 3 inches)
• A black marker or magical black ink and pen
• Your cauldron or a fire-proof dish if using fire
• Material to start your fire (such as pine chippings)

Method

At night time light a small fire in your cauldron or dish. If not using fire then decide where and how you wish to dispose of the paper. Write on your paper the words:
BAD LUCK
   Think hard about when circumstances have not gone well for you and write them all down.

Draw a big X across the paper with the black marker.
   Put the paper into the fire and say three times:

Fire, fire brightly burning
Let me see my luck now turning
Change all that's bad now into good
My life to be then all that it could.

Sit for a few minutes, concentrate on the bad luck being gone and the good luck coming your way.
   Extinguish the fire and dispose of the ashes appropriately. You can use any of the methods shown below to dispose of the ashes. Just substitute the ashes for the paper.

   If you decide to use the Element of Earth then tear the paper into small pieces. knowing that the bad luck can no longer trouble you and say something such as:

Earth dark, cool and strong
I ask you now to right this wrong
All bad luck eliminate
In joy let me participate.

Bury the paper, walk away and don't look back towards it.

If using the Element of Water, find a rushing stream or a source of fast flowing water – at a pinch a flushing toilet can be used. Again tear the paper into small pieces.

As you dispose of the pieces say:

Water, water, rushing pure
Take away bad luck for sure
Charge my senses as you flow
These negatives I will outgrow.

Take time to think about how full your life can be without the bad luck. You no longer need to keep thinking "Poor me".

If using the Element of Air, either get up to a place as high as you can – the top of a tall hill or building perhaps – or walk to a crossroads. At a pinch, a forked road will do.

Tear the paper up into pieces. Throw or blow the pieces to the four winds. Say:

Winds of change, set me free
Take bad luck away from me
Dispel its power within the air
I beg you now grant me my prayer.

Take a deep breath and this time as you breathe in be conscious of the fresh energy you are taking in.

Any of the parts of this technique is enough to dispel the bad luck so a combination of them will be more than enough to change your life. You do however have a responsibility after this to understand yourself and how you draw negative influences towards you.

BREAKING THE HOLD SOMEONE HAS OVER YOU

This spell owes a lot to visualisation and the use of color and in many ways is a learning experience in trusting your own abilities. It can be used in emotional situations, where you feel someone is taking advantage of you, or when you are bound to someone by perhaps a false sense of duty. This technique can be done in more than one sitting, particularly if you do not want any changes to be too dramatic.

You will need
• A strong visual image of the link between you and the other person
• A cleansing incense (such as frankincense, copal or rosemary)

Method
Your image must be one that you feel you can relate to fully. Perhaps the easiest to see

is in the form of a rope joining the two of you together.

If you are good at seeing color then the best to use is something similar to iridescent mother of pearl, because that contains a rainbow of all colors.

You might see the image as a rigid bar, which would suggest that there is an inflexibility in the relationship between you which may require you to deal with the expectations of others.

The incense is used to create an environment which is free from other influences; this is just between you and your perception of the link you have with the other person.

Light your incense and sit quietly, considering carefully the link between you.

Become aware of the flow of energy between you and gently withdraw your own energy, seeing it returning to you and being used for your own purposes rather than the other person's. (This may be enough to bring about a change in your relationship which has a satisfactory outcome for you.)

Next think carefully about how the other person makes calls on your time and energy – whether these are physical, emotional or spiritual. Resolve that you will either not allow this to happen or will be more careful

and sparing in your responses. You might develop a symbol for yourself which you can use when you feel you are being "sucked in".

Preferably use one which amuses you, since laughter is a potent tool. You could use the image of a knot being tied, a cork or a stopcock.

If you decide that you no longer wish to be associated with the person, use a technique which signifies breaking the link. It will depend upon your own personality and that of the other person as to how you do this.

Visualizing the link simply being cut may bring about a more powerful ending with tears and recriminations, whereas a gentle teasing out of the link may be slower but less painful.

It is here that you must trust your own judgement with the thought that it must be done for the Greater Good. If therefore you feel that at least some links must be left in place you can do this, for instance if you would wish to know when the other person is in trouble.

Finally see yourself walking away from the person, free of any bonds between you.

Always ensure that you leave them with a blessing for their continuing health, wealth and happiness. Now you will only become involved with them at your own wish.

You can see from the above that at all points you have a choice for your course of action. This is because each stage must be considered very carefully, and not done in anger. You must remain as dispassionate as you can and always remain true to your own principles.

TO BREAK A SPELL YOU'VE CAST

There are times when we have cast a spell that we should not have done, either because we have not thought it through or because we have reacted in anger and later realize that it was inappropriate. Then we are honour-bound to undo it. This spell is representational and the best time to do this is after midnight at the time of the waning Moon.

You will need
- As many white candles as you feel is appropriate
- Purifying incense (such as benzoin or rosemary)
- Rosemary oil
- Angelica or rosemary herbs
- A bead from a necklace you own - clear if possible (you could use a much loved piece of jewellery or crystal if you don't own a necklace)
- Small square of black cloth
- Cord or thread

Method
Anoint your candles with the rosemary oil, working from bottom to top, since you are sending the spell away. Light the incense and let it burn for a few moments to raise the atmosphere.

Light your candles and as you do so think very carefully as to why you cast the first spell, what it has caused and why you wish it removed. Then say:

Great Mother, I ask a favour of you
On [date] I cast a spell to [insert type of spell]
I now ask for it to be removed and rendered harmless
May it have no further power or gain.

Place the bead or jewellery and the herbs on the black cloth and say:

Here I make sacrifice to you knowing that I must
relinquish this object as token of my good intentions.

Knot the cord around the cloth, saying:

*I transfer the power of the spell to this
   object
And enclose it within its own darkness
So be it.*

Use three knots for finality. Seal the knots
by dripping wax from one of the candles
on them.

   Then take the bag to a source of running
water or a clear space and throw it away as
far from you as you can

   If your first spell was done in anger or
fear, then say:

*Begone anger, begone fear
   It is done.*

*You should find that you have got rid of any
negativity you may have felt. Insofar as you
have given up something which belongs to you,
you have cleared yourself of the law of cause and
effect and of any spiritual difficulty as a result
of your initial action.*

WHEN YOU FEEL THREATENED

We all go through times when we feel that
we are under threat, perhaps at work when
schedules are tight and tempers are about to
snap; or maybe in the home when tensions
are making themselves felt, creating a chill
in the air. This spell, which calls for excellent
visualization skills, protects you by forming
a crystal shell around you, protecting you
from the bad vibrations of ill temper.

You will need
• A clear crystal of quartz or any favourite
one that is full of clear light.

Method
Place the crystal where it will catch the
sunshine. Sit near it and breathe in deeply
through your nose.

   Hold your breath for a moment or two
before exhaling through your mouth.

   Repeat this several times, absorbing the
light cast by the crystal as you inhale and
exhaling any negative feelings, doubts and
darkness. After a minute or two, stand up
and begin visualizing a crystal-like ring
rising around you, from your feet upwards,
getting higher and higher with each breath
you take.

   When the crystal ring is above head
height, see it close over you, forming any
shape in which you feel comfortable to be
enclosed – a pyramid perhaps, or maybe a
dome. Still breathing deeply, feel the "crystal"
form a floor beneath your feet.

Conversely, sense a link between you and the centre of the earth. Stretch your arms and feel your fingers touch the sides of your "crystal".

Look upwards and see the top of the dome or pyramid point. If you can, also try to view yourself from outside the protective crystal in which you have surrounded yourself.

Now say:

Within this crystal, I am safe from
  negative thought,
And am so wherever I might be.

When you feel it is right to do so, return to normal breathing and see the crystal open to allow you to step outside it or perceive it dissolving. This visualisation can then be used wherever you are, perhaps in crowds, a sticky situation or simply under pressure, safe in the knowledge that you can return to it whenever you need to.

Those who have used this spell find that keeping a crystal in the house, office, or wherever they think they may need protection from negativity strengthens the spell's potency. The spell to Protect a Child on page 266 is of a similar sort, and if the idea of being inside a crystal seems strange you could start off with that method instead.

REINFORCING OF A PERSONAL SPACE

In using the Goddess image as a focus this spell is representational. It uses a mirror to represent light and power and also uses numerology (the power of numbers) in the nine white candles. Nine signifies pure spirituality and therefore the highest energy available.

You will need
- Protection incense
- 9 white candles
- An easily held round mirror
- A representation of the Goddess

Method
Light the incense. Place the candles in a ring around the Goddess image.

Light the candles, beginning with the candle most directly before the Goddess image and each time repeat these or similar words:

Light of Luna,
Protect me now.

When all are lit, hold the mirror so that it reflects the light of the candles.

Turn slowly in each direction, ensuring that you throw the light as far as you can in each direction.

Then spin round as many times as you have candles, continuing to project the light and say:

Goddess of love, goddess of light,
Protect this space.

Pinch out the candles and put them away safely until you need to use them again.

This technique is slightly unusual in that you pinch out the candles rather than allowing them to burn down. This is because it is the intensity of light which is required not the length of time it burns. This is a good way of rededicating your sacred space whenever you feel it necessary.

A SPELL FOR THE GARDEN

If you have a garden it is a nice idea to acknowledge the four directions and to make it as much a sacred space as you can. We do this by using the correspondences of the four Elements. Once the garden is blessed it can be used for any of the Sun, Moon and Nature rituals you find appropriate.

You will need
- A compass
- Garden flares or citronella candles to represent fire
- Solar fountain or birdbath to represent Water
- Wind chimes or child's windmill to represent Air
- Small collection of stones and pebbles to signify Earth

Method
Consecrate the objects as you have learned to do. Place the objects in the correct positions asking for a blessing as you place each one. You might call on the Spirits of the Elements, the Nature Spirits or on your best loved deity.

Finally, stand in the middle of your garden, raise your arms and say:

Gaia, Gaia, Mother of all
Bless this ground on thee I call
Make it safe for all within
Peace and tranquillity may it bring.

Obviously you may use your own words if you wish. Spin round three times to seal the energy, then sit on the ground and appreciate the newfound energy.

If you have very little space, we suggest that you combine all of the elements in a terracotta solar fountain and place it in the East. Terracotta represents Earth, the solar aspects suggests Fire, the fountain Water and the East the Element of Air.

PRIVACY SPELL

The word "occult" means hidden. While many witches have chosen over the years to be public about their practices, there is still value in the hidden, the mysterious, the occult.

Some traditions of witchcraft are keen to emphasize that it is a secret, hidden practice that is not for common consumption. They believe that your energy and power ebbs away if, for example, you share a photo of your altar online. It is a belief that the sacred is special and not for everyday mediums such as social media.

It can be hard if you're feeling isolated or you work as a solitary witch to feel a sense of community and online groups often help with giving you that sense of belonging. As a solitary practitioner, you do sometimes have to embrace the solitary, no matter how uncomfortable it feels. The ego wants you to let everyone know how powerful you are and

you may even be excited about the wonderful results you are manifesting.

However, we would do well to remember that all our folklore and mythology has taboos against revealing secrets, turning back to look, or telling a real name. We even say that you shouldn't tell anyone your wish when blowing out your birthday candles because it doesn't come true if you do.

Beyond the mystical reasons for secrecy, there is still a need in life for privacy. This spell will help with this and should be done on a waning Moon.

You will need
- White candle
- 8 white flowers (not roses)
- Bowl

Method
Take the petals from the flowers and put them in a bowl in front of you on your altar. Light the candle and take a deep breath in and then out through your nose. Pick up the bowl and pass it counter-clockwise three times (as if making a circle vertically in the air in front of the candle). Blow three times into the bowl, imagining that all the talk and connections that no longer serve you are being blown into the bowl.

Give thanks to your patron deity and sit in meditation a while. Snuff out the candle and discard the petals in your garden, compost heap or anywhere else where they will break down naturally.

This spell releases unnecessary talk from your life and keeps your private life hidden, but you should also become aware of how you connect with others. Are you just waiting for your turn to talk or are you really listening to what they are saying? Listening is a good way to respect others and will stop you blurting out anything that you later regret telling people.

AMULETS

Amulets are always present, when you're considering protection spells. They have a venerable history of usage throughout the world. This universal usage seems to stem from the human need for protection from what is perceived as evil or not easily understood. It also fulfils a very basic need for some sort of connection to the earth and its gifts.

Most children, for instance, will find or be given a "lucky stone" or object which is cherished for many years without the child being quite aware of the significance of something that might be considered an amulet. It is a natural form of protection that adults give to their children.

The design, shape and understanding of amulets has undoubtedly changed through the centuries but their purpose remains the same. The term "amulet" is derived from either the Latin word *amuletum*, a word of unknown origin probably meaning "to baffle" or "do away with," or the old Latin term *amoletum*, which signifies a means of defence.

In earlier times three types of amulets were recognized; there were objects for protection against trouble and adversity; those which drove away evil influences both medically and from a mental perspective; and those which contained substances such as herbs and oils which were used as medicine. These latter were often worn next to the skin in order to release their inherent properties.

All ancient cultures attached great importance to the use of amulets. The Egyptians employed them almost universally. One of the most notable amulets of ancient Egypt is the Eye of Horus, also called the *udjat* or *wedjat*, the all-seeing eye. Others are the ankh, the Egyptian cross of life, and

the scarab. The scarab signified resurrection after death and protection against evil magic. Ankhs, with their closed top, symbolized everlasting life and regeneration.

Seals in the form of small cylinders were used as amulets by both the Assyrians and the Babylonians. These often contained semiprecious and precious stones. Each stone possessed its own unique magical powers. Various animal-shaped amulets, such as the ram for masculinity and the bull for virility and strength, have also been found.

The Hebrews wore crescent moons to ward off the evil eye and often attached bells to their garments to ward off evil spirits. This is an interesting use of vibration or sound as protection since the sound of the bell was thought to scare off the demons. This usage – similar to the enchantment in a spoken charm – is also seen in Eastern religions in the use of wind chimes and prayer bells.

Cylinder seals used by the Hebrews often contained written prayers, spells and the magical name of God in various forms.

The Arabs too carried on this practice, using the more important characteristics of God – e.g. "God the provider" or "God the just". They would also wear small pouches containing grave dust as protection. In Africa, the fetish, often fashioned from

feathers and shells, afforded the people protection. Beads were largely used in this way, particularly when fashioned from natural objects.

In the 17th to 19th centuries such methods became popular when protection against witchcraft was perceived to be necessary. Interestingly the books of magical instructions called Grimoires, which were used by magical practitioners, were also thought to afford their owners a degree of protection.

The Tetragrammation, the four letters of the Hebrew personal name for God, YHWH and pronounced Yahweh – or, in English,

Jehovah – is believed to be very powerful in magical workings and has been fashioned into amulets by using different spellings.

It was believed to help magicians in conjuring up demons and give him protections from negative spirits – nowadays it is an invocation.

Amulets are also representative of the inherent powers of things – thus an object fashioned in the shape of something else is a manifestation of the latter's power. In shamanistic societies totems and sacred objects are not just specific animals but are representations of mystical powers, and if we can put ourselves in touch with them,

they can be sources of sensible advice, and ways of living our lives.

Animals are often considered to be messengers of the Great Spirit and are on Earth to teach us simplicity. Today, many witches, who in previous times often had a cat as a familiar, are tending to adopt shamanistic practices and so other animals such as bears, deer, eagles and fish can also perform the function of acting as familiars or power animals; they provide us with access to the animal kingdom and let us tap into their inherent power. It is worthwhile recognizing, however, that power animals are not only mammals. Insects and reptiles, for example, are some of the oldest sources of magical power known to humans.

OBJECTS FOR USE AS AMULETS

Below are some definitions of objects that might be used as amulets and as representations of power in modern-day talismans. Talismans form keys to the higher magical realms. In the sense that small articles may also be used as charms, it is worth remembering that charms have had words of power spoken or sung over them whereas amulets have an intrinsic power of their own. These articles may therefore be used as charms, amulets or in talismanic

work. It depends upon your preparation of them for use. Do not be afraid to experiment and find out what suits you best. Remember too that natural objects, such as stones or pieces of tree branch, can be amulets also. When they look like something else such as the head of an animal, they can have added potency. This is why we are so fascinated by misshapen vegetables and fruit. It may just be that the object is under the influence of a greater power and therefore magical!

Acorn

An acorn symbolizes new beginnings and rebirth, also strength of purpose. An acorn anointed with musk oil and carried in your purse, pocket or charm bag will help to attract the opposite sex. To increase your income, anoint an acorn with 3 drops of pine oil when the Moon is waxing and then bury it in your garden as close as possible to the front door of your house.

Amaranth

This is a symbol of immortality, faith and fidelity. It is sacred to the Moon and her Goddesses and is used for enhancement of fidelity and psychic perception.

Anchor

Represents stability, hope and salvation. It favours all matters to do with the sea and

would protect against physical harm.

Ankh

Crux Ansata, the Egyptian Cross of Life, is the key to spiritual wisdom and the hidden mysteries. Representing the Life Force and creative energy, it is a strongly protective symbol. It brings about health and abundance and, through knowledge, gives power over the temporal (physical) realm.

Ant

An amulet in the form of an ant will help the wearer to be industrious and hard working. Placed on the altar it will attract career opportunities.

Antelope

The head of the antelope or ibex is one of earliest known amulets, dating to 4500BCE. It was first associated with speed, then with evil as the God Seth. It is regenerative in its powers and also signifies overcoming – transcending – death and its associated fears.

Antlers (Horns)

Most cultures pay deference to the power of the antler, which suggests power over the forces of nature. They are sacred to the horned God, Pan and represent fruitfulness.

Anvil

This represents physical strength, the primal force of Nature as it manifests Earth and matter. In that sense it suggests the feminine principle and the forging of partnerships and links. It has a connection with all Thunder Gods.

Arrowhead

Carry an arrowhead for protection against enemies, bad luck, hexes, jealousy, evil spirits and all negative forces. Place an arrowhead over your front door (or under the mat) to prevent burglars.

Asp

The asp was an Egyptian symbol of royalty. It carries the same symbolism as the snake from a shamanistic point of view particularly favouring those seeking personal advancement. It also gives help and protection from those in authority.

Axe

This has a meaning similar to that of an arrowhead. It represented the Chief, God or Divine Being and had significance as the double-headed axe, which was said to represent the spiritual journey, in common with the double-headed hammer. It signifies power of all sorts. In the last few hundred years it has been replaced as a symbol of power by the sword.

Badger

The badger's courage is commemorated in the wearing of this amulet. He also represents the balance of negativity and positivity and

the idea of living successfully in the underworld.

Bamboo

This is a Buddhist emblem symbol representing truth, integrity and lasting friendship. Its aspect of wisdom means that it symbolizes a healthy old age and would be a good amulet to use for businesses which have been in existence for some time.

Bat

This creature signifies long-life. In Chinese folklore five bats represent the "five blessings"– Wealth, Health, Love of Virtue, Old Age and Natural Death. It is especially beneficial to educational matters, since it symbolizes arcane knowledge. It is said to bring good fortune.

Bear

The bear is reputedly the guardian of the world and symbolizes inner knowing and healing as well as the watcher. Such an amulet calls on the protection of the energy of the bear clan.

Beads

These are magically significant whether they are made from crystals or ordinary materials such as wood. In African magic, beads were invested with supernatural meaning. Necklaces and pendants even today are worn as amulets, and prayer beads and rosaries in other traditions also make use of beads.

Bees

The bee represents immortality and the soul. It is a messenger of the Gods and as an amulet brings wealth through inspiration and intuition.

Bells

They symbolize the angelic forces and are used to frighten off the Devil and evil spirits. They were put on anything that needed safeguarding (horses, babies, etc) to give them protection against evil actions or thoughts. They can also represent the four Elements and the cycles of the seasons, which is why they are rung at rituals.

Birds

They symbolize the human quest for our utmost potential and the Unconscious. As an amulet it protects the wearer on long journeys and ensures safe travel.

Buckles, Belts or Girdles

These were often associated with Isis or Venus and as such offered divine protection. Symbolizing personal fulfilment, these articles also represent physical well-being and moral strength and were often used as ties for other protective objects. It is for this reason that the girdle is so important in magical workings such as knot magic. You can use them in a variety of ways.

Buddha's footprints

This is an Indian amulet which is said to signify the eight emblems of Buddha – the Wheel of Law (cause and effect), the Golden Fish, (first incarnation of Vishnu), the Lucky Diagram (long life), the Lotus (good luck), the Conch Shell (wealth), the umbrella (majesty), the Vase and the Trumpet of Victory.

Buffalo

The buffalo possesses great strength and also represents the Great Spirit. Sometimes taken also to represent death, this protects the wearer from harm.

Bull

To increase fertility in women and virility in men, wear a bullshaped amulet, or place one under the bed before making love. This also commemorates overcoming the lower urges.

Butterfly

This is a widely accepted symbol of the psyche and the soul. It signifies the continuous cycle of life, death and resurrection. It suggests joy, laughter and pleasure.

Caduceus

This is a powerful image in health matters and is an almost universal symbol for medicine and communication. Representing the wand or staff of Mercury or Hermes, messenger of the Gods, it promotes knowledge and understanding. On a slightly more mundane level, it represents commercial success and safe travel.

Castle

Symbolizing self-knowledge, spiritual enlightenment and esoteric wisdom, the castle is a strongly protective image. It suggests the doorway to knowledge and power.

Cats

A black cat crossing your path is said to be lucky. In Egypt cats were under the protection of the Cat Goddess Bast and hence they are now seen as witches familiars. Worn in the form of an amulet, they seek the protection of the Lunar Goddess in her many forms. They are often worn as small charms on bracelets.

Corn or Wheatears/Sheaves

This representation of Mother Nature signifies abundance, fertility and wealth. Symbolizing the harvest, corn makes a connection with Demeter and other corn Goddesses.

Cosmic Egg

This combines two very potent symbols – a serpent entwined around an egg. It stands for the cycle of birth, life, death and rebirth and is universally recognized. As a health and fertility symbol, it is strongly protective, as are all eggs.

Cow

The cow represents the Mother forms of the deities whose qualities are nurturing and caring. In Egypt, amulets with cows' heads were almost certainly dedicated to Hathor.

Cowrie shell

Because of its shape, which is similar to the cornucopia or horn of plenty, this represents prosperity. In Egypt it was thought to represent the female genitalia, so worn on a woman's girdle it was said to afford her protection. In Polynesian societies it was considered a valid form of exchange token.

Crescent

There is a strong connection between the Crescent and the Moon. As an amulet the Crescent is said to bring success in love and promote good motherhood. The crescent points should always be turned to the right. Any amulet or charm connected to the Moon puts the wearer under the protection of the Goddess and also puts them in touch with their feminine, emotional side.

Cross

This is a protective device against all forms of evil, especially the Devil. It is found in many forms, such as the Egyptian ankh or the equal-armed Maltese cross. The cross is thought to restore good health and is probably the symbol most often worn universally. Esoterically, it stands for the union of opposites: spirit and matter, positive and negative, male and female, sacred and secular, and also for the coming together of all planes of existence. It is much used in talismanic work to represent balance and manifestation in the physical world.

Crow

This signifies justice and fair dealing and in some cultures the creation of negativity. Using this symbol either as an amulet or in talismanic work gives you access to these qualities.

Crown

The crown represents victorious strength and marks authority and rulership. As a symbol it signifies the recognition and reward which success brings.

Crocodile

Wearing this symbol as an amulet is a protection against the powers of the negative. First seen in Egypt, there, it protected against being eaten by the reptile since, if this happened, the dead person could not go onto the afterlife, since the parts of the being would be scattered. It was a general symbol of rebirth in many cultures.

Cupid

An amulet or charm in this form represents love and, as Cupid is the counterpart of Eros,

is used in love charms. It also suggests the breaking of a taboo.

Deer

This embodies compassion and grace. Wearing a brooch or having a representation of the deer in the home calls on the powers of Gods such as Herne the Hunter or Cernunnos.

Dog

Loyalty, and guardianship are qualities inherent in the dog, particularly the domestic variety. Wearing this amulet signifies protection.

Dolphin

Wise and happy, the dolphin suggests the exploration of deep emotion and psychic abilities. It has come to be accepted as initiator of new power and therefore guardian of the human race. It also represents safety in travelling.

Dove

The dove is the soul, the life spirit and transfiguration. The symbol of the turtle dove protects the wearer against death, fire, and lightning. Associated with Mother Goddesses, it brings peace and tranquillity into your home or workplace. It also signifies communication and love.

Dragon

The dragon by tradition symbolizes royalty and riches. The dragon, knowing the answer to many universal riddles, is a symbol of heaven, the Sun and the essence of Nature. The qualities of fire are called upon by the wearing of a dragon symbol. It is a protection against ill-fortune. In Chinese lore the dragon represents luck, material gain and wealth.

Dragonfly

This suggests imagination and breaks through illusions, thus gaining power and understanding through any dreams you may have.

Eagle

The eagle signifies expectation of power, high ideals and spiritual philosophy. It signifies the teaching of higher spiritual aspirations. In China and Japan it symbolizes aggression, fearlessness and courage. It also means good fortune and the highest of Gods. It is the father-principle and the solar emblem of all sky Gods.

Eye of Horus

Also known as the *udjat* or "all-seeing eye", this is an ancient symbol used as an amulet for wisdom, prosperity, spiritual protection, good health, the increasing of clairvoyant powers and protection against thieves. Following on from this symbolism, any eye suggests the Sun, stability and purpose. It is one of the most powerful charms there is. The falcon is another amulet linked with

Horus and is meant to represent the protection of the God. Falcon-headed Gods were important deities in Egypt.

Fan

In Eastern tradition the fan represents protection and safety, so makes a pleasant love charm. It is a lunar symbol depicting life unfolding.

Feather

This is the symbol of the wind and the soul's journey to other realms. It is truth, knowledge and power and is a general omen of good fortune. It is said to help with games of skill rather than strength.

Fingers

Two fingers held across the palm is a symbol of protection and assistance in Egyptian lore. Such a charm represents security. Fingers in talismanic work represent direction.

Fish

Used by most religions to represent the deity, it often signifies the universal mother, fertility and procreation. It stands for the psyche, intuition and the unconscious. The fish also symbolizes gracefulness and going with the flow.

Carp

The Carp represents expansion, particularly from the Chinese meaning. In Europe however – following Celtic tradition – the carp and the salmon are often interchangeable. Wealth, abundance and general prosperity are a more general meaning.

Fleur-de-Lys

This is a stylized lotus or lily which signifies health, wealth and happiness. It is a representation of the Trinity – even perhaps the Triple Goddess – and is also the flower of light, life and love.

Flowers

These are manifestations of developing life and nature, and represent spring and beauty. They often signify the successful completion of a contract, either personal or connected to business.

Fly

In Egypt this may have been used as a protective device. Fly amulets were found with the head of a falcon, the crescent Moon, and an *udjat* eye which would suggest that protection was expected on all levels of existence.

Four-leaf clover

Good fortune is said to smile on you if you carry a four-leaf clover, or if you wear a pin, ring, or pendant shaped like one. The four-leaf clover (a highly magical plant and a powerful amulet of Irish origin) is believed to be the most powerful of all natural amulets. The first leaf signifies fame, the second

wealth, the third faithful love and the fourth health.

Fox

An amulet in the shape of a fox symbolizes elusiveness, agility, cleverness and sometimes deviousness. You might wear this, for instance, if you had to be particularly sharp at a business meeting.

Frog

It is said that to promote friendship or reconcile enemies you should engrave the image of a frog on a piece of beryl and carry it near your heart or wear it as a necklace. A frog amulet is also good for increasing fertility and virility. It is a lunar symbol. In Egypt, the four male creator Gods all had frogs' heads. They were a symbol of regeneration and perhaps a symbol of Hecate in her animal form. This type of amulet was replaced by scarab amulets. It is a symbol of life and the creator, potential life, health and strength.

Fruit (general)

This tends to represent Nature's harvest and earthly fulfilment. It can also suggest worldly desires, reward for past labours and, by association with the idea of the cycle of life, immortality.

Garlic

One of the oldest and most famous of natural protection amulets, garlic has been used throughout the world in a variety of ways.

Witches and shamans use it as a carrier for healing energies.

Gods and Goddesses

An amulet or a representation of any of the Gods and Goddesses, particularly when worn as a bracelet, brooch or necklace, immediately puts the wearer under the protection of that deity.

Grapes

These signify the wine of life, fertility and sacrifice, thus giving the attributes of youthfulness and vigour. At the other end of the spectrum the association is with wisdom and truth, hospitality and peace and prosperity.

Grasshopper

The symbolism of the grasshopper is favourable to agricultural matters, in the sense of abundance and fullness. Signifying riches and wealth, if achieved through effort, this image probably supercedes the dragon fly, in the sense that the grasshopper is more grounded.

Gryphon/Griffin

This is a strongly protective symbol representing moral fortitude and physical strength. A hybrid solar symbol incorporating the characteristics of the lion and the eagle, it can be used most potently in talismans.

Hammer

This representation of the formative,

masculine principle is particularly powerful in techniques of manifestation (having something happen). It signifies victory over one's enemies or obstacles and is especially beneficial for business or career ambitions. Esoterically it is an attribute of all Thunder Gods. The double-headed hammer is said to stand for the labyrinth and for justice and vengeance in equal measure.

Hands

Always important as symbols, hands represent friendship, love and trust. The various types of hands worn as amulets are listed below; any of them avert evil and provide security:

Hand of God represents Divine power

Hand of Fate suggests destiny

Hand of Fatima gives Divine protection

Hare

With a strong connection to the Moon in her form as Mother, the hare stands for regeneration, fertility and rebirth. In Egypt latterly amulets of the hare were always fashioned from green stone. The rabbit, since the dawn of Christianity, has taken on much of the symbolism of the Hare. The energy of the hare is said to favour new enterprises.

Hawk

Similar to the falcon in its symbolism, the hawk signifies allseeing, perception and observation. A hawk amulet would be worn for protection and to give focus to your life.

Heart

In Egypt the heart was said to represent the soul. It also more universally represents the seat of love and therefore devotion. Tradition in amuletic and charm lore used to dictate that a heart should only be fashioned in gold though this now is changing, and many other materials are used. A silver heart given by a woman would acknowledge her own femininity.

Hedgehog

This symbolizes regeneration (after hibernation or a period of stasis). The hedgehog is said to be protective and also is said to conquer death. We still see the protective element depicted today in garden ornaments.

Heron

The image of the heron is similar to that of the ibis (see below) and suggests intuition and organization.

Hippopotamus

As an amulet it warns off bad temper and also stands for regeneration. The hippopotamus Goddesses in Egypt were symbols of female fertility.

Horse

The image of a horse symbolizes freedom, stability and courage. It would also bring you under the sway of Epona, the Horse Goddess.

Hummingbird

This signifies pleasure but also symbolizes the fierce warrior. It can also suggest a spiritual vibration, since the bird achieves stillness by fast movement, thus giving the idea of dynamic stillness.

Horseshoe

The horseshoe is a well known good luck symbol in many parts of the world. It is often taken to represent the Moon in her crescent form. According to superstition, you should nail an iron horseshoe with the convex side up for protection against sorcery and bad luck. For good luck, nail it over your door with the convex side pointing down. Wear any type of horseshoe-shaped jewellery or carry a miniature horseshoe charm in a charm bag to promote fertility.

Ibis

The ibis represents spiritual aspiration and the soul. Always a very important bird to the Egyptians, it was sacred to their God Thoth. It is said to heighten psychic perception and also gives a degree of protection on the physical level.

Jaguar

Symbolizing the wisdom of the shaman and focused power, an amulet or charm in this form would both protect and encourage.

Keys

These symbolize health, wealth and love. As they both open and close, they also signify birth and death, beginnings and endings as well as new opportunities and beginnings. A key can represent initiation and wisdom. To give them away is a token of surrender. An amulet or charm in this form often stands for life itself.

Crossed keys

These suggest power over heaven and earth.

Knot

The knot in the form of the Egyptian figure of eight (known as *tjes*) was supposed to protect the soul from dismemberment in the other world. The intricate Gordian knot was designed to protect the kingdom of Phrygia from fragmentation. The Celtic knot is a protective device when worn as an amulet. The Lover's Knot represents perfect union.

Ladder In Egypt

A ladder was a symbol of Horus, linking with heaven and bringing help when needed. The ladder also represents authority, ambition and career opportunities. When you wear an amulet incorporating this symbol the various options available to you are made obvious often through fresh insight or what may seem like extraordinary means.

Ladybird

This is supposed to represent the Virgin Mary. Because of this association with the Virgin, killing a ladybird will bring bad luck.

Wearing the ladybird as a brooch or pendant brings you under her protection and brings good fortune and money.

Lantern/Lamp

The lantern or lamp is symbolic of the Divine Light and spiritual power. It signifies guidance and protection of the highest order, often that which is generated by faith.

Laurel wreath

This represents worldly success and achievement and a degree of public recognition. From an esoteric viewpoint it is a triumph of life over death and also represents immortality. Used as an amulet or inscribed on a talisman, it opens the way to the right framework for success.

Leaf

Signifying growth, the symbol of the leaf concerns rejuvenation, hope and a revival of energy. Sometimes it can represent recovery from illness and can denote prosperity in business.

Lion

The lion symbolizes nobility and is a symbol of the Sun. It protects through courage, and as an amulet it represents the courage of conviction. It is the fiery principle and sometimes represents the spark of life.

Lizard

An amulet in the form of a lizard is said to give vision in the sense of far-sightedness and the ability to create an acceptable future. It also has connections with the crocodile.

Lotus/Lily

The lotus is a very powerful symbol representing serenity and that which is manifested from purity. The lily often represents perfection and freedom from worry. Symbolizing a change of state, it can be taken as a symbol of death.

Lynx

The lynx is the keeper of confidential information and symbolizes perspicacity. As an amulet it represents a type of instinctive wisdom.

Mistletoe

Revered by the Druids as the Golden Bough, mistletoe is considered to be unholy by the Christian Churches. It represents the feminine principle, but perhaps in its more capricious sense. Mistletoe is also said to establish and maintain family unity.

Mouse

The mouse represents innocence, faith and trust. Worn as an amulet it reminds the wearer of the necessity of an eye for detail.

Mushroom

The mushroom stands for hidden wisdom and mystic power. These are mysterious organisms said to be more akin to animal than plant life. Mushrooms are said to be ruled by the Moon and to bring happiness.

Ouroboros (serpent or dragon biting its own tail)

This universal symbol represents the totality of life, the cycle of continuous energy. Containing integration, disintegration and re-absorption, opposing principles are balanced and held at a tension that promises perfection. It therefore represents life itself.

Owl

To increase knowledge, wear an owl-shaped amulet made of gold, silver or copper. The symbol of the owl (sacred to the Goddess Athena) also brings good luck. The owl is said to work with the psychological shadow, bringing knowledge from hidden places. It also represents wisdom in the sense of knowledge of the Mysteries.

Oyster shell

In Egypt, the oyster shell as an amulet meant "sound, whole and healthy". It is supposed to protect the wearer from harm. Oyster shells today tend more to represent the Moon, because of the association with mother-of-pearl and its luminescence.

Palm branch

This is representative of the triumph of good over evil, and is a solar emblem. It promises victory and acclaim, more usually by hard work than by sheer luck. There is a sense of just rewards here.

Peacock

The peacock is a solar emblem and suggests long life and enduring love. It also symbolizes incorruptibility, immortality and resurrection. Because of the "eyes" in its tail feathers, it is said to link with Horus and the Egyptian pantheon of Gods.

Panther

Representative of the feminine, this is a protective device which brings one under the sway of cat Goddesses such as Bast. As an amulet it is a reminder of the power, speed and grace of the animal.

Phoenix

The symbol of the phoenix as a bird of transformation and regeneration is well known. It represents the continuity of life and the overcoming of obstacles. Ruled by the Element of Fire, since it is from Fire that it regenerates, it also signifies opportunities and benefits. As a solar symbol it also represents renewed youthfulness.

Pineapple

A symbol of fertility also having a connection to the Mother Goddess, the pineapple represents good fortune and fruitfulness.

Pine Cone

An emblem of Cybele, Goddess of plenty, the pine cone with its many seeds signifies abundance, health, wealth and power. Worn

as an amulet, or kept within the home, it is said that you will never lack the good things of life. Miniaturized as a charm, it still has the same significance.

Puma

Said to be the shaman's companion on journeys to other worlds, it is the spirit of grace and inherent power. While the animal is elusive, it is also protective within spiritual journeys and as an amulet personifies these characteristics.

Pyramid

Crystals shaped like pyramids possess the power to balance emotional qualities and are said to bring wisdom. It is thought that wearing an amulet in the shape of a pyramid improves concentration and increases or re-energizes psychic powers. As an amulet it also attracts good luck.

Rainbow

Through its symbolism as the bridge between the physical and the spiritual, the rainbow implies raised consciousness. Representing the seven spiritual centres (chakras) in the body, it also signifies transfiguration and transmutation. On a more mundane level, it indicates success and rewarding journeys.

Ram

The ram or sheep is a symbol of masculinity and also of fertility. In Egypt, the ram's head signified power. Nowadays as an amulet, the ram suggests the astrological sign of Aries.

Raven

The raven represents inner journeys and dreams. Messenger and watcher for the Gods, it also represents mystery, though sometimes in the form of the Trickster. It is sacred to, among others, Morrigan, so wearing this amulet gives protection by this Celtic Goddess.

Rice

Grains of rice are representative of fertility and essential nourishment. Rice finds its place in the contents of witches bottles as amulets and also in some prosperity spells. It also represents domestic happiness. Other grains may also be used for the same purpose, thus linking with the corn Goddesses.

Rose/Rosette

The rose or rosette with four petals signifies femininity and also earthly passions. It was a symbol for the cross and means completion and perfection. This is seen in the symbol used by the Rosicrucians. Roses and rosebuds are often used in love spells.

Scarab beetle

One of the most famous of all Egyptian amulets, the sacred scarab is an emblem of the Great Creator of the Universe. It is a symbol of perpetual renewal of life and

is sacred to the God Khephra. It stands for health, strength and virility. Wear scarab beetle jewellery for good luck and protection against all evil forces.

Scorpion

The wearing of an amulet in this form was a protection against the sting of the scorpion. Much of the sacred imagery was later transferred to the scarab.

Seashells

These are a symbol of femininity and all the Goddesses, particularly the Mother Goddesses.Signifying birth and regeneration, they can be worn as jewellery, placed on altars or kept about the person as a sign of allegiance. They represent prosperity and marital bliss.

Ship/Boat

As the nurturing aspect of the mother principle, there is a connection with the Mother Goddesses. Also, in ancient belief, it suggests the Sun God as he plies his boat across the sky. It has therefore come to represent passage between the various planes of existence. More recently it has come to mean commercial success and personal progress.

Skull

To help break the chains of any addiction, wear a gold skull-shaped charm necklace as a magical amulet. It is said that if you rub the skull three times a day, while focusing your eyes upon it and thinking about the misery that your addiction brings, you may be cured.

Snake

The snake has always stood for transformation and arcane knowledge because of its ability to shed its skin. As an amulet it reminds us of the necessity for constant change and transformation. In Egypt it was thought to protect the wearer against venomous snakes.

Spider

As a representative of Fate, and the weaver of destiny, an amulet in this form reminds the wearer of the intricacy with which life is formed. A lunar symbol of eternal transmutation, it is also representative of the fragility in each of us. It signifies business expertise, insight and astuteness and also unexpected luck concerning money.

Stag

This signifies the masculine power of regeneration. Like the deer it symbolizes all that is natural – it is the giver of spiritual gifts, beauty and mystical signs. It puts us under the protection of the nature Gods such as Pan.

Stork/Crane

As the herald of spring and new life, it becomes obvious why the stork has become the symbol for new babies. In its other

meaning, it signifies a long and fruitful life. In some cultures, it is said to protect households.

Sun

Carry a gold charm shaped like the Sun in a gold or yellow colored velvet charm bag if you wish to acquire wealth, good health, success and/or fame. This is also an effective amulet to use if you feel that others have been causing you unnecessary problems.

Swan

The symbol of the swan is traditionally said to be a guide into dreamtime, giving access to the hidden parts of us that are enclosed in the unconscious. It also suggests dignity and majestic power. As an amulet it calls upon the energy and power that is our birthright.

Sword

The sword represents justice and authority. It is a powerful protection against all forms of harm and also suggests courage and strength. It stands for the masculine principle and therefore for assertiveness arising from belief. It is of assistance in all commercial undertakings.

Thunderbolt

The thunderbolt traditionally represents celestial fire and creative energy. It is sacred to all sky Gods such as Thor and as a symbol is good when aggression is needed. It is said to bring success over business rivals, so as an amulet is worth having when such a vibration is needed.

Torch/Flame

This is the spark of life and has similar connotations to the lantern or lamp (see above). It often represents spiritual illumination and truth. It is obviously a fire symbol and speaks of prosperity and fertility, though perhaps more on a spiritual level than a material.

Tree

This is a universal symbol depicting the inter-relationship between the spiritual and physical planes and sometimes the Underworld. It is the world axis and links with Yggdrasil, the Tree of Life and the Tree of Knowledge. It is the process of birth, death and rebirth. On the material plane, it is success, personal advancement and domestic happiness.

Tulip bulb

Carry a tulip bulb as a natural amulet to bring love into your life. It is said that you should wear one around your neck or sleep with one under your pillow at night to attract a new lover.

Turtle/Tortoise

Said to be a representation of the three planes of existence, the spiritual (upper shell), the

mental (the body) and the physical (lower shell), this is a powerful symbol. For spiritual protection, particularly against psychic attack, stimulation of creativity and strengthening of divinatory powers, wear a gold turtle-shaped charm or amulet. This would also ensure longevity and good fortune and compassion towards others. The turtle also signifies shyness and in Egypt was used as a protective device against evil.

Unicorn

The unicorn is an ancient symbol of chastity and protection, and its fabled horn was said to be used in medieval times as an amulet to detect poisons in the food or drink of kings, queens, popes and other eminent clergy and nobility. A lunar emblem, it is said it can only be seen by virgins and is protective of their virtue.

Vulture

An amulet in the form of a vulture would afford protection by Wadjyit, an Egyptian Goddess. In ancient Egypt the vulture is usually seen side by side with the cobra. Together they are a symbol of sovereignty.

Wolf

A potent power animal, the wolf stands for Earth wisdom, knowledge and protection. As "Leader of the Way" the wolf has some significance and its image used as an amulet

gives a degree of protection. It also gives the wearer speed, agility and power.

Yin Yang

Both an ancient and a modern symbol, the Yin Yang is the embodiment and unification of all opposites. Rather than just representing the feminine and the masculine, it also represents dynamic and passive energy. It is a Chinese cosmic symbol.

Worn as jewellery or kept in the home in larger form, amulets provide powerful protection for a variety of different reasons, as we have seen. You can focus their power more on what you require through using symbols that are culturally or personally more significant for you.

CONCLUSION

SO BE IT

Holding fast to no particular discipline but believing that if it works then do it, we offer this encyclopaedia of spells, techniques and information as a way for you to explore your own magical creativity. Finding the magical self is a journey of exploration, which can become a lifelong task. As always, it is only possible to give guidelines – signposts along the way –as to what has worked for others and what should therefore work for you. For this reason, if a spell doesn't work for you in the way that it has been given in this book, do try it again on another occasion and use your intuition to decide what might be changed or adjusted to suit your own personality.

There are so many spells available across many disciplines that it is only possible to take a few steps along the road of exploration with you. The actions taken during the process of spell-making become so individual that only you yourself know what you actually did to make a particular technique work. For this reason, spell-making is at one and the same time a hidden art and one which needs to be shared – an occupation that is truly creative in its output. You do actually have the ability to make things happen or rather to help in their manifestation You are, however never quite sure what the end result is going to be, but must trust that it will always be for the Greater Good. Someone else may well do exactly the same thing and end up with a totally different result, but one which is right for them

If you are beginning your journey into magic, keep a journal of your thoughts, feelings, spells and the rituals you do, as well as the outcomes – expected and unexpected – that might arise. In the movies, this is always a leather-bound tome that ends up having a significant part to play in the plot, but you can have whatever book you choose. Just pick one that you feel comfortable storing all your spellwork in.

When you have found your book or Grimoire, you should do a ritual to consecrate it. Here is one for you, but do adjust it to your own tastes and beliefs. This is best done on a new or waxing Moon.

You will need
- A book to write in dedicated to magic work and thoughts alone
- A white candle

Method
Bathe and dress in a way that feels appropriate to you. Light the candle – a tealight is fine – and sit still in contemplation of the flame for a while.

Hold the book in your lap for a while and mentally ask Divinity or the Universe that this book helps you on your spiritual journey.

Open to the first page and write down the first word or sentence that comes to mind. Don't think too hard about this. Literally the first sentence. It may be a weird word or what, at first, seems a negative sentence or word. Don't censor or edit yourself.

Over the coming weeks keep an eye open for anything that might help you make sense of the message of your first word or sentence. Write anything that comes up down in your book. This is the start of your connection with your Book of Shadows. You may also write an inscription at the front that gives your family name, if you wish to pass your journal on to future generations of witches within your family.

As you search for knowledge, both esoteric and otherwise, do bear in mind that there are, from our perspective, certain constraints on the use of spells. In our view, spells should never be used to ill-wish or harm someone – it will only rebound on you at some stage. You yourself must take full responsibility for what you do, and indeed of the effect your thoughts can have on your universe, so always think very carefully and be very aware that as you progress and become more proficient, spells are literally Words of Power.

Finally, this book is in reality no more than a reference book. Over the years, spells have come to us from many sources and we share them with you in a spirit of openness and freedom. If we offend anyone then we apologize. If we help someone then we are grateful and if others find tranquillity then "May the Lady and her Lord be praised".

Index of Spells

Friendship, love and relationships

Attracting a new friend..................................... 160

Freeze out 161

To clarify relationships.....................................161

To win the heart of the one you love 162

Chocolate and strawberry delight.................163

To obtain love from a specific person.........164

To focus your lover's interest 165

To bring romantic love to you.........................166

To clear the air between lovers......................167

Herbal Heartease..167

Confidence in social situations.......................168

To create opportunities for love.....................169

To beckon a person..170

To draw a new love to you...............................170

For a lover to come to you 171

To achieve your heart's desires.....................171

To forget about an ex-lover.............................172

To have a person think about you 172

To have your love returned 173

To strengthen attraction..................................174

To stop an argument...175

Garment spell for fidelity 175

To rid yourself of an unwanted admirer...176

To find a new love 176

A lover's token...177

Herb charm to attract love 178

Fidelity charm...178

To bring someone into your life..................180

To rekindle your lover's interest...................180

Resolving a love triangle...................................181

To ease a broken heart 182

To ask for a commitment..................................183

Yemaya's sea love spell.......................................183

Egg roll to forget...184

Building friendships at work.........................185

Reigniting the flames of passion..................186

Finding true love...187

Health, healing and well-being

To form a healthy habit.......................................188

Aches and pains away 189

A healing walk 190

To get rid of warts..190

A light spell...191

A medication spell..192

Ceridwen's spell..193

Cleansing the aura..194

Drawing out a latent talent 195

Fertility spell 195

Healing the body 197

Good health wishing spell...................198

Self-image spell......................................198

Disperse negative emotion.................199

Overcoming your shadows 200

Healing a depression............................201

Healing image spell..............................202

Healing others..203

Physical body change 204

Purifying emotions 205

To cure sickness.....................................206

The spell of the shell 207

Radiant health..208

Balancing your energies......................209

Isis girdle 210

Knot spell 211

Mars water 212

Self-esteem..212

Sleep well..213

To find the truth.....................................214

To remove obstacles..............................215

To slow down a situation 216

A healing technique for someone else 216

Re-enchanting the world ritual 217

Thunder, Perfect Mind Spell...........................218

The evil eye

Diagnosis of the evil eye 220

Removal of the evil eye.......................................220

Antler charm 221

Clove remedy for the evil eye.........................222

Hamsa amulet for the home...........................223

Black cord protection for animals and
    humans...223

Salt method for removal of evil eye............224

Money, luck and career

Basil for business 226

Attracting extra money.......................................227

Footwash for money 227

Money doubling spell..228

How to speed up a happening 228

A case for court...229

A magical pomander..230

Achieving a dream job..231

Activating a wish.................................232

For study and concentration................233

Legal succes.......................................234

Eliminating personal poverty...............234

Fast luck oil.......................................235

Gambling spell....................................236

Money bottle.......................................237

Money charm.......................................238

Money spell..238

Removing misfortune...........................240

Silver spell...240

To banish your debts...........................241

Want spell..242

String spell...243

Open sesame.......................................243

Success in finding a job.......................244

To create opportunity..........................245

To help make a decision.......................246

To improve work relationships..............247

Weaving success..................................248

Reflections...248

Bay leaves of prosperity......................249

The manifesting waterfall.....................250

Grains of wealth.................................250

Cinnamon cake spell............................251

Spell for a promotion...........................252

Pearl money magnet spell.....................253

Santeria bath for success.....................253

Animal ally for business success............254

Honey jar to sweeten colleagues to you.....255

Figs and Honey spell............................256

Blessed nutmeg...................................257

Money Plant Mantra.............................257

Home and personal protection

Animal protection spell.........................258

Animal stones.....................................259

Banishing powder................................260

Animal protection collar.......................260

Blessing for the heart of the home..........261

Cleansing the body of negative energies..262

To reverse negativity or hexes...............263

Household gods...................................264

Invoking the household gods..................265

To protect a child................................266

To prevent intrusion into a building.........267

Fire protection spell.............................268

Protection bottle..269

Protecting your vehicle 270

To protect your luggage....................................271

Protecting yourself prior to the journey....271

To make bad luck go away...............................273

Breaking the hold someone has over you.274

To break a spell you've cast............................276

When you feel threatened................................277

Reinforcing of a personal space 278

A spell for the garden...279

Privacy spell...280

Amulets...281